THE TRADITION OF BOETHIUS

BOETHIUS AND THE ARTS

THE TRADITION OF BOETHIUS

A Study of His Importance in Medieval Culture

BY

HOWARD ROLLIN PATCH
PH.D., LITT.D.

PROFESSOR OF ENGLISH IN SMITH COLLEGE

NEW YORK / RUSSELL & RUSSELL

To H.K.P.

"Haud aliter tristitiae nebulis dissolutis hausi caelum et ad cognoscendam medicantis faciem mentem recepi." *Cons. Philos.*, I, pr. iii, 1-3.

. . .νῦν δέ μοι, ᾿Αγάθων, φάναι,
μετάδος τῶν ταινιῶν, ἵνα ἀναδήσω
καὶ τὴν τούτου ταυτηνὶ τὴν θαυμαστὴν
κεφαλήν . . . .

Plato, *Symposium*, 213 D-E.

PREFACE

THE FOLLOWING essay was first conceived as part of a manual on the writings and tradition of Boethius. It then became apparent that, as is seldom so truly the case with a popular manual, the present work could not depend on a general summary of the results of investigation published in scholarly monographs new and old. It was obvious that the author would be compelled to make a good deal of first-hand research for himself as part of his labours, and to publish this before it had had time to ripen under the hot rays of criticism and review. He had then to choose whether he would attempt a more scientific study of the subject and omit to include much that is already known, or offer an introduction which would indicate the lay of the land and the points at which further investigation is needed. The inaccessibility of certain manuscripts and especially questions connected with the survey of medieval education decided the matter. Much preliminary work regarding the universities of the time would have to be done before one could hope to make anything like a full or accurate estimate of the contribution of Boethius throughout Europe in textbook, training, and lecture. But some idea of the situation as it appears now is needed by students, who may find in the gaps or weaknesses of the present study an opportunity for their own subterranean efforts. Here the author has tried to keep to what, if not at least well established, may be regarded as generally acceptable, and to reserve whatever seems largely theoretical or most open to question for further consideration elsewhere. On the other hand, it is only fair to observe that a considerable proportion of the subject-matter—such as the whole survey in Chapter II and much in Chapter IV—is new.

Although the book contains, therefore, much new material, it also relies on many other studies to which there cannot always be an expression of indebtedness. *Boethius* by H. F. Stewart was naturally a model for some of the presentation here, and served as a guide on many topics where its own discussion was necessarily out of date. The author has leaned heavily on the researches of Graf and Murari and Rand, whose writings have been at once discouraging and inspiring to consult. He has adopted certain suggestions from Miss Helen Waddell and Professor Rand, whose opinions have carried their own authority. To Professor Mary L. Richardson and Professor Charles J. Hill of Smith College he is indebted in various ways. President W. A. Neilson of Smith College helped him when he was in difficulty, and supported his spirits with encouragement. Most of all, perhaps, he is under obligation to Professor Chauncey B. Tinker of Yale University for sympathetic understanding and many of the corporal works of mercy. Courtesies received at the Harvard, Yale, and Pierpont Morgan libraries should have special acknowledgement, as well as favours shown in the tireless co-operation of officials at the Smith College library. Miss Natalie Starr graciously secured photographs of manuscript illuminations in England, and took the trouble to look up a rare book in the British Museum. Other obligations, of which there are many, will be indicated at appropriate places in the pages that follow.

HOWARD R. PATCH

Northampton, Massachusetts
June, 1935

CONTENTS

LIST OF ILLUSTRATIONS

THE TRADITION OF BOETHIUS

INTRODUCTION

THE MODERN TRIBUTE to the memory of the great is usually a biography, but a popular work of that kind is unlikely to be written about Anicius Manlius Severinus Boethius. What name of equal distinction has suffered such wane? Scholars of things medieval know about him, and the booksellers' catalogues list the *De Consolatione Philosophiae*. But when that lover of old books, Mr. A. Edward Newton, discovered a reference to a copy, it took a friend to inform him that what he had found "was the best seller for a thousand years or so."[1] Yet Boethius has been regarded as a Christian saint; his books were indispensable in European education for centuries; his *Consolatio* was translated by important poets and even by monarchs; and his influence has undeniably given an impulse to artistic creation which we cannot fully trace to-day. "The blessed soul that exposes the deceptive world to anyone who gives ear to him," is how Dante characterized his genius.[2] Could the Middle Ages say much more?

It is not surprising, however, that moderns know little of him. An abundance of information about the personal details of his life has not survived. From the line of the Anicii he was born of a patrician family about 480 A.D. He married Rusticiana, daughter of that Symmachus who cared for him when he was left an orphan in his youth. We are informed that he cherished the idea of making the works of Aristotle and Plato accessible to the world of his time, and we know that he partly succeeded in doing so. His religious loyalties appear in his several Christian treatises. Politically he was eminent: he and his two sons became consuls, and he attained the title of Magister Officiorum. In the reign of Theodoric,

---

[1] *The Amenities of Book-Collecting*, p. 90.
[2] *Par.* x, 125-126. Cf. Grandgent's note, *Div. Comm.*, p. 749, for my rendering.

he was exiled in a prison at Pavia under the charge of treason and was put to death in 524 or 525. His father-in-law met a similar end the next year. Beyond facts like these we hear little of his career. But his influence during the centuries that followed his own time was enormous, and his record left in the lives and works of other men has received only scant recognition. This record it will be the attempt of the following pages to discuss. In this way I may hope to contribute something toward a fuller understanding of a great tradition.

While the leaven of Christianity was penetrating the new world that followed the downfall of strictly Roman civilization, it was lucky that Boethius came upon the scene just when he did to help in the formation of the new culture. As a scholar he was fitted to gather up the best of the old, and as a Christian and in a sense a martyr to adapt it to the apprehension of succeeding ages. Thus Henry Osborn Taylor has described him as the transmitter of antique thought, while Arturo Graf, without reference to religion, saw him as the first of the scholastics. How he appeared to his contemporaries we can understand if we turn to a letter which Cassiodorus wrote to him in the name of Theodoric: "In thy translations Pythagoras the musician, Ptolemy the astronomer, are read by the Italians; Nicomachus the arithmetician, Euclid the geometer, are heard by the Ausonians; Plato the theologian and Aristotle the logician dispute in Roman voice; nay, thou hast given back the mechanician Archimedes in Latin to the Sicilians. And whatsoever disciplines or arts the eloquence of the Greeks hath taught through various men, Rome hath received on thy authority alone in the speech of the fatherland. These thou hast rendered clear with such luminous words and marked with such propriety of expression that anyone who had learned them both might have preferred thy work."[1] All that Theodoric wanted

---

[1] *Cassiodori Senatoris Variae*, ed. Mommsen, *MGH., Auct. Antiq.* XII, p. 40, (i, 45), 4, 11-17. My translation leans heavily on that of Taylor, *Mediaeval Mind*, I, pp. 90 f., and that of T. Hodgkin, *Letters of Cassiodorus*, p. 169 (a free rendering).

in this letter was help with a water clock and a sundial, to be offered as presents to the Burgundian King. But there can be little doubt that he realized the substantial and plain truth of what seems like flattery.

Among the most touching of the compliments Boethius received, however, is that from his friend and contemporary in the field of letters, Ennodius: "Thou dost deign to ascribe virtues to me, most exemplary of men, whom in the years of youth without the prejudice of age industry hath made old, who by diligence dost fulfill all that may be required, whose sport in the early part of life is constant study [*lectionis assiduitas*], and whose delight is what would be another's toil, in whose hands the torch with which the ancients glowed shines with doubled fire. For what hardly hath been the share of thy elders at the end of life, abounds in thee at the threshold."[1] The solemnity of the words shows the utter sincerity of Ennodius, who is obviously moved by profound admiration. Not many authors praise each other in this vein.

Precisely what did Boethius write? He composed some pastoral poetry which is lost to us. Early in his career he compiled his Arithmetic based on Nicomachus. Ennodius vouched for his learning in both Greek and Latin: "Thou art one who dost embrace both, and what will suffice when distributed from man to man, thou greedy possessor of the greatest things dost include within thyself."[2] Boethius early launched his project of rendering Aristotle. He began with his commentary on Porphyry's *Introduction to the Categories* (the *Isagoge*) as translated by Victorinus, but later made his own translation and wrote a further commentary. He completed a translation of the *De Interpretatione*, and added two commentaries—a simpler one for beginners, and a later and fuller one for advanced students. For this work he derived material from Porphyry and Syrianus. His rendering of the *Categories* was achieved in the year when

---

[1] Ennodius, *Opera*, ed. Vogel, *MGH.*, *Auct. Antiq.*, VII, p. 236 (*Ep.* vii, 13).
[2] *Ibid.*, p. 268 (*Ep.* viii, 1).

he was elected consul; and, borrowing again from Porphyry, he also furnished it with a commentary. The rest
of the works on logic he translated in due time. He
wrote a commentary on Cicero's *Topics*, on which (as well
as on Aristotle's book of that name) he wrote a treatise,
De Differentiis Topicis. He found time also for original
treatment of certain problems of logic in his *De Syllogismo Categorico*, *De Syllogismo Hypothetico*, and *De
Divisione*. From Nicomachus, Euclid, and Ptolemy he
took material for an important work on music. Euclid
on geometry he rendered in a form which has not at
least fully survived; he also seems to have finished a book
on astronomy, but that is certainly lost. So far his production may seem to have chiefly an educational or philosophical value, as his translation or compilation from
sources would imply. But in the latter part of his life he
busied himself with his four theological treatises—the
Opuscula Sacra, and his famous *De Consolatione Philosophiae*. Besides these a treatise *De Fide Catholica* and
another *De Disciplina Scholarium* have been widely attributed to him. The first is probably his. The *Disciplina*, however, a popular textbook in the later Middle
Ages, was written by one Conradus in the thirteenth
century.

The theological works may have had only a limited
influence, at least in comparison with the philosophical
or logical books. In any case they serve as an anticipation
of later medieval speculations of the kind. Here was
dialectic applied to the use of religion. From his long
study of Aristotle, and from his own borrowings from
other scholars, Boethius had learned the method of sub-
jecting reason to such a discipline even better perhaps
than St. Augustine. In the *Consolatio Philosophiae*,
however, he used a freer hand than ever before. The
work was once regarded as a somewhat mechanical com-
bination of Aristotle with Neoplatonism, in which poems
were interspersed in the manner of the *Menippean
Satires* of Varro. Such was the idea of Usener and

others. But it is clear from the studies of Rand and Klingner that the whole treatise, while it was carefully designed and took much from sources, is anything but a mere composite and is highly original. Its dialogue vaguely recalls the form that Plato and Cicero had made familiar. It gathers up interests of many kinds, some Platonic, some Neoplatonic, much that is Aristotelian, and much that is theological. For example, if Boethius consulted Plato's *Timaeus* for part of his material, it is obvious that he did not stop there but drew on the Commentary of Proclus, and from that moved on to borrow from Plotinus or Aristotle. Yet this is not to urge that he worked with scissors and paste, to lift a phrase here and another there; but that, in default of a library in his prison, he carried with him the riches of genuine learning. Someone has said that he thought as a Neoplatonist; but certainly he did so no more than Augustine or Aquinas or even Cicero. His method, as truly as Cicero's, was that of a student and a philosopher; never that of an imitator. The consolation offered by his masterpiece does not emerge in the same form from any of the Greeks. The Neoplatonists led men to the worship of intellect; Boethius brought them to God. The *Consolatio* embodied what he most generally cared perhaps to set forth. Still more impressive is the manner in which it happens to deal, in one way or another, with what proved to be most of the preoccupations of the centuries that were to follow.

It is not too much to say that the book set the style for a vast amount of subsequent literature. As Battaglia has observed,[1] one of its remarkable features is its at least twofold appeal. To writers of imaginative works it offered inspiration as a work of art through its allegory and through its lyric interludes; on the other hand, to the intellectual it raised interesting questions in an informal and easy manner through its philosophical discussion. The debate on the subject of fate and free will, the treat-

---

[1] *Il Boezio e L'Arrighetto*, p. xiii.

ment of the problem of fortune, the attempt to explain adversity in a universe ruled by a loving God, all show the matter and the manner that were adopted by numerous books in the ages that came after. Taking him as a Christian humanist Rand concludes: "In temperament he is more equable and urbane than Augustine or Jerome, though he can exercise a humanistic tongue, and he is far more profound than Lactantius."[1] How many colloquies and disputes of symbolic figures were to be described after his time until Dante's own sweet discourse with Lady Philosophy, and how many studies of Aristotle "and his philosophye" were to be conducted in a fashion not dissimilar! Seldom has any author pervaded so thoroughly, and even formed, the thought and the expression of his own and later periods. Boethius not only used Greek philosophy to supply a framework for his Christian ideas about life, just as Albertus Magnus and Thomas Aquinas were to do later; but he presented his views in a fashion as graphic as that of the later battles and tournaments of the Vices and Virtues, the harangues of the Liberal Arts, and the adventures of other personifications. The lyrics too men knew by heart; they quoted them occasionally and copied their metres. Like Plato, Boethius had the mind of a poet with which to take his flights, and like Aristotle a rational conscience for ballast.

How much did the Middle Ages derive from him on the artistic side, and how much from Martianus Capella, Prudentius, or some other allegorist? It is often difficult to say, but it is certain that he was a prime source of inspiration. His appeal accordingly reached the world of art as well as that of education and thought. In the chapters that follow I shall attempt to indicate something of the extent of the influence he exerted in the literary and philosophical activity of his time and after. The first chapter will deal with his personal reputation as far as that is revealed by popular stories of his life. The second will attempt to show his place in the realm of education.

[1] *Founders of the Mid. Ages*, p. 157.

In the third, various translations of the *Consolatio* will be discussed; and in the fourth, imitations of that work will be described. In the concluding chapter I shall try to bring together the inferences that seem to follow from the evidence so far presented, although it will not be forgotten that the present survey is not exhaustive, and that revision in detail or in the large may some day require a shift of emphasis in what is here observed. Yet as one reads the works of Boethius himself, one can only feel that, whatever his popularity, we may regard the Middle Ages as especially blest in having for its guide a thinker endowed equally with good sense and learning, a man of letters who was articulate without display.

CHAPTER I

TRADITION AND LEGEND

BOETHIUS was a writer who attained some reputation as a citizen. That he was a political figure meant much to his own day, and that he had intellectual eminence brought its own portion of rather dry fame. But that he had been a loyal Christian and appeared to have suffered martyrdom caught the attention of the Middle Ages. The modern is at once likely to ask whether a cult did not spring up round such a name. If the genius of Virgil as a poet contributed somewhat to the mythical figure of Virgil the magician, who, as Comparetti sought to persuade us, threatened at times to replace him, surely Boethius had some of the qualities of a seer, and a legend might have grown up about him, especially at a time when in the nature of things there could be little proof of careful veracity. But it is thoroughly significant that in this respect there is nothing exciting to record. Perhaps because he did not tamper much with experimental science, he did not become an early Roger Bacon or another Faustus. Locally he was regarded as a saint, but we hear almost nothing of his miracles. What may be described as his legend is rather an erroneous "life," in which the journalism of the day failed to get at the facts and substituted pretty sober if sympathetic invention.

Here, for example, he acquired a new wife named Elpis, reputed author of two hymns. He also studied at Athens —not an impossible idea and one for which some support has been offered. Education at Athens would have led him directly to the founts of wisdom from which he drew so much. Other stories include the vivid one concerning the death of Theodoric, which reasonably suggested that the King had a conscience and that it was troubled by some of the executions he had permitted. According to Pro-

copius,[1] a careful historian, one day after the death of the
supposed traitors the head of a large fish was served to
the King, when suddenly it appeared to him like the
countenance of Symmachus with the teeth set in the lower
lip and the eyes fierce and raging. The King in terror
betook himself to his couch, and ordered that the bed-
clothes be heaped high upon him. He confessed his crime
to his physician, and "lamenting the whole affair and oppressed with grief he shortly died." The King, we remember, was ill at the time. Perhaps this narrative was
founded on fact.

The true life of Boethius is taken from the material
in his own works and in those of his contemporaries. He
himself alludes to his writings, and in the *Consolatio* brief
references to his family and his sufferings break for a
moment the seal of an otherwise dignified reticence.
There were, however, in the manuscripts of what he wrote,
current *Vitae* of the author which offer traditional detail
of their own. Without considerable research in the documents themselves, many of which remain unpublished,
it will be impossible to trace adequately the relationship
among these accounts. A few have been printed by Peiper
in the introduction to his edition of the *Consolatio;* but
at present we can consider only the more important narra-
tives, which, often deriving from the *Vitae* or furnishing
them with further detail, may indicate typical forms that
the legend assumed. Thus the so-called *Anonymus
Valesii,* two fragments edited in the seventeenth century
by Henri de Valois and appended to the History of
Ammianus Marcellinus, may be regarded as sufficiently
ancient to offer something true mingled with false. In
the second of these fragments,[2] which possibly dates from
the sixth century, we are told of the reign of Theodoric,
which seems to have been characterized in general by liber-
ality and prosperity until his last years. In this period, we

---

[1] *De Bello Gothico,* ed. Haury, II, 9-10 (I, cap. i, 35 ff.).
[2] Cessi's edition, p. 19, 2, 26 ff. For an English rendering see Hodgkin's
Italy and her Invaders, III, pp. 298 f. and 518 ff., and Stewart's *Boethius,* pp.
30 ff.

read, there was strife between the Jews and the Christians in Ravenna. The Jews ridiculed the Sacrament of Baptism, and the Christians revenged themselves, even in defiance of their Bishop, by burning the synagogues. This was too much for the King. A religious affront may pass, but material destruction is a menace to everybody. He found it necessary to interfere.

At this time, asserts the fragment, the devil found a way to subvert a ruler who had governed the state hitherto without rousing complaint. Theodoric ordered that the oratory and altar of St. Stephen in the suburbs of Verona be overturned, and forbade any Roman to bear arms. Prodigies of course began to appear. A woman lying under a porch not far from the palace of Ravenna gave birth to four dragons: two were seen carried along in the clouds from the west to the east and then cast into the sea; two, having only one head between them, were captured. A comet shone in the sky for fifteen days, and there were frequent earthquakes.

Henceforth the King seized every possible occasion to show his wrath against the Romans. Cyprian, Reporter to the High Court of Justice and afterwards Count of the Sacred Largesses and Master of the Offices, acted from cupidity and brought accusation against Albinus the Patrician. Albinus, he charged, had sent letters to the Emperor Justin which were hostile to Theodoric. This accusation Albinus denied, and Boethius, Master of the Offices, spoke in the presence of the King in his behalf. "False is the charge of Cyprian," said he, "but if Albinus did it, I and all the Senate too did it with one accord. It is false, my Lord King!" In defense Cyprian produced false witnesses, not only against Albinus but also against his defender Boethius, and the King plotted how he might put them to death. They were taken into custody at the baptistry of the Church. The King summoned Eusebius, Prefect of the city of Pavia, and passed sentence upon Boethius without allowing him a hearing. Shortly after, the prisoner was miserably put to death at Calvenzano.

A cord was twisted round his forehead until his eyes
started from their sockets, and then he was slain with a
club.

Thus died Boethius.   After this outrage the King returned to Ravenna no longer a friend but rather an enemy
of God, forgetful of all His benefits and trusting in his
own arm.   At the same time the religious undercurrent
of the episodes becomes more directly apparent.   Theodoric ordered Pope John to go to Constantinople and bid
the Emperor to restore to their own places of worship all
heretics who had previously been reconciled to the Catholic religion.   But with an obvious reminiscence the Pope
replied, "What thou art about to do, O King, do quickly!"
Such instructions as Theodoric would impose on him, he
said, were impossible to carry out.   The angry King sent
him nevertheless.   Justin agreed to do everything he was
asked, except, he insisted, he could not surrender to the
Arians those who had given themselves to Catholicism.

Meanwhile, fearing the disaffection of Symmachus, the
father-in-law of Boethius, Theodoric had him put to death
as well.   Pope John returned from the east, and feeling
himself in disgrace he died after a few days.   When his
funeral was held, people walked in procession before the
papal bier, and one of the throng, possessed by a demon,
fell down but was miraculously healed when the body
arrived where he was.   At this spectacle the people and
the senators began to cut bits of cloth as relics from the
Pope's garment.   Thus they conveyed the sacred remains
from the city with supreme joy, and on all sides the Pope
was regarded as a martyr to his religion.   Not much later
an order was issued giving the Catholic churches to the
Jews.   But the King's work was over; he was stricken with
a fatal illness and died.   His body was buried in the tomb
he had caused to be constructed for it during his lifetime.

From this account it is easy to see how Boethius was also
thought of as a martyr—at least soon after his day.   He
died an opponent to a great enemy of Catholics.   Little
space is allowed in this story for the imprisonment or for

the preparation of the *Consolatio*.   We do not see him as
even so much of a philosopher as one who might meditate
on the future while he held the poisoned cup.   His was a
brutal death against a turbulent background of religious
controversy and feeling.   Yet apart from certain details
this was doubtless the way the actual events appeared to
the people, who interpreted their history from the rush of
experiences with which they themselves were associated,
culminating in the death of their Pope and the miraculous
manifestations.   Small wonder then that in the *Vitae* we
read that "Boethius was honourably buried in the crypt of
the Church of Pavia, and is called Saint Severinus by the
provincials. . . ."[1] This tribute carries with it a dash of
irony when we learn from his own words that he was con-
demned by the Senate, and that one of the charges against
him was the sacrilege of traffic with evil spirits.[2]   Yet,
after all, is the story so far removed from the facts of the
case?   Boethius belonged to the Catholic party, and his
death was an incident in the course of destruction which
issued from the violent growth of prejudice in Theodoric.
The time he spent in prison was devoted to a consideration
of how his sufferings and those of other people could be
related to the idea of a just and loving God.   His religion
was far more than mere ethics; and the theme of God's
love runs through the *Consolatio*, in no sentimental fashion but with the fervour of sound reasoning.

At any rate such is the memory in which he was held.
Some centuries later King Alfred prefaced his famous
Old English rendering of the *Consolatio* with a brief account of Boethius, taking material from some version of
the *Vitae*.   According to this story Theodoric persecuted
the Romans with "countless crimes" ending with the murder of Pope John, whom he ordered to be slain.   Boethius,
"a man of book-learning and in worldly life most truly

---

[1] "Boetius autem honorifice tumulatus est papie in cripta ecclesie et uocatur
sanctus seuerinus a prouintialibus quod ei prenomen fuit." *Philos. Cons.*, ed.
Peiper, p. xxxv, 16-18.
[2] *Cons. Philos.*, I, pr. iv, 106-110 and 135-145 (*Loeb Libr.* All citations will
be taken from this edition.).

wise," seeing that the King was committing great wrongs against the Christians, considered how "he might wrest the sovereignty from the unrighteous King." "Wherefore, sending word privily to the Caesar at Constantinople . . . he prayed him to help them back to their Christian faith and their old laws." But Theodoric heard of the plan, and thrust him into a dungeon, where he found no consolation and despondency seized him. After this passage the translation of the book itself is introduced.[1] The Old English is specific about the messages which Boethius sent to the Emperor asking for aid. It is the more ironic, accordingly, that Boethius himself in the Latin of the *Consolatio* seems quite as specifically to repudiate the message for which he is here celebrated: "For why should I speak of those feigned letters, in which I am charged to have hoped for Roman liberty?"[2] The point remains, however, that with Alfred as with others the philosopher is something of a martyr who sought to restore the country to an orthodox ruler, and Theodoric is a tyrant working manifold evils against Christendom.

Similar in theme is the form of the story found in the Provençal poem in a manuscript of the eleventh century at Orléans.[3] This interesting work was composed as a warning to youth, holding up Boethius as an example of a reformer to whom the Lord permitted affliction. We young folk, says the poet in the opening lines, have been living in folly:

In ancient days too men were rogues; they were evil then, to-day they are worse. Boethius wished to give them instruction. Before all the throng he made a sermon: they should believe in God, who suffered the Passion; by Him should they all have redemption. Much pains Boethius took but without success. For envy, rather, they cast him into prison. Boethius was a great Seigneur; gallant he was and fair of frame so that Torquator

---

[1] For the Old English see the edition of Sedgefield, Oxford, 1899. My quotations are mostly taken from his rendering of Alfred's version into modern English, published the following year, (*King Alfred's Version*, pp. 1-2).

[2] *Cons. Philos.*, I, pr. iv, 89-90. Loeb trans. p. 149.

[3] *Das altprovenzalische Boëthiuslied*, ed. Hündgen.

Manlius loved him much. In wisdom he was not slothful; so much he derived that he was never at a loss. So good an example he has left among us that I do not believe there was in Rome another of his intelligence. Count he was of Rome, and had great influence with Manlius the King and Emperor. He was the best among all virtuous men; he was regarded as lord of the whole empire. But for one reason he had a more shining fame: they called him doctor of wisdom.

Torquator Manlius died, and Boethius grieved. In his place was Theodoric who "believed not on God, our Creator." Boethius did not want him for overlord, nor would he receive dignities at his hands. He lashed the new King with his speech, and Theodoric took such action ill. From sheer malice he wanted to make him appear a wicked man:

He caused a letter to be written with great deception, and had Boethius's name inscribed on it. Thus he sent it to the land of the Greeks. In the name of Boethius he recommended to them a plan: they might cross the sea, armed for strife; he will treacherously surrender Rome to them.

But Theodoric had the messenger followed, captured with the letter, and cast into prison. At the Capitolium at daylight arrived the King to fulfill his evil plan. There he reproached Boethius and his companions for treachery, and without a hearing his victim was again thrown into prison, where he lifted his voice in prayer. So we are led to a lament which is similar to the first part of the *Consolatio*.

It is evident that the introduction is made up of material suggested by the *Vitae* and the *Consolatio*, somewhat coloured by the general tradition. But the prayer itself is so remarkable that it will be worth while to repeat it in full in translation:

Lord, Father! in whom I have so much trusted—in whose mercy stand all sinners—my muses who have lost their song—I was going to sing of wisdom! I weep all the day, I follow the manner of a child: all into weeping turn my desires.

Lord, Father! Thou who art wont to govern me, in Thee

am I accustomed always to trust.   Thou didst make me stand
in so much great wealth!   Of all Rome did I possess the rule.
Wise men I garbed with fitting ornament, with the justice which
I had liberally to bestow.   I did not serve Thee well, nor wouldst
Thou suffer me further.   Therefore Thou didst let me endure
imprisonment.   I have nothing that I may take, nor can I give
anything.   By day and night I do nothing but ponder in sadness.
All into weeping turn my desires.

The picture of Boethius on his knees in this fashion shows
how he was established in the popular imagination at the
time.

All this is quite in accordance with the local tradition
that grew up concerning his tower of imprisonment and his
tomb.   He was first buried in the ancient Cathedral of
Pavia near the tower of the Baptistry.   In 721 Liutprand,
King of the Lombards, enlarged and endowed the Church
of San Pietro in Cieldoro, and possibly it was he who
translated the body thither.   Here the inscription at the
right side of the high altar included the following lines:

> Ecce Boetius celo magnus
> et omni mundo mirificandus homo.
> Qui Theodorico Regi delatus iniquo:
> Papiam senium ducit in exilium.
> In quo se mestum solans dedit inde libellum.
> Post ictus gladio exiit e medio.[1]

The idea of martyrdom obviously appeared early; and in
time, following the ecclesiastical tradition that he had been
decapitated with a sword, Boethius was depicted like certain other saints carrying his head in his hands.   In fact
sometimes he was thus represented receiving the Holy
Eucharist.   His name was registered in certain lists as that
of a saint; the Bollandists in the *Acta Sanctorum* give him
the title, and his cult was sanctioned for the diocese of
Pavia by Pope Leo XIII in 1883, where his feast day falls
on the twenty-third of October.   Several times moved to

---

[1] Gualla, *Historiae suae patriae*, etc., iv, 16 (p. 55ʳᵒ).   For further notes on
this inscription see the Appendix to this chapter.

a new resting place, his bones are now in the crypt of the rebuilt Church of San Pietro in Cieldoro. The site of the tower where he was confined is marked to-day by a marble monument.

One may properly insist that all the details which we have reviewed give a one-sided picture of the medieval idea of Boethius. One should never forget his tradition as a man of letters and learning, a mellower one perhaps to the scholar, and one reflected in such lines as those of the praise accorded to him by Gerbert of Aurillac (later Pope Sylvester II, born about 940) or those of John of Salisbury. As we shall see, the student in the Middle Ages probably thought of him as a schoolman rather than as a saint. Gerbert wrote an inscription in 996 for a statue erected by the Emperor Otto III, but even his tribute includes the following verses:

> . . . That intellect divine
> Compels for thee the world's *imperium*.
> So by the Gothic Bacchanalian sword
> Died Roman freedom. Consul and exile, thou
> Laid greatness down to win it in thy death.[1]

And we must recall the famous lines of Dante in the *Paradiso* where he refers to him in the sphere of the sun as the "anima santa":

> Lo corpo ond' ella fu cacciata giace
> Giuso in Cieldauro, ed essa da martiro
> E da esilio venne a questa pace.[2]

In general one may well marvel at the restraint which governs the medieval tradition of such a figure. Graf's theory that the cult went no further than it did because

---

[1] Trans. Waddell, *The Wandering Scholars*, p. xxvii. I have restored the lines to their original order. Thus the Latin:
> . . . Sed mens diuina coercet
> Imperium mundi; gladio bacchante Gothorum
> Libertas romana perit. Tu consul et exsul
> Insignes titulos praeclara morte relinquis.

See *Œuvres de Gerbert*, ed. Olleris, pp. 294 f.

[2] *Par.* x, 127-129.

everybody knew of the philosopher's imprisonment and death hardly seems cogent. After all Virgil's tomb was popularly identified. Rather the fact seems to be that something in the very moderation of Boethius's personality gave a quality to his memory among men, and this fact has its own significance. On the other hand Theodoric became the centre of an important saga, and Graf has described the legend in Italy that showed him as a figure among the damned for killing a Christian martyr.

Incidentally there has been one strange offshoot from the whole tradition in the modern world. In a seventeenth-century controversy, centred in the embarrassing problem of Roman Catholics in England, a book by Nicholas Caussin containing a rather extravagant life of Boethius was translated into English by the papist Sir Thomas Hawkins and others to deduce new lessons from history. This was entitled, "The Holy Court, or the Christian Institution of Men of Quality. With Examples of those who in Court have flourished in Sanctity." Here Theodoric, of course, is a tyrant; Opilio and Basilius correspond to Oates and Bedlow. One remarkable feature is the story of Boethius's speech to the Senate. It is earier, he says, to fly than to speak. He has attempted to cure Theodoric of his error "by all the sweetest ways."[1] Now that he is forced to speak he attacks the corruption of the court and the two favourites. "Since nature hath not created us like crocodiles, who are said to have eys [sic] to weep and not a tongue to complain," it is hard to be silent in so great revolutions of affairs. "Out alas, Sir, if we exclaim against witches who poison fountains, how can we be silent, seeing endeavour is used to invenom the soul of the Prince, who is the source of all counsels, to the end we may hereafter find poison, where we hoped for remedie?" He appeals to Theodoric to remember his people. "Sir, onely behold and imitate your self; re-assume that spirit which made you reign in our hearts, as well as in our

---

[1] *The Holy Court*, London, 1650, [II], pp. 288b ff. The petition of Rusticiana is on pp. 293-294.

Provinces; distinguish flatterers from true friends. . . ."
"This Oration greatly enkindled minds, and King Theo-
dorick was so much amazed at this libertie, that he seemed
not wel setled in his countenance, he onely said in a few
words, he would give all satisfaction to the Senate. . . ."
   The hero is, however, accused of conspiracy. Basilicus,
Opilion, and Gaudentius come as witnesses, "men of lost
conscience and reputation." Boethius is not allowed to
speak further; Rusticiana addresses him, and to her he
bids farewell. To the King the forlorn Rusticiana deliv-
ers a moving petition. "Alas, Sir, said she, if you once
more deign to behold from the throne of your glorie the
dust of the earth, cast your eyes upon a poor afflicted creature, which is but the shadow of what she hath been. I
no longer am *Rusticiana,* who saw palms and honours
grow in her house, as flowers in medows. . . ." As for
her husband ". . . calumnie hath depainted his innocency
. . . with a coal, to inflame you with choler against a man,
who ever held your interests as dear unto him as his own."
But as well present "musick to the ears of Tygers"! The
tyrant commanded her to withdraw. So Boethius makes
an apostrophe to Rome to the effect that it may be "puri-
fied by [his] bloud"; and he "died partly for the defense
of the Catholick Church against the Arians." How much
this narrative added to the veneration of the martyr we
cannot know, but the striking fact is that in the seventeenth century Boethius still seemed available as the central figure in such an appeal.
   On the other hand modern scholars have felt prompted
to inquire whether the philosopher was in truth a Christian
at all. As for the *Consolatio* we are told that it might
perfectly well have been written by Cicero, at least so far
as its substance is concerned. As far back as the tenth
century Bruno of Corvey thought he detected heresy in
the work, and in the twelfth century John of Salisbury
noted that it did not set forth the Incarnate Word. From
Obbarius to Nitzsch and Graf the names have been many
of those who thought that Boethius was not even Christian

in his views. But this is not the place to follow the long history of this particular debate. Apart from the evidence of the *Anecdoton Holderi* that Boethius was author of the religious Tractates, tradition is a powerful witness. After all, the matter of the *Consolatio* is not wholly unlike much of the argument in the works of St. Thomas Aquinas, and with this consideration the evidence drawn from popular memory has its own value which should not be ignored.

CHAPTER II

MEDIEVAL THOUGHT

To HENRY ADAMS the great structures of Mont-Saint-Michel and Chartres were symbols of the range of medieval interest. He might equally well have used Avignon and Vézelay; and yet here again, as before, there would have been a great omission. Oxford, Paris, or Bologna, some symbol of the activity of the intellectual life should be included if one is to view the period fairly. As a beginning let us take Pavia and Monte Cassino. In the first Boethius wrote works which pointed the way for learning during the next thousand years, and in the second St. Benedict laid a strong foundation for the powerful tradition of monasticism in which that culture was to flourish. The seeds of the Lord did not fall upon stony ground in either case. Of the *Consolatio* Taylor remarks in words that are as just as they must have been carefully weighed: "Deep must have been the effect of that book so widely read and pondered on and loved . . . with its intimate consolings, its ways of reasoning and looking upon life, its setting of the intellectual above the physical, its insistence that mind rather than body makes the man. Imagine it brought home to a vigorous struggling personality—imagine Alfred reading and translating it, and adding to it from the teachings of his own experience. The study of such a book might form the turning of a mediaeval life; at least could not fail to temper the convulsions of a soul storm-driven amid unreconcilable spiritual conflicts." [1]

Yet Boethius wrote other works. In considering the whole development of medieval philosophy one thinks first of all perhaps of its enormous indebtedness to the Greeks. No one has a better right to sum up the entire

[1] *Med. Mind*, II, pp. 162-163.

period than Haskins, and as he has observed: "It is perhaps evading the question to say that the mediaeval mind had a natural affinity for Aristotle, since this mind had been early formed on the Aristotelian logic of Boethius; but it is true that the later centuries turned with avidity to Aristotle's dialectic and stretched themselves on the frame of his thought."[1] Overlooking for a moment the problem as to whether the frame served as a couch or a rack, we may well ask why the later centuries showed this tendency. Why, unless for the reason that the habit was already established, and from long years of discipline a suspicion of anything less systematic was ingrained. At any time it is easy to forget how much one's thinking is conditioned by the presuppositions and method of approach, indeed by the type of logic, which the fashion of the period takes for granted and inculcates in its training. The air may be saturated with all sorts of ideas that have long been regarded as axiomatic and can rarely be traced to their real source. In the Middle Ages, however, the way is plainer; the general indebtedness on all sides to the instruction or the bare hints received from Boethius is apparent.

In the first place, when learning was scarce his manuscripts were copied in comparative abundance. No properly equipped library was without one or more of his works. In the second place, what he wrote furnished the basis for education in various subjects in the schools and universities during the many centuries until the Renaissance, whatever modifications and crosscurrents changed the course of thought. The *Consolatio* itself—according to Gibbon's famous comment "a golden volume not unworthy of the leisure of Plato or Tully"[2]—has enjoyed a steady popularity until the present time, and occasionally

---

[1] *Renaissance of the Twelfth Century*, pp. 342-343.

[2] *Decline and Fall*, chap. xxxix (ed. J. B. Bury, London, 1901, IV, p. 201). It is only fair to note that Gibbon dealing with the subject-matter adds (p. 202): "Such topics of consolation, so obvious, so vague, or so abstruse, are ineffectual to subdue the feelings of human nature." Cf. Spence, *Notes and Queries*, 9th, II (1898), pp. 462-463.

has had a profound influence. Finally, through commentaries written by others on his various treatises, through quotation and borrowing, the tradition of Boethius has been maintained, indirectly perhaps but no less potently and in ways more subtle and in the present connection more significant.

The number of manuscripts of Boethius available at any one time in all the libraries of medieval Europe would be impossible now to ascertain. Apart from the question of ordinary wear and tear and the copies lost to us through burning, even the collections of medieval documents left to us to-day have not all been canvassed. Schepss recorded the fact that he knew of more than three hundred copies of the *Consolatio* alone; Engelbrecht speaks of almost four hundred. There are doubtless more. Of exceedingly popular works like Geoffrey of Monmouth's *Historia* there are about a hundred and ninety; of the *Roman de la Rose* some three hundred. When we remember the importance of the first of these documents in medieval romance, and that of the second in allegory— especially the allegory of the Court of Love, the meaning of these figures becomes clearer. From lists we know that the works of Boethius were found at Durham and York. For the latter we have the famous testimony of Alcuin. I quote the whole passage concerned, in West's translation, partly for its own interest as a list of outstanding authors in a library of the eighth century, and partly to show the arrangement:

> There shalt thou find the volumes that contain
> All of the ancient fathers who remain;
> There all the Latin writers make their home
> With those that glorious Greece transferred to Rome,—
> The Hebrews draw from their celestial stream,
> And Africa is bright with learning's beam.
>
> Here shines what Jerome, Ambrose, Hilary thought,
> Or Athanasius and Augustine wrought.
> Orosius, Leo, Gregory the Great,
> Near Basil and Fulgentius coruscate.

Grave Cassiodorus and John Chrysostom
Next Master Bede and learned Aldhelm come,
While Victorinus and Boethius stand
With Pliny and Pompeius close at hand.

Wise Aristotle looks on Tully near.
Sedulius and Juvencus next appear.
Then come [Albinus], Clement, Prosper too,
Paulinus and Arator. Next we view
Lactantius, Fortunatus. Ranged in line
Virgilius Maro, Statius, Lucan, shine.
Donatus, Priscian, Probus, Phocas start
The roll of masters in grammatic art.
Eutychius, Servius, Pompey, each extend
The list. Comminian brings it to an end.

There shalt thou find, O reader, many more
Famed for their style, the masters of old lore,
Whose many volumes singly to rehearse
Were far too tedious for our present verse.[1]

Manuscripts are recorded as being at Nevers, Freising, St. Gall, Lorsch, Reichenau, and Murbach, in the ninth century; at Fleury, Bobbio, and Cremona, in the tenth. At Durham, Richard de Bury, who celebrates at least himself as a lover of books, knew the *Consolatio* and *De Musica*, and could quote from them in his *Philobiblon*.

Boethius was on the shelves at Paris and Chartres and Cologne and many other places. Bishop Leofric presented a copy of the *Consolatio* in Latin and one in English to the Church and monastery of St. Peter's in Exeter, and of these the Latin is now to be seen in the Bodleian Library at Oxford. We cannot attempt here a systematic survey of even the important copies, or discuss their circulation in the distribution and reassembly of great libraries. A scholar of the ninth century asks a friend to lend him a copy of *De Musica* and hopes it will be accompanied with notes. Servatus Lupus of the same period acknowledges the loan of the commentary on the *Topics* of Cicero.

---

[1] West, *Alcuin and the Rise of the Christian Schools*, pp. 34-35. For the original see Dümmler, *Poet. Lat. Aevi Carolini*, MGH., 1, p. 203, ll. 1535-1561.

Dr. Dee, the Elizabethan Astrologer in England, mentions Planudes's Greek translation of the *Consolatio*, a copy of which he presented to the library of Cracow, and the *Arithmetica*, which he acquired from Bury St. Edmunds. The latter codex also contains the *De Musica*, and found its way to the Lambeth Palace library. It is safe to say that wherever there were good books in the Middle Ages there too could be found a copy of one or another of the works of Boethius. The observation that Haskins makes with special reference to the twelfth century may with justice be applied to the whole period: "Another group of essential books, 'without which no gentleman's library is complete,' comprised the transmitters —not transmuters!—of ancient learning: Martianus Capella, Priscian, Boethius, Isidore, and Bede." [1]

Apart from the fact of intensive study several of the *carmina* of the *Consolatio* were set to music at various times. What this may have meant in the way of disseminating the ideas or at least of making the book more widely known the reader may judge for himself. But advertisement of this kind was hardly necessary. The work was quoted *verbatim* in almost every connection, and, it is perhaps fair to say, thousands of times, if we may judge by the instances that have been listed. From casual reference and extensive borrowing, Boethius is everywhere recognized as an authority, fully as eminent as one of the Church Fathers, but more versatile than most of them. Hrotsvitha, Hincmar of Rheims, Gerhoh of Reichersberg, Petrus Cantor, Helinandus, Abailard, Alanus de Insulis, John of Salisbury, Walter Map, William of Malmesbury, Roger Bacon, Robert Holkot—one must call the roll of practically everyone of account in the Middle Ages if one is to include those who show indebtedness to him. Albertus Magnus and Thomas Aquinas had of course occasion to transmit much of his material to others in their lectures and treatises; on the other hand, Jean de Meun introduced

---

[1] *Renaissance of the Twelfth Century*, pp. 80-81. For a list dated about 1100 cf. *ibid.*, p. 7.

Plate 1, Boethius and Philosophy

extensive quotation into his part of the *Roman de la Rose,*
including the long passage on free will. Brunetto Latini,
to whom at one time a translation was attributed, borrowed
material for his *Tesoro*. Lists have been collected to
show numerous examples of specific indebtedness in Dante,
which appear in such a way as to show that he knew the
Consolatio thoroughly and embodied as well as quoted its
ideas. Boccaccio uses it in *Il Filostrato,* in the *De Genealogia Deorum*—that remarkable manual of mythology—
and elsewhere; and Chaucer shows almost constant evidence of what he derived from the same source. Lydgate
took over much, at least indirectly, through Boccaccio and
others; Gavin Douglas in Scotland acknowledges influence; the militant suffragist Christine de Pisan in France
pays proper tribute; and Giovanni Pontano and Pico della
Mirandola and others in Italy continue the same tradition.
It is significant that in the twelfth century Otto of Freising
uses the words of Boethius to say "that 'the greatest sol-
ace' in life is to be found in handling and thoroughly
learning all the teachings of philosophy. . . ." [1] As the
nineteenth-century Englishman flavoured his speech with
Horace, so the cultivated man of the Middle Ages found
it decorous or illuminating now and then to take a phrase
or two from the *Consolatio*.   In making an observation of
this kind Peiper nicely remarks: "Ita factum ut cum Ver-
gilio Horatio Lucano atque Statio Boetius penetraret in
consuetudinem hominum. . . ." [2] which we may render
as meaning that thus Boethius pervaded men's ordinary
intercourse.

But here a difficulty at once arises for him who would
further trace the philosopher's influence. When a medieval writer discusses a topic like true nobility or free will
in the language or at least according to the general argument of the *Consolatio*, we cannot tell to-day, so far as his
opportunity is concerned, whether he derived his thoughts

---

[1] *The Two Cities,* trans. C. C. Mierow, ed. A. P. Evans and C. Knapp, p. 90.
For the Latin see the Appendix to this chapter. The echo, though intentional, is
vague: cf. *Cons. Philos.* III, pr. i, 3-6.
[2] *Philos. Cons.,* p. lxiv.

from Chaucer or Dante or the *Roman de la Rose* or from Boethius himself; for they all contain something of the same material. But it hardly matters after all whether the borrowing is direct or indirect; the moral is pretty much the same. Of the words of Boethius it may be said more truly than of most that he scattered them not in ears "but grafted them to grow there and to bear."

With the invention of printing it was clear that there had been no waning of interest at the coming of the Renaissance. The *Consolatio* was first printed, apparently at Savigliano, in 1471. What seems to be the first edition furnished with a commentary (and a translation) left the press of Coburger in Nürnberg in 1473. Other printings or editions appeared frequently thereafter, at Toulouse, Cologne, Louvain, Ghent, Lyons, Venice, Basel, Strassburg, and elsewhere, usually with a commentary, and often with a translation. The first collected edition of the works of Boethius appeared at Venice in 1491-1492. Of later editions of the *Consolatio* we should note that of Vallinus in 1656 (of which a copy found its way into Dean Swift's library), and that of Obbarius in 1843, in both of which the apparatus is of historical importance. The first edition to be published in England is that of the seventeenth-century "S. E. M.," whom, as we shall see later, we now recognize as Edward Spencer. The collected edition in Migne's *Patrologia Latina* appeared in 1847. Scholarly treatment marked the Teubner text of Peiper's *Consolatio* with extensive apparatus, and the edition in the Loeb Library in 1918, as well as that of Fortescue and Smith in 1925.

But entirely aside from popular enthusiasm for the great book, there was a professional attitude sustained throughout the Middle Ages in intellectual circles, where not only the words of Holy Writ but those of other important volumes were subjected to closest scrutiny. Nothing could have been more generally effective in spreading the influence of a writer, as well as in bearing witness to his standing in the community, than the commentaries which his words evoked, and which in turn carried his *dicta* into new channels to draw the fresh attention of the universities. Of these portentous works Dr. Silk, the latest student in the field, remarks: ". . . so from the ninth to the fifteenth century the works of commentators on the *Consolatio* gradually acquired an importance almost overshadowing that of the utterances of Boethius himself. The student's logical approach to the *Consolatio* was through a commentary. There he found strange words, allusions to Greek myth and Roman history, etc., all amply explained; Boethius' Greek quotations rendered in easy Latin; most interesting and important of all: discussion of the religious, philosophical, and scientific matters broached by Boethius, the latter accompanied by illustrative charts and diagrams." [1]

Before the tenth century there were at least two commentaries on the *Consolatio* which doubtless furnished the groundwork for those that followed. One has been confidently attributed to Remigius of Auxerre. Moreover, there was the famous work of Servatus Lupus of Ferrières (ninth century) on the *metra*. When King Alfred came to write his translation he had the help not only of such documents as were then in existence and, as Schepss has made clear, made use of some of them, but also of the suggestions of the Welsh monk, Asser, his biographer, to whom indeed a commentary has been attributed. In the tenth century Bruno of Corvey, as we have already noticed, wrote a treatise on the ninth poem of the third book for the edification of Bishop Bovo, attempting to show that in these verses there was much to found against the Catholic faith of its author. In the twelfth century we have the work of the gifted grammarian William of Conches (a disciple of Bernard of Chartres whom John of Salisbury described as a great Platonist), of special significance because he taught in the schools of Paris as well as at Chartres, and for one of his students had John of Salisbury. It may also be significant that he wrote a

---

[1] *Trans. and Proc. American Philol. Assoc.*, LXII (1931), p. xxxvii.

commentary on Plato's *Timaeus*. William's study of the *Consolatio*, based on what had gone before in the way of treatises, was extensively utilized by Nicholas Trivet, an English Dominican of the late thirteenth and early fourteenth centuries in Norfolk, who was associated with the universities of Paris and Oxford. According to Jourdain what Trivet wrote "occupe une place honorable parmi les travaux qui attestent l'érudition de l'auteur et son activité laborieuse."[1] He also wrote commentaries on the Scriptures, St. Augustine, Valerius Maximus, Aristotle, Seneca, Ovid, Juvenal, and others, and his work was known abroad even in the fifteenth century. His material on the *Consolatio* was used by Chaucer in his translation of the book, and had direct influence on the famous commentary long attributed to Thomas Aquinas but now generally assigned to Thomas Walleys (c. 1332), which in turn was enormously important partly perhaps on account of the great name attached to it. Other significant works of the kind include that formerly ascribed to Robert Grosseteste, the thirteenth-century Bishop of Lincoln, and that of Pierre d'Ailly (1350-1420).

Besides these studies there were others devoted to the interpretation of the *Opuscula Sacra*, of which the first was probably that attributed to John the Scot. Others have been assigned to Alcuin, Remigius of Auxerre, Hincmar of Rheims, and Gilbert de la Porrée. Gilbert's story is illuminating. According to Poole he is "the first medieval writer who was at once taken as a recognised authority on logic, as the immediate successor of Boethius and Isidore. . . ."[2] John of Salisbury heard Gilbert lecture on logic and divinity, and says of him that he "was a man of the clearest intellect, and of the widest reading; he had spent some sixty years in study and the exercise of literature, and was so ripe in liberal culture as to be surpassed by no one, rather it was believed that in all things he ex-

---

[1] "Des Commentaires Inédits de G. de Conches et de N. Triveth," etc., in *Excursions Historiques*, p. 46.
[2] *Illustrations of the Hist. of Med. Thought*, p. 132.

celled all men." [1] His commentary on *De Trinitate* was attacked by no less a figure than the great St. Bernard of Clairvaux, who, it appears, was not so much interested in intellectual freedom as in the faith of his people.

Gilbert's material was based ultimately on the work of John the Scot, but certain doctrines brought suspicion upon him, especially his distinction between "substance" and "subsistence." Did he mean to imply a difference, say, between "God" and "Divinity"? A Council was summoned at Paris to examine him for heresy in 1147. Whether unworthy motives moved the prosecution, whether indeed Bernard himself was fairly actuated, writes John of Salisbury, opinion varied; but John's personal judgment is that a man of such sanctity is moved by a zeal for God, and that a bishop of such importance and learning as Gilbert de la Porrée would not set down anything in his writings from which Bernard would have to dissent. Adam du Petit Pont, a logician, and Hugh of Champfleury, later chancellor to the King of France, also Bishop of Soissons, supported the charge. For his own witnesses Gilbert called men who were "once his scholars, now his fellow-bishops." Then the Commentary itself was sought, but could not be found. The Council adjourned for a year. To the prosecution were added Robert of Melun and Peter Lombard. John of Salisbury and Thomas Becket were present. Poole observes that the conflict was really one between the Pope and the cardinals, on Gilbert's side, and the prelates of France and England, on the other.

Gilbert was exonerated and his Commentary too. He wrote a new preface to prove its harmony with the confession of faith which St. Bernard had put before the Council. Bernard and his followers did not own themselves defeated, but the accusation was withdrawn. The modern may find the whole dispute trivial, and yet an important principle was involved. Perhaps the last echo

---

[1] *Ibid.*, p. 188. For the Latin see the *Hist. Pontif.*, ed. Poole, cap. 8, pp. 17-18, and the Appendix to the present chapter.

of this dramatic scene may be heard in Matthew Arnold's sonnet on "the Divinity," in which he refers to Gilbert as "the obscure opposer" Bernard "outweighed."[1] For Arnold the issue has still some degree of vitality. How like him to insist (against Gilbert): "Wisdom and goodness, they are God!"

Among the group of the prosecution was a certain Clarenbaldus, a student of Hugo of St. Victor and Thierry of Chartres, who was provost of the Church of Arras 1152-1153, and who wrote a commentary on *De Trinitate* to oppose certain opinions of Gilbert and favor Bernard. It appeared from time to time in editions of Boethius, but for genuine importance during the next fifty years did not compare with Gilbert's. Finally we must mention the work of Thomas Aquinas, which appeared in the next century, and is genuinely his own.

The significance of all these commentaries can hardly be overestimated at the present time. As the history of medieval philosophy receives more thorough investigation, there is little doubt that the far-reaching influence of such documents in education and thought will draw more and more attention. Dr. Silk tells us that the body of manuscripts to be surveyed is "immense." Just as the commentary of Servius on Virgil was of use to Dante, and that of Trivet on the *Consolatio* helped Chaucer, so all through the development of the discussion of the schoolmen these studies had their place, and without doubt profoundly affected the formation of thought in the period. Possibilities of this sort will become more apparent as we consider the place of Boethius in medieval education and see the importance of his own commentaries on Aristotle.

It is with much hesitation that the present writer approaches that subject. In itself it is one for several volumes. Full consideration of it is dependent not only on a thorough knowledge of the schools and their libraries, but also on an extensive understanding of the medieval arts and sciences. In a field, then, where there is still

[1] *Poems*, p. 398.

much pioneer work to be done, a preliminary sketch must
have its own serious defects, and these, we hope, will be
pardoned.   Rashdall has pointed out in his account of the
universities that in a general way the arts were known
from three writers: Martianus Capella, Cassiodorus, and
Boethius; and we may observe that from Boethius Cassiodorus himself derives somewhat.   About these two
Cesare Foligno has made the not wholly flattering remark
that "with them there became established the peculiar
tendency of later Roman culture to reduce into set schemes
the sum total of what the ancients knew and the men of
the time could use," [1] a comment that seems more sugges-
tive than accurate.   How far Boethius penetrated the
minds of scholars we may infer from the complaint of the
eleventh-century Otloh that sometimes clerks gave more
credence to him than to Holy Scripture.   It is like St.
Gregory's objection to classical studies: the same lips
cannot sound the praises of Jupiter and the praises of
Christ.   Even women, says Specht in his history of education, diligently studied the pages of these writers.

A modern tribute to Boethius observes that his "educational writings had profound importance" and that his
"books on music, arithmetic and Euclid, his commentaries
on the *Isagoge* of Porphyry—an introduction to Aristotle
which nearly every student used—his works on logic and
his translations of Aristotle, imperfectly known for a long
time as they were, made Boethius the greatest name
among the teachers of the Middle Ages. . . ." [2]   It is
not too much thus to divert the praise commonly bestowed
on the Arabian scholars and say that Boethius introduced
the knowledge of Aristotle in the western world.   To his
translations men turned from the beginning of the period
to the end; not, ordinarily at least, to the renderings of
Avicenna and Averroes.   In the early centuries his version of the *De Interpretatione* (the *Perihermeneias,* as it
is usually called in medieval lists), the *Categories,* and the

---

[1] *Latin Thought during the Middle Ages,* pp. 46-47.
[2] Mallet, *History of the University of Oxford,* I, pp. 6-7.

Isagoge, were known and used; his rendering of the other logical books of the *Organon* came to light in the second quarter of the twelfth century as the "New Logic." An explanation for this generally recognized fact is offered by Haskins: "One may easily suppose that in an age which had use for only elementary logic . . . the advanced treatises fell into neglect and the manuscript tradition was correspondingly attenuated. In the revival of dialectic in the twelfth century men begin to seek additions to the store of logical writings and they discover the Boethian text."[1] With evidence from the manuscript itself Haskins suggests that the version referred to by Robert of Torigny as the "antiquior translatio" is this text. But in the thirteenth century Roger Bacon could still say of the translations: "We do not now possess either the half or better part."[2]

While it is true, however, that our author's name will be primarily associated with the tradition of Aristotle, and, as we have seen, the sympathy of the Middle Ages was primarily in that direction, his contribution did not end there. It is important to remember that the *Consolatio* means to the period not only something of Aristotle's metaphysics but also a good deal of Plato's *Timaeus.* Of the latter, A. E. Taylor remarks that the first two-thirds were known in the Latin of Chalcidius, ". . . the other two principal sources being apparently the *Consolatio* of Boethius and the exposition of Cicero's *Somnium Scipionis* by Macrobius, both works in which the *Timaeus* is very largely drawn upon. This explains why Platonism means to the great schoolmen of the thirteenth century principally the *Timaeus.* . . ."[3] Speaking of the influence of Boethius, John Burnet says: ". . . it is here we find the earliest point of contact between English literature and Platonism."[4] To this consideration should be added another, namely, that here one

---

[1] *Studies in the Hist. of Med. Science,* p. 233.
[2] *Opus Majus,* trans. Burke, I, 30; for the Latin see the edition of Bridges, I, 27.
[3] *Commentary on Plato's Timaeus,* p. 2.
[4] *Essays and Addresses,* p. 269.

who had a taste for Neoplatonism would find something not wholly uncongenial though much modified. Many of his ideas harmonize with those of the pseudo-Dionysius; when they reappear in Dante's *Divine Comedy* it is hard to tell from what source they really came.

Secular education in the schools and universities dealt with the Trivium—grammar, rhetoric, and logic or dialectic. The classics including Boethius were studied in the twelfth century at Tegernsee with an apparatus of grammatical and linguistic exegesis. His rendering of Aristotle was used for rhetoric and logic. Roger Bacon cites the *Disciplina Scholarium* as evidence that Boethius placed a proper emphasis on the knowledge of terms. As I have already indicated, we now recognize that this work was mistakenly attributed to him, popular though it was; but it cites his Aristotle and Porphyry for textbook purposes. In the allegorical *Battle of the Seven Arts*, written by the thirteenth-century trouvère Henri d'Andeli, it is exceedingly interesting to find our author as the champion of Dame Logic and her cohorts against Grammar. This work represents a medieval battle of the books, an educational controversy of first-rate significance for an understanding of the period. Aristotle on the side of Logic makes Grammar tumble backward. Persius, Juvenal, Horace, Virgil, Lucan, Statius, Sedulius, Propertius, Prudentius, Arator, Homer, and Terence, all smite Aristotle, but he stands "firm as a castle on a hill." Priscian tries to beat out his eyes; but the Old and New Logic, Ethics, Necromancy, Medicine, and others, with Sir Boethius and Sir Macrobius "Dressed in a caitiff garb" and Porphyry too come on a run to bring aid. Dame Grammar is defeated, but the author hopes that scholars will return to her, as was the manner when "Henri d'Andeli was born." It is a fundamental problem of culture we find laboured in this work. It is the strife of the Aristotelians against the Platonists, scientific against "liberal" scholarship, the ancients against the moderns, *mutatis mutandis*, a strife that was reawakened centuries later in Oxford and Cam-

bridge. As the editor, Professor Paetow, notices, it is
significant that Logic, not Theology, is the commander of
the forces of Paris which here overwhelm the authors
of Orléans led by Grammar. Here too we see the ex-
citement caused by the "new Aristotle," and obtain a clue
to the contemporary fashion of scholastic discipline, especially in the change of temper in the twelfth and thirteenth centuries.

The part played by Boethius in the history of dialectic
is really fundamental. In this field, as a great authority
on the subject, Dr. Prantl, remarks, one can easily observe "how often they went back to Boethius and no further." [1] At one time or another his versions of the prior
and posterior *Analytics*, his translation of the *Isagoge* of
Porphyry, and his commentaries, were generally used.
As we have seen, the Old Logic—comprising the *De
Interpretatione* and the *Categories*—was studied in the
early Middle Ages. These, Richard de Bury tells us in
the fourteenth century, beardless boys gabbled "with
childish stammering." [2] The New Logic—the *Analytics*,
the *Topics*, and the *Elenchi*—was added in the period
from the twelfth century on. At Rheims, however, in
the tenth century Gerbert of Aurillac used the Porphyry,
the *De Interpretatione*, and the *Topics*—more, says Taylor, than any man before him or for a hundred and fifty
years after. Most important of all, perhaps, he adopted
the Aristotelian division of philosophy into theoretical
and practical, which afterward spread to many other students and obtained generally. The praise then which he
wrote for Boethius, in the inscription to which I have referred, came from a scholar whose own works testify to
his devotion:

[1] *Gesch. der Logik im Abendlande*, I, p. 679: "Allbekannt ist es, von welchem
ausserordentlichen Einflusse auf das Mittelalter die Werke des Boethius . . .
waren, und wir werden uns im weiteren Verlaufe der Geschichte der Logik noch
hinreichend davon überzeugen können, wie oft man auf Boethius, und nicht weiter
zurück, recurrirte."

[2] Trans. Thomas, *The Love of Books*, p. 69 (cap. ix). For this reference I am
indebted to Miss Waddell.

Roma potens dum iura suo declarat in orbe,
Tu pater et patriæ lumen, Seuerine Boeti,
Consulis officio rerum disponis habenas,
Infundis lumen studiis et cedere nescis
Græcorum ingeniis. Sed mens diuina coercet
Imperium mundi. . . .[1]

Gerbert shone in zeal and wisdom, we are told, and restored the study of the old philosophers.

But the most far-reaching contribution of Boethius is yet to be mentioned. From a sentence in his translation of Porphyry, together with his commentary thereon, sprang the great controversy among the schoolmen which divided them into so-called realists and nominalists. Beginning in the ninth century with John the Scot it continued with Roscellinus and Abailard, and lasted at least until the fourteenth century with William of Occam. Do "genera" and "species" have what we should call an objective existence? The details of this long debate must be followed elsewhere, but anyone may guess how fundamentally important it is. In the twelfth century Godfrey of St. Victor looked back over the fray and complained:

> Sits Boethius quite stunned by this disputation,
> Listening to this and that subtle explanation,
> But to side with this or that shows no inclination,
> Nor presumes to give the case sure adjudication.[2]

Which is as much as to say that, in his opinion, Boethius sat comfortably on the fence. Boethius, however, was a realist, as we discover in *De Trinitate*, ii, 42 ff. How much of the logic of Thomas Aquinas is to be inferred

---

[1] *Œuvres,* ed. Olleris, pp. 294 f.

[2] Rand, *Founders of the M.A.,* p. 146. For the Latin see Godfrey's *Fons Philosophie,* ed. Charma, p. 42 (st. 59):

> Assidet Boetius stupens de hac lite
> Audiens quid hic et hic asserat perite
> Et quid cui faueat non discernit rite
> Non presumit soluere litem diffinite.

The passage is quoted by Hauréau, *Hist. de la Philos. Scholast.,* I, p. 120.

from his method of dealing with universals? Properly, then, Dame Philosophy appears in sculpture at Laon and at Sens as he represented her! Who had a better right to tell us how she really looks? In the Quadrivium his contribution was equally important, especially in the fields of arithmetic and music. Of the first, a modern writer remarks that the *"De Arithmetica* of Boethius held its place as an authoritative textbook for a thousand years after its first appearance in 502; the printed editions issued after 1488 were innumerable."[1] It is literally true that evidence for the use of the book appears throughout the entire period. What seems like an extravagant statement is only another way of saying with Specht that "The common instructor of all these writers [Bede, Alcuin, Rabanus, Helperich, and others] in arithmetic was Boethius, from whose *Institutio Arithmetica*—a translation of the Arithmetic of Nicomachus—the Middle Ages mainly formed their knowledge of the art of numbers."[2] The *Computus* of Rabanus Maurus was thus derived. It must be admitted that the use of Boethius was common in the early period, and that the treatises of Gerbert assumed an important place later, as the Abbé Clerval points out; but we already know how much Gerbert himself was indebted to his master. Hrotsvitha also borrowed his learning in arithmetic and music for her *Paphnutius* and *Sapientia*. Honorius of Autun in his allegory *De Animae Exilio et Patria*, tells how the soul, exiled from its true fatherland Sapientia, finds its way back on the road Scientia:

. . . scientia enim in rebus physicis: sapientia uero consideratur in Diuinis. Per hanc uiam gradiendum est non passibus corporis, sed affectibus cordis. Haec quippe uia ducit ad patriam tendentes

---

[1] Adamson, "Education," in Hearnshaw's *Med. Contrib. to Mod. Civilization*, p. 204.

[2] *Gesch. des Unterrichtswesens*, p. 130: "Der gemeinsame Lehrer aller dieser Schriftsteller war für die Arithmetik Boetius, aus dessen *institutio arithmetica*, einer Uebersetzung von Nikomachs Arithmetik, überhaupt das Mittelalter seine Kenntnisse in der Rechenkunst schöpfte."

per decem artes, et libros sibi adhaerentes, et quasi per totidem
ciuitates et uillas sibi seruientes.[1]

In the city of Arithmetic "Boëtio docente, par et impar
numerus multipliciter se complicant." In the city of
Music a chorus partly of youths and partly of their elders
instructed in the doctrine of Boethius praises God. The
full allegorical, tropological, and anagogical meanings of
this story are set before us, and the dire results of remain-
ing in exile. By the Arts, we gather, one is brought
home to the full wisdom of Holy Scripture; incidentally
we have here a striking testimony to the importance of
Boethius. Somewhat similarly in the twelfth-century
Apocalypsis of Bishop Golias, when Pythagoras leads the
dreamer to another world where he sees Priscian, Aristotle, Tullius, Ptolemy, and Euclid, "Boetius was there,
and did his nomber tell."[2] Emile Mâle is correct in his
suggestion that Boethius may be the figure representing
arithmetic in the sculpture of the west porch at Chartres.
In Gregory Reisch's fifteenth-century Tower of Learning
he appears with the inscription that identifies him with this
specialty.

In geometry too he was an authority, and here again
Alcuin and Gerbert made use of him. The latter also
refers to his work "de astrologia"; in the English pageant
to honor the entry of Prince Arthur in 1501 he appears
in the guise of astronomer. But of all the Arts it was in
music perhaps that he held the least disputed sway, and
in a "royal entry" of 1432 in England the personification
is represented with "Boece, her clerk." Here once again
Specht ventures to speak superlatively of his contribution:
"The teacher of the Middle Ages in music was Boethius."[3] It is interesting to remember that Chaucer's

[1] Pez, *Thesaurus Anecd.*, II, pt. 1, cols. 227-234 for the whole allegory. The
quotation is taken from col. 228 A-B. See also Migne, *Patr. Lat.*, cols. 1241-1246.

[2] Wright, *Latin Poems commonly attributed to Walter Mapes*, p. 272, translated in the reign of Elizabeth or in that of James. For the Latin see *Die Apokalypse*, ed. Strecker, p. 18, st. 11.

[3] *Gesch.*, p. 143: "Der Lehrer des Mittelalters in der Musik war Boetius."
He shows how many other works were based on *De Musica*.

eagle in the *House of Fame* has evidently been taught from *De Musica*, and the greatest praise that the fox in the *Nun's Priest's Tale* can bestow on Chantecler's crowing is to say that he has in music "moore feelynge" than had "Boece, or any that kan synge."[1] The textbook was read at St. Gall, Chartres, and many other places, and its use continued well into the modern period.

At this point we may stop to consider some of the places where, as we have ample evidence to show, the various books written by our author were utilized. Walter of Speyer tells us that in the cathedral school of his town in the tenth century the reading included the usual classics, Martianus Capella, and the *Consolatio*. At St. Gall the situation is pretty much the same according to Ekkehard IV, and it is well known that Boethius manuscripts were often copied and used there. The Abbot Grimald (841-871) augmented the cloister library out of his own collection, contributing works of Alcuin, Augustine, Rabanus Maurus, Virgil, Vegetius, and others, and notably the *Consolatio*. Notker Labeo not only translated the *Consolatio*, but compiled a textbook on rhetoric with excerpts from Boethius; there too were known the *Arithmetica*, *De Musica*, and other works. It is interesting to have Ekkehard's eulogy of the author, if the ascription of the following verses is correct:

> . . . requiescas, sancte Boeti,
> cuncta docendo pia socio sermone sophia
> qui bybliothecas uestisti lumine cecas.
> tandem pro Christi nec amore pati timuisti.[2]

The scholar, then, did not forget the martyr. Thus in one of the earliest and greatest of medieval centres of education the works of our author were of outstanding importance, and clearly recognized as such.

Moving elsewhere we find a similar state of things. In Paris the *De Interpretatione*, Porphyry, the logical

---

[1] *Cant. Tales*, B. 4483-4484.
[2] *Zeits. für deutsches Altertum*, XIV (1869), pp. 72-73, ed. E. Dümmler.

works, the Arithmetic, *De Musica,* all are used. We
have already seen what Gerbert did at the restored school
at Rheims. The studies of the Abbé Clerval show us
the importance of Boethius in medieval Chartres. At
Montpellier his works are used with those of Terence,
Virgil, Cicero, and Juvenal, as a basis for the *ars oratoria.*
At Toulouse the *Divisions* or the first three books of the
Topics are a part of the assignment for the four years in
the arts course. At Oxford the Old Logic was to be read
for the bachelor's degree; the *Topics* was not required.
The course for the Master of Arts included a study of the
Arithmetic, *De Musica,* and logical works, which held at
least until the fifteenth century. One difficulty in our
survey is that we cannot consider the detailed history of
each institution—to indicate, for example, when Boethius
was introduced, and how far his works were used in comparison with those of other available authors. We may
recall, however, that most of the authors who were consulted were nearly always indebted to him, and thus we
may gain a proportionate sense of his influence. So we
might go on: at Vienna, Paderborn, in fact all over
Europe, his works were cited for study. On July 31,
1438, the Chancellor of Oxford issued an order to break
into the room of one Master T. Cooper in Brasenose Hall.
Here among other books were found the Porphyry and a
commentary of Boethius on Aristotle. So we catch a
glimpse of the typical student's collection.

The situation in the universities is parallel to what we
find when we investigate the lives and special interests of
the great scholars. Trained from the start as they were
in textbooks written by Boethius, they went on to careers
in which in most cases they had frequent recourse to one
or another of his works, and perhaps on the side found
diversion and inspiration in the *Consolatio.* We know of
Alcuin's interest, who was introduced to our author
through the works of Isidore of Seville. We have also
noted the indebtedness of Rabanus Maurus, Albertus
Magnus, and Thomas Aquinas, too subtle and extensive

to be traced adequately here. To these names must be added that of Michael Scot, certainly one to conjure with, and Roger Bacon, who finds Boethius a master of the languages of the original documents from which he translates, and Grosseteste a master of the sciences. Grosseteste himself was a disciple. Here too we should mention Alexander Neckam, a great figure in medieval education who wrote of Boethius as follows. He is speaking of Pavia:

> Fertur in hac magnus dormire Boetius urbe,
>   Felix sub tanto consule Roma fuit.
> Transtulit interpres quam plura uolumina fidus,
>   Insuper obscurum luce serenat opus.
> Qui clarum sidus logices commenta peregit,
>   Qui magnæ fructus utilitatis habent.
> Urbs felix radiat tam claris clara patronis,
>   Exultat tantis curia summa uiris.[1]

Most of all perhaps we take pleasure in the memory of John of Salisbury, trained in the logical works, onlooker at the trial of Gilbert de la Porrée, who wrote in discriminating praise of the works of our author: "Without difficulty he is profound in doctrine, without levity striking in expression, fervent in speech, effective in demonstration."[2] Eulogies of this sort are not uncommon in medieval treatises, and lists of them have been compiled by editors of the *Consolatio*, celebrating its writer's philosophy, intellect, and wisdom. Dante, we recall, placed him in the *Paradiso* with the doctors, Aquinas, Albert, and Dionysius.

Allusions of this variety, however, with any number of parallel passages cited to prove influence have something of the weakness of statistics, which notoriously may prove anything or nothing. The reader is likely to suspect that

---

[1] *De Laudibus*, v, 405-412 (*Neckam, Rolls Series*, pp. 449-450).

[2] "Sine difficultate profundus est in sententiis, in uerbis sine leuitate conspicuus, orator uehemens, efficax demonstrator. . . ." *Policrat.*, vii, 15. For the whole passage see the Appendix to this chapter.

Plate 2, BOETHIUS THE TEACHER

the cards are stacked against him, especially if the case in question is one of the first magnitude. It will be worth while, then, to examine for a moment some of the obvious effects which the writings of Boethius had on the prevailing ideas of medieval philosophy, to see how much his work counted, not merely as a discipline in education, not merely for verbal suggestion in literature, but in the intellectual scheme.

From the preceding discussion it is already clear that hints from Boethius led to the medieval classification of the sciences, or fields of intellectual activity. The general effect of his books, moreover, was to direct thought to the patterns or formulae of Aristotle. The problem of universals, to which his translation of Porphyry's *Isagoge* and his commentaries ultimately gave rise, had to do with the whole approach to the problem of reality. But down through the centuries after his day, in the scope of what concerned physical and metaphysical man, scarcely anything occupied the attention of the philosophers more steadily than what is really the central problem of the *Consolatio:* chance in its relation to God and Divine foresight, and in relation to man and his longing to shape his own destiny. Does the fault really lie in the stars or external circumstance or in ourselves that we are underlings? Whenever a writer attempts to justify the ways of God to man he has to face this question. Aristotle argued that chance provides for the free will of man, which a ruthless and ineluctable destiny will not permit. Borrowing the Neoplatonic idea of the spiritual cosmos as an orb with God as centre and Fate in control of the circumference, Boethius suggested that Fate or chance— all that is apparently casual and changeable—is in the last analysis under the control of a rational God. This is the theme of the argument in the *Consolatio,* IV, pr. vi, 63 ff. His solution was acceptable to Albertus Magnus. Thomas Aquinas insists, of course, that to regard Fortuna as an independent living reality is erroneous, because all things are ruled by God Himself; and yet his conclusions are perfectly harmonious with the same figure. Dante's conception, by which chance is personified as the ministering angel of God (*Inferno*, vii, 67 ff.) is a literary derivative based on the same solution. How many times Fortuna appears in medieval literature in passages inspired directly or indirectly by Boethius no one can probably tell, and few who have not looked into the subject can remotely guess.

As a logical consequence from the ideas in the *Consolatio* the proposition holds that the free will of man has some reality, without destroying the force of God's grace which is effected through external or internal circumstance. This the orthodox solution is found with variations from Augustine to Thomas Aquinas and still later, sometimes in combat with the libertarianism of Pelagius and sometimes opposed to the other extreme of determinism. Into this matter Boethius goes with comparative brevity, but with singular balance he helps to establish what became the Christian doctrine. In this connection he also took what was to be the normal position with respect to stellar influence. As Thorndike observes, "his constant rhapsodizing over the stars and heavens would lead [Christians] to regard the science of the stars as second only to divine worship. Indeed, his position was the usual one in the subsequent Middle Ages." [1] For him as for others—above all Dante— planetary or stellar influence is only one form of the general distribution of Divine grace, and involves the same problems with respect to free will. But with him as with Dante and those who held to orthodoxy on this point, although God never for an instant loses control of the whole universe, mankind also has a sufficient degree of free will to retain moral responsibility. Nothing could more profoundly affect any interpretation of the meaning of life than the solution one way or another of this question. Its inferences in the field of aesthetics and criticism cannot here be traced. The answer adopted by

[1] *Magic and Experimental Science*, I, p. 622.

Boethius is the answer of the Middle Ages as a whole and of Christianity.

The discussion of free will in the *Consolatio* was directly taken over by Jean de Meun for his part of the *Roman de la Rose* (ll. 17302 ff.). Dante was extensively influenced by it. Chaucer incorporated a long section of it in the soliloquy of Troilus in *Troilus and Criseyde* (iv, 960 ff.), where the despairing young lover tries to put all the blame for his affairs on God or circumstance, and omits the corrective supplied by Boethius and implicit in the Epilogue of the poem itself. The argument of the *Consolatio* that nobility is a moral matter and depends on character rather than family or wealth (II, m. vii and elsewhere) is extended by Dante in the *Convivio* (IV, *canz.* iii) and in the *Purgatorio* (vii, 120 ff.); and from him in turn it is borrowed by Chaucer's Wife of Bath in her story of the loathly lady and her sermon on democratic ideals delivered to her reluctant husband. So one might follow the social influence of Boethius, apart from strictly philosophical interests. In Chaucer's case it is possible that his enthusiasm for the "common profit," that slogan of fourteenth- and fifteenth-century socialism, derived something from the *Consolatio*, as his friend the poet Deschamps was led from time to time to write on the perils of wealth. Deschamps never seems quite to get away from his memories of Boethius.

But it is impossible to arrive at a complete estimate of his influence on writers like Dante and Chaucer. The philosophical implications which these writers found in the *Consolatio* and which grew in their minds with tangible results are often hard to describe. Murari has suggested how much kinship Dante found in the political prisoner and spiritual exile of so many centuries before his own. Boethius and Dante both took comfort in philosophy and celebrated the personification in much the same way. In the *Convivio* (ii, 16) we see Dame Philosophy as a gentle lady "full of sweetness," and when we think of Dante and the Beatrice of the *Divine Comedy* we may agree that here is another and even more important parallel. The figure of the orb of destiny, whether the great poet got it from Plotinus, Boethius, or the pseudo-Dionysius, crowns the *Paradiso* (xxii, 55-63, etc.), in which we find the flaming souls aspiring to that centre of stability and eternity which is God. Hitherto the universe appeared with earth as the centre and the heavens around that; but now in eternal values all is turned inside out, and the ephemeral and earthly are farthest from the true centre. Probably no single author or work had so profound an effect on Chaucer as Boethius and the *Consolatio*. Not only did he reproduce sections of the latter in his *Balade* on Fortune, in the *Former Age*, in *Gentilesse*, in *Trouthe*, and elsewhere, but obviously he knew it thoroughly and quoted it at will. In the *Troilus* it furnishes the underlying philosophy, and lends the poem dignity as well as beauty in the passages celebrating love and deploring Fortune. The problem of chance is dealt with by Chaucer in Boethian terms more than once in his career. But of all this we shall say something further when we discuss his translation of the *Consolatio* itself.

So in the thirteenth and again in the fourteenth century a poet of first-rate importance shows deeply and extensively the influence of Boethius in his intellectual as well as his artistic life. It is a perilous thing when a man has such power over his fellows. But clearly he led them in the right paths for their own good and for many of the riches of the fruitful life. Of the *Consolatio* Burnet acknowledges that it is "the book that made [its author's] name precious to educated men for centuries, and which it is hardly an exaggeration to call the source of all that is best in the literature of western Europe." [1] In one or another of his works he gave hints or salutary discussion to help in solving the problems of the day. After all is there any other writer whose effect in so many departments of thought, in so many fields,

---

[1] *Essays and Addresses,* p. 268.

among so many varied writers, and over so wide a period, has been as extensive as his? In dealing with the different subjects touching medieval education much of his versatility, one may urge, is inherited from Plato and especially Aristotle; but aptitude was first required for transmitting their material. And he was not limited to these authors. His work on music, for example, carried his interest elsewhere; and this too has been important till modern times at Oxford and Cambridge. Small wonder that his sayings invaded the *florilegia* or books of extracts. With reference to the later medieval sermons and their allusions Dr. Owst observes, "We notice . . . the continued popularity of 'Boyicius, the grete clerke in hys time'. . . ."[1] Here too we must recall the large number of translations and imitations of the *Consolatio*, which form the subject of the following chapters, and which had their own contribution to make to literature and thought. Clearly this mass of evidence shows that we are unlikely to overestimate the significance of Boethius among the truly great of all time. Of his works men shall say, here is wisdom; and his words run to and fro like sparks among the stubble.

[1] *Literature and Pulpit in Med. England,* p. 86.

CHAPTER III

TRANSLATIONS OF THE CONSOLATIO

SAMUEL JOHNSON had a high opinion of the learned and illustrious Mrs. Elizabeth Carter, two of whose essays he published in the *Rambler*. Boswell's *Life* tells us that, according to Mr. Cave, Johnson advised Mrs. Carter to " 'undertake a translation of *Boethius de Cons.* because there is prose and verse, and to put her name to it when published.' "[1] Evidently this was a sufficiently distinguished task for a bluestocking of the period. In the same place we learn that Johnson himself translated effectively a part of III, m. ix; and one may suspect that a gentleman of the eighteenth century, particularly the great lexicographer, would find a quality suited to his taste in the *Consolatio Philosophiae*. But the fact that this advice was offered in the age of classicism is interesting when we recall that centuries before, in what is still sometimes referred to as the Dark Ages, William of Malmesbury comes pretty close to a smile at the idea of translating Boethius at all. In Asser's time, he admits, one needed such a version to interpret the text: "in those days it was necessary, in our days ridiculous."[2] Mrs. Carter did not, however, make the attempt, possibly because, as Boswell suspects, she thought the work would not have had a popular sale. One can hardly suppose that she was aware what a royal line she might have joined, or that she was right in her estimate of contemporary taste. King Alfred had made his version for the education of his subjects; Jean de Meun, decidedly an elegant man of letters in the thirteenth century, offered one in French, which was used beyond the limits of his country; Chaucer took great pains to make an accurate

[1] *Boswell's Life of Johnson,* I, p. 95.
[2] ". . . labore illis diebus necessario, nostris ridiculo." *De gestis pontif. Angl.,* ii, section 80 (ed. *Rolls Series,* p. 177).

46

rendering for the fourteenth century; and in the Renaissance Queen Elizabeth sustained her reputation for learning by trying her fluent pen in the same way.

Yet with these names the catalogue is by no means at an end. What the significance of the long history of translations from Boethius may really be we can at least guess. Not only writers of the first rank but minor poets and the other lesser geniuses who "sat under them in sees" found it advisable to make some sort of rendering of the *Consolatio* in the vernacular. Obviously there was a popular demand for the work, at least in many centuries, and it was not merely the demand of learning. For during most of the time under consideration the cultivated class knew enough Latin to get along without such assistance. Men wanted, therefore, not merely a reasonable knowledge of the book, but intimacy with it. That so many in all ages turn to philosophy for consolation is not, perhaps, surprising; but that they should turn to the form of it offered by Boethius in the sixth century is remarkable, especially when we observe that they went to the extent of putting his thoughts into their own words. There is a kind of impertinence involved in leading others to wisdom, unless one is very certain that the fountain is pure; but clearly these writers wanted to make the benefit accessible to others, lay as well as learned. One can imagine the careful use of some of those manuscripts, which also contained Jean de Meun's version or perhaps Chaucer's, with a commentary of some sort and an illumination or two by way of ornament. How richly they were prized! Were the philosophical treatises of Alcuin or Abailard or Thomas Aquinas translated before the nineteenth century? Not for popular sale in any case. But the *Consolatio Philosophiae* was pondered over and passed about for admiration in royal halls as well as in the gloom of a medieval study.

King Alfred

THE life of Alfred the Great was marked by a deeply religious dedication and by a love of his people. Because of both of these characteristics he included the *Consolatio* among the books that he translated or arranged to translate for his people's benefit. Stewart's words can hardly be bettered, that "It gives additional lustre to the name of Boethius that such a king as Alfred, inquiring after those books which might with most advantage be set within his subjects' reach, should have chosen the 'Consolation' to represent philosophy in the little library he was preparing for their use."[1] While one may recognize the truth of this statement, and add its counterpart that the King was not likely to escape Boethius during the ninth century, we may be tempted to observe that the choice contributes a certain lustre to Alfred himself. Of all his selections this was perhaps the best fitted to spread some idea of culture among his contemporaries. And there is another point of importance regarding the nature of his work itself which makes it have a special quality. This is what Professor Sedgefield calls the "personal note" in the translation, a note "such as we look for in vain in English literature for hundreds of years after."[2]

To understand this quality we must consider what we may learn of the King's temperament. What sort of man was he? I venture to say that in some ways his personality is clearer than that of any other man of equal antiquity. In any case his activity in political, philosophical, and literary fields showed the depth of his serious purpose. He went daily to Mass; he contributed to religious foundations; and he studied Holy Scripture. For many years, Asser tells us in his famous biography, he was the victim of an unknown malady, and suffered acutely from it. The *Consolatio* thus offered him the kind of food for reflection which a man of his temper

---

[1] *Boethius,* p. 171.
[2] *King Alfred's Version . . . Done into Modern Eng.,* p. viii.

would naturally seek. Simeon of Durham preserves for us the not unlikely item that Alfred used to repeat II, m. iv (*Quisquis uolet perennem*) by heart:

> Who with an heedful care
> Will an eternal seat prepare. . . .[1]

Small wonder that the book commended itself to him for general use; it was such a work as might furnish many a quotation for his own *Handbook*. According to William of Malmesbury, Asser helped him by making the original plainer to him with comments. According to the proem "King Alfred was the interpreter of this book, and turned it from book Latin into English, as it is now done. Now he set forth word by word, now sense from sense, as clearly and intelligently as he was able, in the various and manifold worldly cares that oft troubled him both in mind and in body."[2] It was indeed, as Professor Sedgefield further observes, "a love's labour. It satisfied his intellectual cravings and stimulated his uncultured but vigorous mind. . . ."[3] And clearly his purpose was mainly to give his people the same nutriment that he enjoyed.

In a previous chapter we have already considered the life of Boethius which Alfred sets forth in his preface. Perhaps the most pervasive change in his rendering, however, is the definitely Christian colouring which he introduced. He mentions Christ, and refers to Christian men and the angels and the devil. Instead of Dame Philosophy's appearing to him, we find Wisdom and sometimes Intelligence; Wisdom conducts the dialogue. For Boethius we sometimes have the Mind. Fate is properly Wyrd for the Old English, and Fortune becomes *woruldsælda* (a plural abstract noun). In place of five books with alternating prose and verse we have forty-two sections of prose with proem and epilogue. The change

---

[1] *Hist. Regum Angl.*, dccclxxxvii (ed. Surtees Soc., I, p. 60). Stewart and Rand, *Boethius*, p. 195.
[2] Sedgefield, *King Alfred's Version*, p. lvi.
[3] *Ibid.*, p. viii.

in substance is considerable: so much so that one might fairly describe the work as somewhat of a paraphrase with emendations and additions.   Alfred expands, for example, the story of Orpheus and Eurydice; he introduces new illustrations from history; comments, similes, and metaphors are brought into the narrative or developed.   The famous example of the *Ubi sunt* formula in Boethius—"Where now are the bones of Fabricius?"—becomes in the Old English "Where now are the bones of Weland?" for the sake, no doubt, of including the more familiar figure from Teutonic mythology:

Where now are the bones of the *famous and wise goldsmith, Weland? I call him wise, for the man of skill can never lose his cunning, and can no more be deprived of it than the sun may be moved from his station.*[1]

For some of his changes he derived suggestions, as we have seen, from the commentaries.   Thus the simile of the egg and the developed figure of the wheel of destiny owe something to this source.   The whole work is shorter than that of Boethius, despite these modifications; but it is cogent and vivid.   Whether or not one feels that Alfred has in some respects improved on his original, one point is clear: namely, that every touch of originality shows its author's concern to make the meaning entirely plain to his subjects.

Although we cannot be sure of the date of this performance, the general impression which the book gives is that of something done late in Alfred's career.   It shows a judicial and wise attitude toward life.   This quality we find, for instance, in his rendering of the first speech of Fortune:

"How wilt thou answer [Fortune] if she say to thee, 'Why dost thou reproach me, O Mind? Why art thou enraged against me? In what have I angered thee? 'Twas thou that first desiredst me, not I thee; thou didst set me on the throne of thy Creator, when thou lookedst to me for the good thou shouldst seek from

[1] Sedgefield, *King Alfred's Version*, p. 48.

*Him. Thou sayest I have deceived thee, but I may rather
answer that thou hast deceived me, seeing that by reason of thy
lust and thy greed the Creator of all things hath been forced to
turn away from me. Thou art indeed more guilty than I, both
for thine own wicked lusts and because owing to thee I am not
able to do the will of my Maker. He lent me to thee to enjoy
in accordance with His Commandments, and not to perform the
will of thine unlawful greed.*

"*Answer us both now,*" *said* [*Wisdom*], "*as thou wilt; both
of us await thine answer.*" [1]

Or we may consider the simile of the wheel of destiny,
replacing that of the orb in the original:

The wheels of a waggon turn upon its axle, *while the axle stands
still and yet bears all the waggon and guides all its movement.
The wheel turns round, and the nave next the wheel moves more
firmly and securely than the felly does. Now the axle is as it
were the highest good we call God, and the best men move next
unto God just as the nave moves nearest the axle. The middle
sort of men are like the spokes, for one end of each spoke is fast
in the nave, and the other is in the felly; and so it is with the
midmost man, at one time thinking in his mind upon this earthly
life, at another upon the divine life, as if he looked with one eye
heavenwards, and with the other earthwards . . . and so also
those men are most free from care, both in this present life of
tribulation and in the life to come, that are firmly fixed in God.*[2]

The figure is worked out in much more specific detail than
we have space to represent in quotation here. It is again
interesting to see that the King took such great pains to
make his symbolism comprehensible and to drive home
the moral. If he does not seem gifted with poetic expression, he is nevertheless moved with considerable zeal.

Among the works presented by Bishop Leofric to
Exeter Cathedral in the eleventh century was, as we have
noticed, the "Book of Boethius in English." Probably
this was a copy of Alfred's translation of the *Consolatio*.
To-day his version survives in two principal manuscripts:

[1] *Ibid.*, pp. 16-17.
[2] *Ibid.*, pp. 151-152.

one of the tenth century in the great Cotton collection in
the British Museum; the other of the twelfth century
in the Bodleian Library at Oxford. The first of these
was considerably damaged in the fire which did so much
harm to the Cotton manuscripts in 1731. But the seventeenth-century antiquary and scholar, the famous Dutch-
man, Francis Junius, had made a transcript of the
Bodleian manuscript, to which he had added important
variants from the Cotton version together with a copy
of the *metra* from that source. Thus we fortunately
have readings preserved from that manuscript before it
suffered injuries from the fire. Besides all this material,
we also have a fragment of a third manuscript discovered
by Professor Napier of Oxford in a leaf which at some
time previous had served as part of a bookbinding. In
the Cotton version, which is the oldest, the *carmina* of
Boethius are rendered in a metrical form (except for three
in prose, and omitting six altogether), while in the Bodleian manuscript these appear in a prose translation
(omitting the same six). Moreover, a verse proem has
been preserved in the readings of Junius from the Cotton
manuscript; in the Bodleian manuscript the proem is in
prose. Much controversy has been expended on the
authorship of these metrical portions, and entire agree-
ment has not yet been reached as to whether the King
wrote the verse as well as the prose. In his proem of the
Bodleian manuscript he states definitely that he first wrote
the prose and then turned it into verse; the metrical form
was almost certainly rendered on the basis of the other.
All in all it would seem that the burden of proof is on
those who would deny Alfred's authorship, especially
since to do so they must also demonstrate that he was not
the author of the proem in question.

The King's translation, no doubt important in its own
day, has had a distinguished history in more recent times.
In 1698 it was published by Christopher Rawlinson at
Oxford, with assistance in the editing from Edward

Thwaites, a Fellow of Queen's College. The text was based on that of the Bodleian manuscript through the transcript made by Junius; readings and *metra* were added from the Cotton version, and *testimonia* from various sources. This production was praised and utilized by the Rev. George Hickes, who is chiefly remembered to-day for his *Thesaurus*, and who published some of the metres in 1705. Indebted to Rawlinson's edition is the one published by J. S. Cardale in London in 1829, with a translation, and in the appendix a literal rendering of metre XXVI (IV, m. iii) with notes. The *metra* were printed by the Rev. Samuel Fox in London in 1835 as a supplement to Cardale's volume, together with a translation, of which the author said (p. vii): "I have endeavoured to give a literal version, and at the same time to preserve in the translation a portion of the rythm [*sic*] which is found in the Saxon. . . ." In 1864 under the auspices of the Bohn Antiquarian Library the same author published a complete edition apparently based on Rawlinson with "a literal English Translation." Here the "Editor has availed himself of the kind permission of Martin Tupper, Esq., D.C.L., &c. &c., to substitute his excellent poetical translation of the Metres for his own literal one," and tenders his sincere thanks (p. vii). Of Mr. Tupper's work it will be worth while to examine some samples.

For the first we may take the translation of lay IV^c (I, m. v):

> O Thou, that art Maker of heaven and earth,
> Who steerest the stars, and hast given them birth;
> For ever Thou reignest upon Thy high throne,
> And turnest all swiftly the heavenly zone.

> .   .   .   .

> For ever, Almighty One, Maker, and Lord,
> On us, wretched earthworms, Thy pity be poured;
> Why wilt Thou that welfare to sinners should wend,
> But lettest weird ill the unguilty ones rend?

> Evil men sit, each on earth's highest seat,
> Trampling the holy ones under their feet;
> Why good should go crookedly no man can say,
> And bright deeds in crowds should lie hidden away.
> (Pp. 270-272.)

The next is from Tupper's rendering of XVIII[r] (III, m. vii):

> Alas! that the evil unrighteous hot will
> Of lawlessly wanton desire should still
>   Be a plague in the mind of each one!

> The wild bee shall die in her stinging, though shrewd,
> So the soul will be lost if the body be lewd,
> Unless, ere it wend hence, the heart be imbued
>   With grief for the deed it hath done.
> (Pp. 303-304.)

From lilting melodies like these it is a far cry to "O stelliferi conditor orbis" or even to "Habet hoc uoluptas omnis." Perhaps we should be grateful for the fact that Victorian England could be lyric in this fashion about its morality; but one thinks ruefully instead of the dignity of Alfred and his "Æala, ðu scippend scirra tungla," and, earlier still, of the power and compactness of the lines in the original *Consolatio*. Tupper's verses, however, were published separately and appeared also in the Jubilee edition of the *Whole Works of King Alfred*. Thus Boethius was able to contribute something, however indirectly and in whatever respects modernized, to the Queen's celebration. We should add that of certain portions of Alfred's work there have also appeared a Dutch, a French, and a German rendering.

Notker Labeo

FROM the St. Gall of to-day one could hardly guess what an intellectual centre it was in the early part of the Middle Ages. Now the monastery is pretty well secular-

ized, and the library itself does not fairly suggest the sort
of books once collected among its treasures and their significance for the older period.   To a heritage from Irish
and from Old English culture the monks added a wealth
of Biblical and classical material; even Greek manuscripts
were preserved, and the Greek language was known and
read by some of the clerks.   Here we cannot dwell on
the musical and artistic importance of the school or on its
achievements in the field of early drama.   In the course
of time, some of the manuscripts were scattered, extensive
additions were made in new books, especially after the
invention of printing.   But for centuries the importance
of the institution was generally recognized, and it is not
likely to be ignored by the modern historian.

Among the scholars of St. Gall few attained to the
learning and distinction of Notker Labeo (not to be confused with Notker Balbulus of musical fame, or with
Notker the Physician).   He lived from about 950 to
1022.   Related to several other eminent figures associated with the monastery, among whom was probably
the author of the *Waltharius,* he was possessed with an
extraordinary zeal for advancing the education of his
world.   For his efforts to teach Latin by means of rendering Latin works in German he earned the soubriquet
of Teutonicus.   In a letter to Hugo Bishop of Sion he
explains that it is necessary for the proper study of ecclesiastical works read in the schools to have them in translation: "While I should like our students to have access
to these works, I have dared to do an almost unprece-
dented thing in that I have attempted to translate Latin
writings into our language, and to elucidate syllogistic or
figurative or dialectic phrases with the help of Aristotle,
Cicero, or some other writer."[1]   According to his own
list he managed to finish the *Consolatio,* the treatise *De*

---

[1] The letter is printed in Piper's edition of Notker, I, pp. 859-861. See p. 860,
10ff.: "Ad quos dum accessum habere nostros uellem scolasticos ausus sum facere
rem pene inusitatam. ut latine scripta in nostram conatus sim uertere et syllogystice
aut figurate aut suasorie dicta per aristotelem uel ciceronem uel alium artigraphum
elucidare."

Sancta Trinitate, the Distichs of Cato, the Bucolics of Virgil, the *Andria* of Terence, the *De Nuptiis Philologiae et Mercurii* of Martianus Capella, the *De Interpretatione* and *Categories* of Aristotle, an arithmetic, the whole Psalter, and a third of Gregory the Great's Homily on Job. He is half-apologetic for his labours. Yet so much is here claimed that for a while modern scholars were inclined to question whether it was he or his followers who actually accomplished the task. Still there is no real reason for denying his authorship; and he goes on to assert that he has also written a rhetoric, a "computus," and various other Latin *opuscula.* Of his translations five have come down to us, including the *Consolatio.*

In his letter to Bishop Hugo he made the following revealing comment: "It is necessary to know the fact that, since German words with the exception of articles must not be written without accent, articles alone are pronounced without accent, acute or circumflex. . . ."[1] He is most conscientious in living up to the principle herein embodied, as to written accent, and his procedure has been of the greatest value to modern investigators of the development of the German language. As the spellings in the *Ormulum* assist the student to-day in determining the quantity of Middle English vowels, so Notker's acute accent for short syllables and his circumflex for long have special importance for the scholar in the field of Old High German.

In the prologue to his *Consolatio* we read an account of the general state of things in Rome in the days of Boethius, we have a brief *Vita,* and then we proceed to the body of the work. Here he first quotes the original, and then he translates and explains or comments, relying somewhat on the available commentaries. His notes vary in length and resemble pretty much those that appear in

---

[1] Piper, *op. cit.,* I, p. 861: "Oportet autem scire quia uerba theutonica sine accentu scribenda non sunt. preter articulos ipsi soli sine accentu pronuntiantur acuto et circumflexo. . . ."

the later great studies and glosses on the book. The
Latin itself he turns about for greater clarity, and he re-
tains its phrases at times when a German equivalent seems
to fail him. Where King Alfred obviously meant to
have his readers enjoy the Old English version for its
own sake, Notker plainly wishes to lead his students to
an understanding and appreciation of the original. "Any
comparison must of course be decided in the King's
favour," observes Dr. Naumann. "His work is much
more delightful and popular than the monk's in expression, as well as in the peculiar ideas and themes scattered
through it. . . ."[1] Illuminating as this comment is, it
seems to embody the old complaint against textbooks:
namely, that the very apparatus they wear frustrates their
main purpose. But it is true that in their respective versions Alfred appears the philosopher and Notker shows
himself the scholar. Incidentally we may observe that
the last three books of Notker's rendering have somewhat longer comments, and that for this and other reasons
modern investigators at one time thought that these books
might have been written by his disciples under super-
vision. This view is now generally abandoned and the
whole work is ascribed to him. It is conceded that Notker's efforts benefited the German language: he was never
slavish to Latinisms, and he enriched the German vocabulary. It is a pity that he could not have added a knowledge of Greek to his other accomplishments. In any
case his influence was pretty much cut short by the
Cluniac reform which had little use for his variety of
humanism.

He died in the plague (along with Ruodpert, Anno,
and Erimpert) which the army of Henry II had brought
from Italy. Just at the time of his death he had finished his translation of Gregory's Homily on Job. His
thoughts, however, were not occupied with his contribu-

[1] "Der Vergleich müsste freilich sehr zugunsten des Königs ausfallen. Noch
viel köstlicher und volkstümlicher in der Sprache, wie auch in eingestreuten eigenen
Gedanken und Motiven ist sein Werk als das des Mönches. . . ." H. Naumann,
Notkers Boethius (*Quellen und Forschungen*, CXXI, 1913), p. 115.

tions to learning or with his share in the great fellowship
of scholars, but with his own sins and with charity to
others.   His work in life had been truly prompted by his
love of his pupils, as was narrated of him by Ekkehard
IV, who was among their number.

Other medieval German versions of the *Consolatio* include one attributed to Peter von Kastel and assigned to
the year 1401.   Among several in the modern period
we have one in which the prose parts were written by
no less a man than Francis Mercury van Helmont.   Of
this the title for the Sulzbach 1667 edition reads:
"Des fürtrefflichen hochweisen Herrn Sever. Boetii weil.
Burgermeisters zu Rom, christlich-vernunftgemesser Trost
und Unterricht, in Widerwertigkeit und Bestürtzung über
dem vermeynten Wohl—oder Uebelstand der Bösen und
Frommen, in fünf Büchern verdeutscht und mit beyge-
fügten kurzen Anmerkungen über etliche dunkele Ort
desselben. . . ."   A second edition, in which the preface
was signed with van Helmont's initials, appeared with
certain omissions at Lüneburg in 1697.   It is interesting
to reflect that the *Consolatio* offered something to the
intellectual equipment of this strange character, the
"scholar gypsy" of Matthew Arnold.   It is further interesting to learn that the second edition was published
at the request of Sophie Charlotte, Electress of Brandenburg, wife of Frederick I, and friend of Leibnitz, who, as
we shall see, was responsible for a rendering of his own
in French.

The Provençal Boece

THE story of Boethius in Provençal verse of the tenth
century (MS. eleventh century) we have already outlined
at some length, giving the material of the *Vita* which is
here incorporated.   As we have seen, the poem is written as a warning to youth.   Only a fragment of a little
over thirty-two stanzas remains to us, in which the ten
syllable lines are bound together by rime or, in the case

of a fair number of lines, by assonance. The world, we
are told, is getting more evil; and Boethius wrote to give
instruction for his day, but he was cast into prison. The
account of his experiences follows, and then a moral disquisition. In youth one should give oneself to God, trust
in Him alone and not in possessions. As mist covers
the light at dawn, so riches cover the Christian heart.
Boethius reproaches his friends, those who formerly
praised him. One does not well who stands on a weak
ladder. Who is it who has a strong ladder?—the good
Christian who cherishes a strong faith. When Boethius
was in prison and lamented his sufferings and sins, a lady
visited him, the daughter of the King of great might.
Her beauty illumined all the palace, and when she en-
tered a house it was made so bright with her radiance
that no light had to be kindled—one could see forty
towns away.

This lady could change her stature at will, grow tall
and pierce the very heavens. None could conceal himself
before her glance, and she could read the hearts of men
across the sea. Who trusts her need not fear death; but
she casts her enemy into Hell and she carries the key of
Paradise. Beautiful are her clothes, of good and fine
material; she made them herself more than a thousand
years ago, but they do not deteriorate. She wove the
garment, which no man can cut. Even the hem which
hangs down to the ground, one could not buy for a thousand pounds.

She holds a pleasant converse with Boethius. Her
clothes, it seems, are sewed with love and faith. They
are so white and shining that they blind Boethius. *Pi* is
embroidered on the hem, and then a ladder and above
it *theta*. *Pi* means life on earth, and *theta* heavenly law.
The steps of the ladder are no less precious than gold,
and on them go a hundred thousand little birds, some up,
some down. Those that reach *theta* are of a different
color. The steps are made of Alms, Faith, Love, Goodness, Fidelity, Largesse, Joy, Truth, Chastity, Humility.

The birds who climb to the top are the good men who have faith and who cherish no longing for earthly things. The birds coming down are those men who begin well and then turn to evil desires. In her right hand the lady holds a book of burning fire. This is the King's book of judgment. With this she sets fire to the impenitent sinner. In her left hand she holds a royal sceptre showing her power to punish sinners.

This extensive paraphrase may be pardoned if it shows the remarkable touches of originality and charm in the piece, sometimes improving on suggestions in the Latin itself, and sometimes branching out on a different tangent. The moral implications are obviously developed; and the meaning of Lady Philosophy is shifted to signify something very much like the medieval idea of Wisdom, the second person of the Trinity. The symbolic use of the ladder, not uncommon in medieval literature, appears now in a most unusual fashion. As to the further length of the poem conjecture may now be futile, but from the character of what we have it would seem unlikely that many stanzas have been lost.

Simund de Freine's Roman de Philosophie

In the poem just considered a truly extravagant poetic license may seem necessary if we are to include such an adaptation among a group of translations of the *Consolatio*. It is, however, clear that few of the early renderings fall strictly within any such category. Simund de Freine's *Roman de Philosophie* (of the late twelfth century) may seem even less appropriately included in this chapter. It is nevertheless something more than a mere imitation; the direct borrowings and echoes of its original are very extensive indeed. Of the author's life almost nothing is known except that he was Canon of Hereford in the thirteenth century, and a friend of that lover of the rare and the curious, Giraldus Cambrensis.

The poem of some sixteen hundred and fifty lines in

competent Anglo-Norman begins with an introduction setting forth Simund's name in an acrostic.   Here we find
stated its general theme: man should not complain of mis-
fortunes, nor rejoice unduly in good things—much the
same idea as that which the author expressed in a poem
to Giraldus:

> Si uariat fortuna uices sit mens tua talis
> Ut neque laeta bonis sit neque laesa malis.[1]

A clerk complains against Fortune that first she exalted
and then she abased him.   While he speaks, Dame Philosophy appears, accompanied by her seven daughters, the
seven Liberal Arts, and shows him that *la richesse* is only
a frivolous illusion which comes and goes.   The familiar
characteristics of Fortune are then set before us.   The
clerk describes his own history, how Fortune exalted him
and made him rich, and how she then made him fall again
—the trial reserved for all mortals.   Direct borrowing or
close imitation of the *Consolatio* begins at about line 149
and continues with generous if scattering selection.   Material is drawn from other sources: from the lapidaries, for
example.   Steadily the same moral is presented, that
Fortune's gifts are worthless; that true treasure comes
from God—dignity, honour, and good estate.   Nor does
God rob man of free will.

The interesting detail of the companions of Philosophy
seems not to have been original with Simund.   In a didac-
tic vision described by Adelard of Bath perhaps a century
earlier, the same lady appears with the seven Arts, debates
with Philocosmia (who represents appropriately change
and decay), and explains the nature of the Arts.   The
same companionship occurs also in the *Elegy* written by
Henry of Settimello in the latter part of the twelfth century, and in the less familiar treatise *De Consolatione
Rationis* by one Petrus of Compostella (c. 1140), where
Reason is substituted for Philosophy.   But to these docu-

---

[1] *Les Œuvres de Simund de Freine,* ed. Matzke, (*Soc. Anc. Textes Fr.*), p. vii.

ments we must return at a later time. In any case Simund's work has, it must be noted, chiefly the interest of the ingenious. The great lyric "O stelliferi conditor orbis" (I, m. v) is rendered without much sense of its opportunity for a religious poet:

> Sire Deu omnipotent,
> Par ki cil haut firmament
> Dedenz une nut e jur
> Une fez se turne entur,
> Par ki al chef de quinzeine
> Pert la lune runde e pleine,
> E quant al solail se joint
> L'um ne veit de lui un point;
> Sire, par ki poësté
> Sunt si lung li jur d'esté.
> E de ki cunseil ceo mut
> K'ivern ad si lunge nut,
> Vus ki guvernez si bien
> Le ciel l'amunt e tute rien,
> Mesestance adrescez une;
> Mès ne suffrez ke Fortune
> Pusse enginner bone gent
> Par sun faus blandiement.
> Hom est vostre criature;
> Ne soffrez k'il eit leidure.   (Ll. 149-168.)

"Lord God omnipotent, by whom the firmament on high turns once about in one night and a day; by whom at the end of a fortnight the moon appears round and full, and when it is united with the sun, one can not see it at all; Lord, by whose power the days of summer are so long, and by whose counsel it is moved that the winter has such long nights; You who govern so well the heavens on high and everything, repair one injury: permit not that Fortune deceive good people by her false blandishment. Man is Your creature; suffer not that he have evil."

Here we have almost the impression of listening to a courtier on his knees. But if the lyrical value of the poem is not great, the verses have their own charm in the strange conceits occasionally introduced and in the neat

Plate 3, Jean de Meun Presents his Translation to Philippe le Bel

phrasing of the thought.   Thus Simund compares the claw of a chicken, which can be opened and closed by pulling its sinews, with the hand of the covetous man, which opens to take something but is closed against giving.   His use of the figure of the spider is well known: the spider spins thread for its web from its own belly, and all its labour is to catch a fly.   So he who loves wealth drains his own heart and poisons his own soul.

Jean de Meun

THE translation of the *Consolatio* in French prose now generally attributed to Jean de Meun is a businesslike rendering from the end of the thirteenth century or the beginning of the fourteenth.   It was written for Philippe le Bel, who greatly encouraged the cultivation of letters, and to whom personally the author seems to have given his newly written manuscript, if we may trust the miniature that depicts the scene.   From his work in translation and from his part in the *Roman de la Rose* Jean may fairly be styled humanist, and it is interesting to see that he chose Boethius for special attention both in the allegory and here.   His version sometimes appears with the Trivet commentary, and in this form doubtless was discovered and used by Geoffrey Chaucer, who found this somewhat pedestrian version handy for checking the Latin original, imitated the insertion of glosses in the text, and borrowed from both Jean de Meun and Trivet.

Frère Renaut de Louhans

> Fortune, mere de tristesce,
> De douleur et de affliction,
> Mettre m'a fait en ma jeunesce
> Mon estude et m'entenc*i*on
> De faire un Romant sur Boece
> Que on dit de consolac*i*on
> Qui donne confort *et* leesce
> A ceulx qui ont tribulac*i*on.

Thus writes the Dominican Frère Renaut de Louhans in his *Roman de Fortune et de Felicité*. This work was finished in March 1336 at Poligny, a paraphrase of the *Consolatio* in French verse signed by the author in acrostic, like Simund de Freine's *Roman*, to which it is vaguely comparable. Renaut has used Jean de Meun's translation together with a commentary which he ascribes to another "frere prescheur." He begs his critics to be gentle and not to find fault with his French:

> Pour ce qu'en mon commencement
> Je ne fu point nourriz en France.

He was not reared, he means, in the Île de France but in Louhans in the Department of Saône-et-Loire. He does not always give the original word by word, but its substance is here. He tells the story of how Fortune showed her dark countenance to Boethius.

Besides the material drawn from his source, the "escript," the author has introduced digressions based on his own invention. He is more of a poet than Simund de Freine, perhaps, and writes more freely, dealing with the prose and the metres with about equal facility; but he shows no great inspiration. We may examine the beginning of his version of "O stelliferi conditor orbis" (I, m. v):

> O, creerres de firmament
> Et de toutes chose creable,
> Qui te siez sans ton mouvement
> En ton hault siege perdurable!
> Ly cieulx tourne ysnellement
> Et unies toutes choses muables.
> Estoillez variablement
> Euvrent selon ta loy estable.
> Tu ordennas par lay certaine
> Toutes les choses de cest monde:
> La lune du solail lointaigne
> Est sans cornes toute ronde;
> Adonc est elle toute plaine
> Et la lumiére moult habonde,

Mais qua*n*t du solail est p*r*ouchaine
Com*m*ent que sa clarte estande. . . .

Other translations in French of about the same period
are noted by Delisle, including one in prose and verse
which was extremely popular judging by the manuscripts,
and one by an Italian writer, who incidentally says that he
has already produced an Italian rendering. Still another
version, which did not appear until the fifteenth century,
may possibly be assigned to the authorship of Colard
Mansion, the famous printer of Bruges. A copy of this
from the press of Antoine Vérard was presented to Henry
the Seventh of England. Among still later French renderings is a résumé of the first two books by the philosopher Leibnitz, a friend of the Electress of Brandenburg,
Sophie Charlotte, whose interest in the *Consolatio* has
already been noted.

For some years a translation into Italian was attributed
to Brunetto Latini, the great Florentine to whom Dante
owed so much, and who, Dante himself says, taught him
"come l'uom s'eterna" (*Inferno* xv, 85). But apparently the whole idea is founded on a blunder with reference to an actual work by Alberto della Piagentina, a
Franciscan who became mixed up in politics and spent
some time in prison in Venice. In 1332 he produced his
version of the *Consolatio* but it was not printed until 1735
in Florence. Among later Italian translations one may
note that of Ludovico Domenichi, written at the instance
of Cosimo de' Medici, and published in 1550.

A Catalan *Consolacio* was finished by a Dominican of
Barcelona, Fra Antonio Ginebreda, in the fourteenth century, and also a translation was written afterward in Spanish.
The Spanish was several times reprinted, and other versions
in the same language followed. In the low countries in the
fifteenth century and later, Flemish and Dutch versions
appeared. In 1585 from the Plantin press in Leyden
came one by Coornhert in Dutch "van de Vertroosting der

wysheyd" with music for the portions in verse. Here
too perhaps we may note a translation into Greek by
Maximus Planudes, a monk of Constantinople in the
fourteenth century, who added some interpretative notes.
He was the author of various other works, and the manuscripts of his rendering of the *Consolatio* are by no means
rare. In the later period there are as well versions in
Hebrew, Hungarian, and Polish.

Chaucer

To-day we are likely to enjoy the work of Geoffrey
Chaucer most for his art as a teller of tales or for his
humour or for his realistic picture of life. We forget that
Hoccleve lavished praise on him as a universal father "in
science" (by which he meant knowledge), and called him
a "Mirrour of fructuous entendement" (fruitful understanding). Indeed we read with a smile the first line of
Deschamps's complimentary poem to his English friend:
"O Socrates, plains de philosophie!" Yet no work seems
to have had such a profound or at least far-reaching effect
on Chaucer as the *Consolatio*. From French literature
he perhaps derived style, and from Italian he learned
much about narrative. The Latin classics afforded him
much in material and in general guidance. Dante touched
deeply his imagination and his thought. But, as we have
noted in a previous chapter, the influence of Boethius is
pervasive and almost at all times tangible, from the time
when Chaucer used the *Consolatio* through the interme-
diary of the *Roman de la Rose* until practically the end
of his career. Many of his special interests, like that in
the nature of true gentilesse, that in the problem of fate
and free will, or that in the problem of chance, may have
been prompted by material in the *Consolatio,* and were
certainly considered in the light of its discussion. If
Dante inspired him in his religious life, Boethius certainly
interpreted philosophy for him.

He made his translation, it seems likely, in the general

period in which he began his *Troilus and Criseyde*—let us say in the years following 1380. One cannot help conjecturing that he was led to the task, less by any early discovery on his part of the ample borrowings in the *Roman de la Rose,* when he translated that poem, than by the philosophical problems which come lightly or seriously into the *Teseide* and the *Filostrato,* where a concern for the fate of human characters engaged his attention. Speaking of the *Knight's Tale* and the *Troilus,* Dr. Jefferson observes that, "In each Boccaccio furnished the tale, but Boethius, in *Troilus* especially, gave an impetus of thought, which, among other things perhaps, prompted Chaucer to mould Boccaccio's tales into something different and to recast the characters." [1]   It is also possible that in studying the Italian poems the English writer conceived the idea of getting a more thorough knowledge of the *Consolatio,* and of making the remarkable book more accessible thereby to his contemporaries. In any case his procedure was characteristically thoroughgoing. He used not only the Latin original, but, as he often had recourse to a French translation in working over a Latin document, he drew on the version ascribed to Jean de Meun as well as Trivet's commentary. From these sources he included explanatory material as glosses in the text, and apparently inserted notes of his own. The metres he put into prose. He seems really to have studied more than one text, and is at pains to be accurate and clear. The result is not without its defects; mistakes have been found in his rendering. Thus he is now and then guilty of totally misrepresenting the sense of the original, sometimes because he followed errors in the French or perhaps because the manuscripts he used were faulty. But on the whole his version is workmanlike and eminently useful. The style, marked as one would expect by a considerable use of a Latinate vocabulary and generally diffuse,—in contrast to Alfred's version it is half again as long as the original, —is nevertheless clear.

---

[1] Jefferson, *Chaucer and the Cons. of Philos. of Boethius,* pp. 131-132.

Dr. Jefferson, from whose study of the work as a whole many of these observations are borrowed, has finely put the matter thus: "Chaucer's prose, then, is marked by a fullness, a sense of measure and proportion. A consideration of the sections of this chapter which deal with his inconsistency of phrasing, his cumbersome handling of indirect discourse, and his misconstructed sentences precludes any idea of a precise application of mechanical principles such as came later to characterize the prose of John Lyly; yet, Chaucer, gifted with a sensitive ear, feeling the spirit of his original, has reproduced its enthusiasm, its dignity of expression, and, as best he could, its symmetry of style. His translation is the translation of a poet." [1]

As a sample of the work let us take the rendering of the verses "Felix nimium prior aetas" (II, m. v):

Blisful was the firste age of men. They heelden hem apayed with the metes that the trewe feeldes broughten forth. They ne destroyeden ne desseyvede nat hemself with outrage. They weren wont lyghtly to slaken hir hungir at even with accornes of ookes. They ne coude nat medle the yift of Bachus to the cleer hony (*that is to seyn, they coude make no pyment or clarree*), ne they coude nat medle the bryghte fleeses of the contre of Seryens with the venym of Tyrie (*this is to seyn, thei coude nat deyen white fleeses of Syrien contre with the blood of a maner schellefyssch that men fynden in Tirie, with which blood men deyen purpre*). They slepen holsome slepes upon the gras, and dronken of the rennynge watres, and layen undir the schadwes of the heye pyntrees. . . .[2]

This passage cannot be taken as fully typical of the whole *Consolatio;* for the original itself varies in style, from verse to prose, from lighter treatment to close argument, and Chaucer's translation varies with it. It may be illuminating to see what he does with the material quoted when in a short poem he puts it into verse:

[1] Jefferson, *op. cit.,* p. 46.
[2] *Complete Works,* ed. Robinson, p. 393.

> A blisful lyf, a paisible and a swete,
> Ledden the peples in the former age.
> They helde hem payed of the fruites that they ete,
> Which that the feldes yave hem by usage;
> They ne were nat forpampred with outrage.
> Unknowen was the quern and eek the melle;
> They eten mast, hawes, and swich pounage,
> And dronken water of the colde welle.[1]

And so on.   The prose is not without its music; one feels only that in the verse, apart from the question of details from other sources and metrical fluency, the poet shows a freer hand and feels more at home.

For lyric power, however, few passages can compare with Chaucer's rendering of II, m. viii (*Quod mundus stabili fide*), which is worth close examination.   The prose reads as follows:

That the world with stable feyth varieth accordable chaungynges; that the contrarious qualities of elementz holden among hemself allyaunce perdurable; that Phebus, the sonne, with his goldene chariet bryngeth forth the rosene day; that the moone hath comaundement over the nyghtes, whiche nyghtes Esperus, the eve-sterre, hath brought; that the see, gredy to flowen, constreyneth with a certein eende his floodes, so that it is not leveful to strecche his brode termes or bowndes upon the erthes (*that is to seyn, to coveren al the erthe*)—al this accordaunce of thynges is bounde with love, that governeth erthe and see, and hath also comandement to the hevene. . . .[2]

Sings the possessed Troilus at the top of his bent:

> "Love, that of erthe and se hath governaunce,
> Love, that his hestes hath in hevenes hye,
> Love, that with an holsom alliaunce
> Halt peples joyned, as hym lest hem gye,
> Love, that knetteth lawe of compaignie,
> And couples doth in vertu for to dwelle,
> Bynd this acord, that I have told and telle.

[1] *Ibid.*, p. 629 (*The Former Age*, 1-8).
[2] *Ibid.*, p. 398.

> "That that the world with feith, which that is stable,
> Diverseth so his stowndes concordynge,
> That elementz that ben so discordable
> Holden a bond perpetuely durynge,
> That Phebus mote his rosy day forth brynge,
> And that the mone hath lordshipe over the nyghtes,—
> Al this doth Love, ay heried be his myghtes!"[1]

And more to the same effect. Is this a compromise of the purport of the song in the *Consolatio*, which celebrates something more than love *paramours*? Hardly, for Troilus here wishes to link his passion with the force that, according to Plato as well as Boethius, moves the stars; and only the irony of the present setting of the passage touches its splendour. One cannot think that because youth here speaks, engaged in a temporary affair, the beauty of the lines is less genuine. Such music one hears again at the beginning of Swinburne's *Tristram of Lyonesse:*

> Love, that is first and last of all things made,
> The light that has the living world for shade. . . .[2]

But the infidelity of Criseyde, the dolorous end of Troilus's attachment, marks Chaucer's scene with genuine if not profound tragedy. The love which Troilus felt is marred. A plague on both houses! He fails to keep his desire for Criseyde on this level after all. "Swich fyn hath, lo, this Troilus for love!" (V, 1828).

Incidentally we may note Chaucer's masterly rearrangement of material for lyric purposes. But short selections cannot represent the merits or the qualities of his translation, and may quite unfairly expose its defects. That he caught the spirit of the original is obvious, and that he was imbued with it appears in his subsequent quotation or echo of line after line in most of his works, usually in words that suggest his own *Boece*. He drew from nearly every part of the *Consolatio* in a way that shows his com-

[1] *Ibid.*, pp. 515-516 (*Troilus and Criseyde*, iii, 1744-1757).
[2] *Tristr.*, Prelude, 1 ff.

plete mastery of it; he introduced its material not only in less significant moments in his plots but at important places where the philosophical meaning becomes apparent. Thus he shows a Boethian influence when he writes about true nobility, moral responsibility, divine intervention in human affairs, the really solemn problems of human life. When the plot of the *Teseide* depended too much on chance, the poet turned to the *Consolatio* for material which would assist him in getting rid of the weakness in the *Knight's Tale*. Viewed in one aspect the *Troilus* seems almost like an illustrative document furnished for a proper understanding of Boethius's teaching.

Chaucer had already considered, perhaps, the problem of tragedy in an early form of what was to be the *Monk's Tale*, where he offers a succession of stories of people who have fallen from high estate after the stroke of Fortune, and where his definition is based on a gloss in a manuscript of the *Consolatio*. He considered the problem of chance in the *Knight's Tale* and in the *Balade* on Fortune, where he borrows from Boethius and Dante to describe chance as an angel of grace subservient to God; the same idea is twice presented at important moments in the story of the *Troilus*. Now, in the *Troilus*, we see the tragic case of a young hero and heroine. Their fate seems linked with that of Troy itself, and their doom is hinted early in the poem. Irony is thus derived from the intention of the characters and their method of dealing with their own desires. Troilus, after a long resistance to love, succumbs; and Criseyde, calmly looking at the situation with an eye to her own advantage, concedes him all he asks. She manages to seem to herself the victim of circumstance; and yet her character comes to the same decision respecting Diomede in an even less creditable situation. "To Diomede algate I wol be trewe!" (V, 1071), she says. Troilus blames Fate, Divine Providence, everything. He is a noble youth, but, alas! it will not do. God has doubtless foreseen his disaster but not because he played no part in it himself. Anyone well versed in the

Consolatio knows that much.　His soul takes its flight, ascends to the stars, and there it learns laughter.　Such is balance and proportion.　We return to a proper evaluation of earthly love and love celestial.　So too at the end of the *Consolatio* we are told to lift our hearts to God. It is a *sursum corda* which Chaucer sees fit to direct to young people for whom he had an immense sympathy. "O yonge, fresshe folkes, he or she,"—his voice seems to linger—

> . . . of youre herte up casteth the visage
> To thilke God that after his ymage
> Yow made. . . .[1]

The solution of tragedy in Boethius is the same: "areise thi corage to ryghtful hopes; yilde thou humble preires an heygh" (V, pr. vi).　The poem tells of all the high preoccupations of youth, but like a good romance in the Middle Ages it ends with a prayer.

　　After Chaucer had finished *Boece* and the *Troilus* as well, he did not forget the *Consolatio*.　Even when he was reading the satirical Deschamps, and the star of the Wife of Bath was distinctly in the ascendant, he turned back to what was one of his "old bokes" for material. Perhaps there he had learned how to "flee fro the prees." How far his version served his contemporaries we cannot tell; but, as we shall see, it was used later by Walton, by Walton's printer Thomas Richard, and by Colville the Elizabethan.　It was pirated too.　The first book was taken over, disguised, and set forth as a new work in a fifteenth-century manuscript now in the Bodleian Library. "I take in purpose to telle the menynge of it as I am disposide be grace of the good lorde above," claims the writer, but his labours were spent chiefly to hide his indebtedness.　Perhaps too Chaucer's work was at one time mistakenly attributed to the industrious monk of Bury St. Edmunds, John Lydgate, who has been repeatedly cited as the author of a translation.　Nothing of that sort

[1] V, 1835 ff.

by Lydgate has survived; and the idea more likely sprang from a confusion in regard to the extant version assigned on good grounds to John Walton, Canon of Oseney.

John Walton

IN 1410 John Walton, Augustinian Canon of Oseney and Papal Chaplain, completed his translation of the *Consolatio,* of which some nineteen manuscripts have survived. It was written at the instance of one Elizabeth Berkeley, probably the daughter of Lord Thomas de Berkeley of Gloucester, who was a patron of letters, and whose daughter Elizabeth married Richard Beauchamp, Earl of Warwick and patron of Thomas Malory. The book was printed in 1525 by Thomas Richard, monk of Tavistock, who introduced numerous changes. It is significant that with Chaucer's rendering available Walton's should have been so much in demand.

The reason may perhaps be found in the fact that Walton's is a translation entirely in verse. The general reader, for several centuries at least, liked to take his philosophy that way. The first three books in this version are in eight-line stanzas *(ottava rima)*; the last two, with a special preface explaining the difficulties of the shift to loftier matters, are in the seven-line stanza of Chaucer's *Troilus (rime royal):* "The sentence [doctrine] for to saue in metre trewe" (st. 576, 4). On the whole the performance is adequate. Chaucer has been widely used; and, where he errs, sometimes the error is overlooked and retained and sometimes correction is introduced. Certainly the verse is easier to read than the prose, even in those parts (perhaps one may say especially in those parts) where the argument is involved.

The book begins with a translator's preface, avowing a purpose to keep close to the thought of the original, and containing tributes to Chaucer and Gower. Here the writer speaks of several other English translations, some in verse and some in prose, of which he himself has seen "sumwhat." A prologue follows, in which he gives an account of Boethius obviously derived from the manuscript *Vitae* together with an interesting touch from the tradition of the damnation of Theodoric. The translation is reasonably faithful, never stirring or exalted, but considering the task imposed on the author remarkably competent. For purposes of comparison we may examine some of the passage based on the eighth Metrum of Book II, part of which Chaucer used so effectively in the *Troilus:*

> That þus þise worldly enter[ch]aungementes
> Acorden alway in þaire variaunce;
> And also þat þise fletyng elementes
> Halden þe bondes of þeire aliaunce,
> Thogh þat betwene hem be contrariance;
> And þat þe Phebus with his chare of golde
> The rosye day haþ in his gouernaunce,
> þat is so cleer & lusty to beholde;
>
> And be þe mone þe nightes ben gouerned
> As Esperus haþ broght þeym in cumpace;
> Also þe wode see þus is be-werned
> His propre boundes not for to overpace,
> þat he beflowe noght þis erthely place;
> All þis accordaunce doþ þe bond of loue,
> þat see and lond doth clippen *and* enbrace
> And may comaunden in þe heuene aboue.
>
> . . . .
>
> This loue it is þat holy bondes knytteth
> Of mariages full of honeste;
> And loue it is þat trewe lawes setteþ
> þat felawes haue in theire comynalte.
> But ow mankynde, full blisfull myght ȝe be,
> If þise ȝoure hertes had in gouernaunce
> þat heuen haþ set in suche tranquillite,
> That þere-ynne may be no contrariaunce! [1]

[1] *Boethius: De Cons. Philos. trans. John Walton,* ed. Science, stanzas 321-322 and 324.

Chaucer's verse is simpler. This is cumbersome, yet not without fluency and some degree of eloquence.

About 1479 appeared Caxton's edition of Chaucer's Boethius, for which the printer said in his epilogue[1] that the author "hath deseruid a perpetuell lawde and thanke of al this noble Royame of Englond. . . ." He called Chaucer "first translatour of this sayd boke into englissh & enbelissher in making the sayd langage ornate & fayr." In 1525 was printed Walton's version, as we have seen. It is interesting that Richard altered many readings to bring them closer to Chaucer's.

George Colville

THE translation by George Colville came out in 1556, with a second edition in 1561. Of the writer little is known. His work is dedicated to Queen Mary: as health of body and health of mind are both desirable, and she is worthy to have both, so he offers her this book of wholesome doctrine. "And gentle readers . . . consyder that my onelye purpose was nether for prayse of men, nor for any reward, but to contente the myndes of the wise, and to instructe the ignoraunt vnlearned people with the holesome doctryne of Philosophye, or wysedome, that is conteyned in this boke, and soo to cause men to cesse, and leue of and gape no more soo gredylye as they do for worldlye and transytorye thynges, but to ensue and folowe vertue in godly lyuynge, and fynallye to ascend from thys lyfe actyfe in thys worlde, vnto the lyfe contemplatyfe whych neuer shal fayle. . . ."[2] He insists on his unworthiness to attempt the task, and then he gives us a prose rendering, borrowing expressions often from Chaucer, introducing glosses, and writing in a fluent, even rhythmical style without the ornamentation fashionable a little later. In general it is a faithful performance, but he is no slave to the Latin, as one could see from the original text which was

---

[1] Spurgeon, *Five Hundred Years of Chaucer Criticism and Allusion*, I, pp. 58-59.
[2] *Boethius' Cons. of Philos., Trans. . . . Colville*, ed. Bax, p. 9.

printed conveniently in the margin. He uses marginal notes and synonymous expressions to make his meaning clear. The notes have an interest of their own: "Pryde is lyke unto the lightening, for it beareth the mynde so high as thoughe it passed men of the earth, and yet it can not reache ye heuen." [1] "The Sirians do take it for a prayse, to eat theyr parentes, when they be deed, rather then wormes shoulde." [2] As a sample of his translation we may take his rendering of part of Metrum vi, Book IV. He does not indicate the shift from prose to verse in the original.

If thou wylt behold wyselye the ordynaunce of god in thy pure mynde and thought, loke vpon the altitude of the hygh heuen, for there the sterres do kepe their olde course and concorde by the iust bande of thynges. For the sonne moued with his redde fier and hete letteth not the cold compas of the mone, nor the sterre called the beare (that turneth his swift courses about the north pole, beyng neuer washed in the depe Occean sea) couetethe to drenche hys flames in the same sea, seinge other sterres to be drowned therin. And the sterre Hesperus, that is to say, Venus, sheweth always by euen courses of tyme, the late darkenes, that is to saye, the nyghte. And the sterre called Lucifer, bryngeth agayne the cleare daye. Euen soo the loue euerlastynge of gods prouidence, makethe the enterchaungeable courses of the sterres. And by suche mutuall concorde, troublesome warre and varians, is expulsed from the mouths of the sterres, that is to saye: from the regions celestiall that beareth the sterres. [3]

With the last sentence we may compare Chaucer's equivalent: "And thus maketh Love entrechaungeable the perdurable courses; and thus is discordable bataile yput out of the contre of the sterres." [4] If Colville has taken hints from Chaucer, he has also been independent even to the point at times of not being so close to the original. On some matters he is closer. In his avowed purpose to use the book to lead men to the contemplative life he seems to stand pretty much alone.

[1] *Boethius' Cons. of Philos., Trans.* . . . *Colville*, ed. Bax, pp. 17-18 (margin).
[2] *Ibid.*, p. 48 (margin).
[3] *Ibid.*, p. 112.
[4] *Complete Works*, ed. Robinson, p. 433, 21-24.

Sir *Thomas Chaloner*

A MAN of letters and translator, sent as ambassador to Spain in 1561, Sir Thomas Chaloner was a conspicuous figure in the English diplomatic world of his day. About 1563 he wrote an English metrical version of all the *carmina* of the first book of the *Consolatio*, and the first two of the second book. His work is remarkable in its fidelity to the original and in its skill of expression. Take for instance his translation of I, m. v (*O stelliferi conditor orbis*):

> O maker of the starry Skye,
> That sitting on thy steddy seate above;
> Incessantlye
> Doste swiftlye welde the Heven rounde:
> And makste the Starres that by a lawe they move
> To order bounde:
>
> That now all rounde & full of lighte
> The farther from her brother, dame *Diane*
> Doth dymme the sighte
> Of all the lesser Starres abowte:
> But nygh to *Phoebus*, aye more pale & wane,
> Her lighte goth owt
>
> .   .   .   .   .
>
> So nothing brekes thy statutes olde,
> But in the werke thow hast them tasked to,
> Their order holde
> Thus ruling all to certen ende,
> Save only men; thow lettest what they do
> Vnbridled wende
>
> For whie hath Fortune thus her will
> In turnyng thinges now vp, now downe, so ofte
> Withowten skill?
> The payne that for offence besittes,
> The Gilltless have: and wickedness alofte
> In honour sittes.[1]

[1] *Queen Elizabeth's Englishings*, ed. Pemberton, pp. 154-155.

At the end of his work the author remarks, "Ther is no more of this yet done, my busynes otherwise occupieng my hedd & all my leys*ure*. . . ." If encouraged he will complete his task. "I here that he is well translated late, all in prose"[1]—referring possibly to Colville's performance.

Queen Elizabeth

QUEEN ELIZABETH's command of Latin is part of her fame, and everyone knows how she silenced the ambassador from Poland with an extemporaneous reply in that language. After delivering it she turned with a laugh to her council for their approval; a *tour de force* it was, no doubt. Nichols in his *Progresses* tells us that "At Windsor she amused herself with translating 'Boethius de Consolatione, 1593'. . . ."[2] A graver motive for the task was, however, suggested by William Camden. After the news had come that Henry of Navarre had made his profession of faith at St. Denys in the Roman Catholic Church, the Queen was plunged into grief. "This her great Grief," says Camden, "she sought to allay by reading the Sacred Scriptures and the Writings of the Holy Fathers, likewise by frequent Conferences with the Archbishop; and whether out of the Philosophers Books also, I know not. Sure I am that at this time she had Boëtius his Books *De Consolatione* daily in her Hands, and translated them very handsomely into the English Tongue."[3] The picture of the great Elizabeth with the *Consolatio* daily in her hands impresses the mind and stirs the imagination. How handsomely she translated the work we shall presently see.

Three separate sheets of letter paper in the British Record Office, written "by different persons at different times," assert that the Queen finished her performance at amazing speed, the time varying (according to the sheets)

---

[1] *Queen Elizabeth's Englishings*, ed. Pemberton, p. 160.
[2] *Progresses of Queen Elizabeth*, III, 564, n. 1.
[3] Camden, *Hist. of the . . . Princes Elizabeth*, Book IV, p. 475.

from twenty-four to twenty-seven hours. One of them
says that she translated at the rate of one page to every
half-hour. Most of the metres she wrote in her own
hand, but apparently she dictated much of the prose to a
secretary, Thomas Windebank, who was Clerk of the Sig-
net in 1568. She followed the original almost word by
word, making a mistake now and then but getting the
right order even if she failed to make sense. One sees
her plowing grimly ahead to the gallant finish. Let us
take her rendering of I, m. v. (*O stelliferi conditor
orbis*):

> O framar of starry Circle,
>> who lening to the lasting grounstone,
> withe whorling blast hevens turnest,
>> and Law Compelst the skies to beare;
> Now that with ful horne,
>> meting all her brothers flames
> the Lessar stars the mone dimmes,
>> Now darke and pale her horne,
> Nar to Son Loseth her Light.
>> And she that at beginning of night,
> Hesperus [her] frosen rising makes,
>> And Luciphar palled by Phebus vpriseth
> Againe her wonted raines exchangeth.
>> thou, by the Cold of Lefe falne shade
> straightist thy Light with shortar abode:
>> Thou whan the fervent sommar comes,
> Easy nights houres deuidest.[1]

And so on. It sounds hurried, something of a stunt; but
her translations from Sallust, Plutarch, and Horace show
that she was taking her work seriously. The "groun-
stone" depends on a mistake in her reading of the Latin.
If the exigencies of verse were hard on her hand, her
prose is about as laboured: "While of al this alone in
silence I bethought me, and tearesful complaint in stiles
office (*stili officio*) ment, ouer my hed to stand a woman
did apeare of stately face, with flaming yees, of insight

---

[1] *Queen Elizabeth's Englishings*, ed. Pemberton, p. 13.

aboue the comun worth of men. . . ."¹ Thus Philosophy arrives on the scene. Sometimes the meaning is
utterly remote, as when (II, m. ii) we read:

> What raignes can drawe bak
>   hedlong desiar to stable end,
> Wha*n* thirst of getting inflames
>   The flowing ma*n* wit*h* largist gifts?

Yet we can see how the words found their present place
if we turn to the Latin:

> Quae iam praecipitem frena cupidinem
>   Certo fine retentent,
> Largis cum potius muneribus fluens
>   Sitis ardescit habendi?

The Queen kept straight on to the end, in spite of the
affairs of state and many bewilderments. Most remarkable of all, however, at least for us to-day, is the fact that
a potentate with interests so multifarious should have
chosen this special document for her particular attention,
to assuage perhaps her great grief and to beguile the time.
In spite of her haste and even in spite of her blunders, the
translation has its merits. From the original something
of the dignity is retained with ragged splendour.

The seventeenth century reveals no falling off in the
general tradition of the *Consolatio*. Rather it enjoyed
at this time a renewed vogue, as Dr. Houghton's survey
of the field informs us. It is quoted by many of the poets
—Thomas Heywood, John Donne, Giles Fletcher, and
others; and the metres are translated by Vaughan and
by Phineas Fletcher. In the period 1604-1608 a certain
John Bracegirdle translated the whole book into English
verse. He was no poet, and his rendering of the prose
is better than that of the *metra*. His work, called the
Psychopharmacon, was never published, but the title is not

---

¹ *Queen Elizabeth's Englishings*, ed. Pemberton, p. 2.

Plate 4, Boethius and Philosophy

without its significance for the period and for the author's understanding of Boethius.

"I.T."

ONE of the best of the modern translations appeared in 1609 with a dedication to "the Most Vertuous Lady, the Countesse of Dorset Dowager," widow of the Thomas Sackville who is famous for his part in the *Mirror for Magistrates* and *Gorboduc.* The Preface to these "Five Bookes of Philosophicall Comfort, Full of Christian Consolation," states that Sackville himself had also had in mind a translation, and insinuates some apprehension that in its "speculatiue points" the book may be above the understanding of the Countess.

How this particular age took its Boethius we may gather from other remarks of the writer:

It is an old saying, and not so old as true, that *uino uendibili non est opus hædera:* I would it were as true, that the best thinges are alway most esteemed, then I would not doubt but that this golden booke of *Boethius* would be in great request; for I cannot imagine, what fault any man can find with it, that is delighted with Vertue. . . . And yet this I will adde more; that the noble, learned and pyous wits and minds, will take most benefite and pleasure in *Boethius.* The reason is, for that *similis simili gaudet.* . . . Finally he was truely *Boethius,* that is, an helper and relieuer of all innocent and distressed people. And least his Benefite should liue no longer then himselfe, he committed it to writing, and sendeth it to thee, in this his noble, learned, and pyous worke.

The writer explains that the translation is in prose and verse to increase the enjoyment of it. One may easily guess how difficult the task of rendering it was:

since our prince of Poets, *Chaucer* turned it only into prose. Which will be a sufficient motiue to take this labour in good part; and to beare with such faults as cannot easily be amended.

To the Countess he says in particular:

And yet also (Madame, for I had rather you should wisely feare,
then I foolishly flatter) looke into it as a glasse, not so much to
see if most parts be much, as if any bee lesse beautifull. Weigh
if in all things and at all times, you haue truely preferred the
veritie of goodnesse of God, afore the vanitie of vice of the
world; if you haue, continue therein, so much more carefully, as
remaines for you a lesse time of this combersome carefulnesse.

It may be surmised that the Countess did not take this as
foolish flattery.

The Preface, signed "I.T.," appears on the face of it
to be the work of the translator. Who was "I.T."? A
commonly favored suggestion is that he was John Thorie,
a Fleming, born in London 1568, B.A. of Christ Church
Oxford in 1586, and friend of Gabriel Harvey; but
Thorie's authenticated translations are from the Spanish.
Dr. Houghton has, however, shown that in all likelihood
the author of the present work was Michael Walpole, a
Jesuit. It was dangerous for a Roman Catholic to publish a book in England at this time, and hence the finished
work was entrusted to "I.T." to see it through the press.
Incidentally it is illuminating to see that papists like Sackville and Walpole had a special liking for the *Consolatio*,
a book to which Queen Elizabeth seems to have had recourse for different reasons, and which so many moderns
have regarded as not essentially Christian in character.

As for the rendering itself, in this case it is most exact.
With slight modification it is that which is used to-day in
the edition of the Loeb Classical Library. Anyone may
compare for himself the clear argument of the prose or
the fine poetic lines of the *carmina* with the Latin original.
Consider for instance the beginning of I, m. v (*O stelliferi
conditor orbis*):

> Creator of the skie,
> Who sitst on thine æternall throne on hie,
>   Who doest quicke motion cause
> In all the heau'ns, and giu'st the starres their lawes.

That the pale Queene of night,
Sometimes receiuing all her brothers light,
   Should shine in her full pride,
And with her beames the lesser stars should hide;
   Sometimes she wants her grace,
When the sunnes rayes are in lesse distant place.
   And Hesperus that flies
As Messenger before the night doth rise,
   And oft with sodaine change
Before the Sunne, as Lucifer doth range.

The last four lines show a difference, arbitrary in its way, from the Latin, but marked with the adroit turn of a true master. "Nunc obscuro pallida cornu" does not find a precise equivalent in "Sometimes she wants her grace," but the spirit of the original is preserved in the English. The verses are all truly poetic in their own right.   Or again take the beginning of IV, m. vi (*Si vis celsi*):

If thou wouldest see
   Gods lawes with purest mind,
   Thy sight on heau'n must fixed be,
Whose settled course the Starres in peace doth bind.
      The Sunnes bright fire
   Stops not his sisters teame
   Nor doth the Northerne beare desire
Within the Oceans waue to hide her beame.

The metrical form is changed but conveys the solemnity of the original, or even increases it.

Illic iusto foedere rerum
Veterem seruant sidera pacem.

Here is the original for the fourth line quoted above; it is rendered more compactly, and with the force of added climax.

The prose is managed in general with a neat fidelity, and the involved argument is nearly always easy to follow. But while the style is notably simple, not burdened with Latinisms as one might expect, the rhythms of Boethius are nevertheless often preserved, and the whole discourse moves forward with its own vitality. Take, for instance, the fine rendering of a difficult passage in V, pr. ii:

> But the minds of men must needes be more free, when they conserue themselues in the contemplation of God, & lesse, when they come to their bodies, and yet lesse when they are bound with earthly fetters. But their greatest bondage is, when giuing themselues to vices, they loose the possession of their owne reason. For hauing cast their eyes from the light of the soueraigne truth to inferiour obscurities, forthwith they are blinded with the cloud of ignorance, molested with hurtful affections, by yeelding and consenting to which, they increase the bondage, which they layd vppon themselues, and are after a certaine manner captiues by their own freedome.[1]

Here "when they conserue themselues in the contemplation of God" shows a little gain over "cum se in mentis diuinae speculatione conseruant"; and on the other hand "minus uero cum dilabuntur ad corpora" is replaced more simply by "and lesse, when they come to their bodies." But, clause by clause, and phrase by phrase, the English gives an almost literal rendering of the Latin.

Other seventeenth-century translations deserve perhaps less notice. In 1626-1631 R. Fanshawe achieved an admirable version of the metres. In 1664 Sir Harry Coningsby published the whole book in English verse, in which, as was the case with Bracegirdle's work, the prose is rendered more successfully than the *metra*. In 1674 appeared the *Summum Bonum* by Edmund Elys, offering books I-IV in prose and verse (with certain omissions) and indebted to Walpole. In 1695 or thereabouts was published a translation by Sir Richard Graham, Lord Viscount Preston, whose life was a tragedy, and who under sentence for high treason spent some time in the Tower and in Newgate. His edition includes notes from Val-

---

[1] Pp. 123$^{vo.}$-124.

linus; the design of the book was taken from Elys's; and his verse employs all the standard metrical forms, including blank verse. This work enjoyed great contemporary popularity. In 1698, we recall, appeared King Alfred's translation published by Christopher Rawlinson from a transcript made by Francis Junius.

Mention should also be made of a curiosity of literature —a supposed translation by one "S.E..M." which came out in 1654-1655. The volume is in fact made up of two books, containing critical material by S.E.M. and the Latin text. But except for a few illustrative passages (chiefly taken from "I.T.") no translation is here; instead we have the first edition in England of the Latin text with notes. The author, as Dr. Houghton has discovered, is Sir Edward Spencer. His initials were reversed, and the added "M." probably stood for "Miles" (Knight). In his dedication to the fourth Earl of Southampton, Spencer says that he has studied Boethius "these forty yeares"; that he once saw a translation, "a very good one," dedicated to "my Lady your mother" in manuscript, but that that was thirty years ago; and that he sent one for his lordship to peruse which was signed "G.G." He gives a descriptive prologue in Latin and English of the first four books of the *Consolatio*. The material is derived from the pseudo-Aquinas commentary. Later follows an essay in Latin on III, m. ix and other passages, and a life of Boethius based on Bertius and Rota. In at least one copy discussion of the fifth book is appended at the end of the volume. The Latin text is really independent, and was taken from the Plantin edition of 1562.

The reputation of Boethius did not wane in the eighteenth century. In 1730 appeared a translation of the *Consolatio* by William Causton; in 1785 one by Philip Ridpath; one by R. Duncan in Edinburgh, 1789; one of the metres only, published anonymously in 1792. I quote a passage from the middle of Ridpath's version of IV, m. vi:

Nightly, the beaming pole around,
The northern Bear conducts his train,
Nor strays from his appointed bound,
To rest him in the rolling main.

Fair Vesper, to his office true,
At eve renews with light his horn;
And shaking from his locks the dew,
Bright Phosphor ushers in the morn.

Kept firm by love's eternal chain,
Th'etherial lamps their rounds revolve;
No strife disturbs the radiant train,
No force their concord can dissolve.[1]

Cardale's version of King Alfred's translation was published, as we have seen, in 1829. But our present survey must fall short of exhausting all the material on the subject in these periods, which would form a library in itself. The best we can do in the present compass is to indicate the immense popularity of the work as testified by these numerous renderings from the time of the author himself until the present day—wherein we may perhaps note that of H. R. James (New Universal Library) 1897 and that of W. V. Cooper (Temple Classics) 1902. Here too we may mention among a few recent versions of some of the *metra* those skilfully turned by Miss Helen Waddell and Mr. Howard Mumford Jones. Thus has the leaven of Boethius been at work through the Middle Ages and the Renaissance and even the modern period. Writers have not been content to read him for themselves alone, but have been inspired to present anew the sixth-century author in versions suited for their friends and contemporaries.

[1] Ridpath, *Cons. Philos.*, pp. 178-179.

CHAPTER IV

IMITATIONS AND INFLUENCE

THE MOST STRIKING TESTIMONY of all to the power of
the *Consolatio* appears in the attempt through many centuries to interpret its meaning in various adaptations and
imitations. Something like this we have already observed,
in varying ways, in King Alfred's rendering and the Provençal *Boece* and especially in Simund de Freine's *Roman
de Philosophie*, where invention to a greater or less degree
has certainly distinguished translation. Indeed on these
terms it is hard to find much difference between Simund's
work and the poem written by Henry of Settimello which
we shall presently examine, except that Simund's *Roman*
aims at keeping a little closer to the original. Most of
the early versions are adapted in some fashion to their
times, and even the later and fairly close translations introduce some measure of change in form or content.
Simund tries to reproduce the scheme of the original; and
it is fair for us to pay some consideration to the author's
own purpose, as well as to take account of the traditional
method of classifying these documents. In any case the
moral to be derived from the material remains perfectly
clear. The full extent of the influence enjoyed by the
Consolatio is beyond our power to estimate.

This influence appears in a number of works where it
would seem that the authors were inspired by Boethius
mainly to appreciate the form of his treatise. The variety
gained by a shift from prose to verse commended itself
apart from his special purpose. The allegorical method,
also, of setting forth a discussion of serious problems was
particularly to the taste of the Middle Ages; and, although it was familiar in the works of Prudentius and
others, surely it gained some of its popularity from the
little book which became so widely known. The Socratic

style too of dealing with problems in dialogue, of showing the "sic et non" by question and answer, was certainly less familiar through the works of Plato than in the pages of Boethius. Furthermore the content of the book permeated, as we have seen, the thought of men for at least a thousand years; and it found new expression in various forms, offering consolation for ills other than those specifically of prison and exile. At all times men have assumed the vocation to justify the ways of God to man; or, if they concede that at least part of the time human disobedience is at the root of suffering, they are likely to search for remedies in counsel not unlike those suggested by the *Consolatio*. So Philosophy, if not always justified of her children, seems through the ages to have many of them.

The imitation of the form of the *Consolatio* in the mere alternation of prose and verse is not easy to identify. It is, for one thing, the manner of the *satura*, and it appeared earlier than Boethius in the exceedingly popular work *De Nuptiis Philologiae et Mercurii* of Martianus Capella. On the whole the *Consolatio* was perhaps more likely to be the instrument which effected the plan, especially where we find its metrical patterns reproduced; but absolute certainty in the matter is out of the question. With this proviso we may cite the *De Rectoribus Christianis* (855-859) of the poet Sedulius Scottus, who composed this regimen of princes for Lothar II, setting forth the duties of his monarch in this tactful way in twenty chapters, and managing at the same time to make a considerable display of his own learning. Here too belongs the Norman History in three books, intended by its author Dudo of St. Quentin (fl. c. 1000) to celebrate the Normans; but, more resplendent with learning than reliable historically, it introduces the Muses who sing in the measures of Boethius. Neoplatonic inheritance appears in the allegorical *De Mundi Uniuersitate* of Bernard Silvester (fl. xii century) on the creation of the Megacosmus and the Microcosmus, a sort of Christian *Timaeus* in which symbolic figures set forth the material. Natura complains to Nous that matter is still formless, and we then follow the beginnings and the process by which the universe receives its order, with every detail listed. The journey of Natura through the spheres and to the lower world to obtain the aid of Urania and Physis for the creation of man is dwelt on at length. In this complicated task Bernard has been obviously assisted by Martianus Capella, the *Somnium Scipionis* with the commentary of Macrobius, and Boethius.

It is significant to note that Adelard of Bath and Alanus de Insulis were pupils of Bernard. We have already referred to Adelard's *De Eodem et Diuerso*, a prose allegory with two passages in verse. In this treatise Philosophy appears with the Seven Liberal Arts, holds converse with Adelard, and disputes with Philocosmia (representing change and decay), whose handmaids are Riches, Power, Honour, Fame, and Pleasure. In the Second Book of the *Consolatio* Boethius had dealt with the "falsely seeming goods" of Fortune which these handmaids represent; now with Adelard they become "oppressed as if with shame" and can not "bear the gaze of the opposite seven," the Liberal Arts. Thus even as early as the twelfth century culture was supposed to weaken the hold of secular interests; salvation presumably comes by education! The Arts themselves may be ultimately derived from Martianus Capella, but the work is also richly indebted to Boethius. Incidentally we may also take note of the *Fons Philosophie* of Godfrey of St. Victor, written in the same period. According to this poem the author goes on a visionary journey past the seven poisonous streams of the mechanical arts to the mountain-spring whence flow the clear rivers of the Liberal Arts; and Boethius himself is mentioned along with the other great masters of philosophy who drink of the waters of Dialectic. He listens to the strife regarding

Aristotelianism and Platonism, and the controversy between nominalists and realists, but according to Godfrey, as we have seen, shows no preference.[1]

From the impulse derived from Bernard Silvester came the further transmission of things Platonic and Neoplatonic in the well-known writings of Alanus de Insulis, which have been often described. His *De Planctu Naturae* carries on the tradition of Martianus Capella and Boethius in its verse and prose, in which Dame Nature, elaborately described, bewails the unnatural vice of the time. She talks with the author, and the sins are discussed. Further symbolic figures appear, and the poet visits the house of Nature, wisely cautious, however, about daring to enter such intimacy. His *Anticlaudianus*, written entirely in verse, deals with the creation of man. In Nature's garden a meeting is held to discuss the project of making a perfect man, and Prudence, prompted by Reason, and assisted by her daughters the Liberal Arts, goes to heaven to obtain the soul. Nature makes the body. The house of Fortune, part dazzling with splendour, part in ruins, must be sought out for proper gifts from the fickle Goddess. The complications of the allegory only serve to furnish an abundance of material for later productions of the sort. Both works of Alanus were utilized by Jean de Meun in composing his *Roman de la Rose*, where the dwelling of Fortune appears again, and where borrowings of that kind are equaled only by the indebtedness to Boethius. Jean de Meun, as we have seen, was a close student of the *Consolatio*, which he translated and also rifled. In a similar way Chaucer used the French poet's work as well as that of Alanus, made his own translation of the *Consolatio*, and borrowed from Boethius. His *House of Fame* shows the benefit of hints received from the abode of Fortune in the *Anticlaudianus;* his *Parlement of Foules* takes much from *De Planctu Naturae*.

We cannot attempt here to indicate all the developments of this sort. The history of medieval allegory is as intricate as its plots. One other outstanding instance may, however, be briefly considered. The *Anticlaudianus* is also in part responsible for the Spanish *Visión Delectable* (1430-1440) written entirely in prose by Alfonso de la Torre. This ponderous narrative relates how Understanding, repelled apparently by the corruption of the world, seeks knowledge of the truth. Accompanied by Instinct he goes to a lofty mountain and comes to the abode of the Arts, from whom he gets instruction. One thinks immediately of the mountain-springs in the *Fons Philosophie;* and here too there is something of the tradition from Martianus Capella. At the top of Alfonso's mountain are Truth and her three sisters: Nature, Wisdom, and Reason. This is the realm of the Earthly Paradise, and in this pleasant region dwell the Four Cardinal Virtues. It is to be noticed that Reason's height at times touches the heavens and occasionally she assumes normal stature, a familiar trait of Philosophia in the *Consolatio.* The idea is older than that, however, although that is the probable source for its use in this instance, as well as with reference to Fortune in the *Roman de Fauvel* (where we find a long account of Boethius) and perhaps in the passage describing Fame in Chaucer's *House of Fame.*

But it is impossible to trace all the details of indebtedness. Works which show an alternation of prose and verse, in addition to the instances already discussed, might be further listed, and some will be mentioned in the course of this chapter; but the connexion of many with Boethius is tenuous. For example, the fourteenth-century *Voir Dit* of Guillaume de Machaut, in the tradition of love poetry with inserted letters in prose, almost certainly bears no relation to our theme. On the other hand, Dante's *Vita Nuova,* which reveals the many ways in which Beatrice became the poet's friend and guide and indeed his philosopher, is not entirely remote in substance. Still more remarkable is the parallel in the *Convivio,* where Dante gives some account of Lady Philosophy and several references to Boethius. After losing Beatrice, he set himself, he tells us, "to read that book of Boethius, not known to many, wherein, a captive and an exile, he had consoled himself."[1] When he speaks of the book as not known to many, he refers perhaps to the knowledge of intimate understanding. In the *Convivio* as in the *Vita Nuova* and the *Consolatio* the prose interprets and expands on the verse; in this case indeed it becomes even a direct commentary. Dante's work inspired Boccaccio, whose *Ameto* shows a similar form, telling how the young hunter whose name furnished the title met Lia (faith) and was led by Venus to the awareness that it is love which teaches and reveals all things. In this instance, however, the verses as songs constitute a part of the narrative, which, though exalted in purpose, cannot quite lift its delicate feet from the solid earth.

Closer than most of the compositions just considered, however, are the works whose theme is in some definite way allied to that of the *Consolatio*. Perhaps because their influence was restricted or their aim narrow, some of these are lost or difficult of access. The *Consolatio siue Laterna Monachorum* by Ekkehard of Aura († 1130) has not survived, but we are told that it was written in imitation of Boethius. Lawrence of Durham's *Consolatio de Morte Amici* (c. 1100-1154), in which Lawrence tells his troubles in prose and a Consoler replies in verse, remains in manuscript. The *Consolatio Nostri Exemplo* of Pier della Vigna [Petrus de Vineis] (1190-1249), minister to Frederick II and a man of great power in his day who fell into disgrace with Fortune and men's eyes, has not survived. On the other hand, the *Consolatio Theologiae* of the exiled Johannes of Dambach [Iohannes de Tambaco] (1288-1372) had enough popularity to be reprinted many times, excerpted, and translated, at least in

---

[1] *Conv.* II, xiii, 2: "e misimi a leggere quello da molti non conosciuto libro di Boezio, nel quale, cattivo e discacciato, consolato s'avea." (Temple Classics trans., p. 111.) Cf. Baur, *Boetius und Dante*, p. 11.

part, into Dutch, Spanish, and English. In the original
Theologia is accompanied by *Puellae* and *Milites*. The
dialogue is conducted between a crowd of sufferers and
the separate damsels who answer their complaints. In
fifteen books of prose Johannes sets forth ample remedies
for all disturbances of public and private peace. The
causes of such disturbance are taken up systematically:
adverse fortune, persecutions, injuries, exile, loss of
friends, lack of exterior joy, silence, sadness, loss of freedom, physical defects, everything. Quotations from
various authors, Augustine, Jerome, Gregory, Chrysostom, Cato, Seneca, Valerius Maximus, Boethius, and many
more, afford the solution of all difficulties. Such a com-
prehensive work may have been in part inspired by
Seneca; one wonders if there is any possible connexion
between it and another essentially different compilation
of remedies, that of Petrarch.

Not so close to Boethius in title, the prose *Synonyma de
Lamentatione Peccatricis* of Isidore of Seville (c. 570-
636) offers an undoubted parallel to the *Consolatio*.
This work presents a sort of dialogue between Homo,
who bewails the age in desperate outbursts, and Ratio,
who instructs and comforts him. The remedy for ills is
to be found in the spiritual life and contemplation.
About 1140 another Spaniard, Petrus of Compostella,
wrote his *De Consolatione Rationis* in two books of alternating prose and verse in which the debt to Boethius is
also obvious. Here Petrus sees the World in a vision
as a maiden who lures him. Impelled by the Flesh and
about to yield to World's charms, he beholds another
gentle creature, Nature, who by showing him the wonders of created things leads him to perceive the indwell-
ing spirit. Reason then appears leading the Seven
Liberal Arts, berates the others, and gives Petrus an in-
structive discourse. Further complications follow which
introduce material on divine prescience and human free
will, and various religious and theological subjects. The
point of the whole treatise is that God gave man reason

to achieve understanding. The similarity of the allegory to Adelard's *De Eodem et Diuerso* is of course inescapable. Martianus Capella has contributed here as well as Boethius.

A more famous work, however, is the *Liber Consolationis et Consilii* in Latin prose of the thirteenth century by Albertano of Brescia. Anyone who has diligently read Chaucer's *Tale of Melibee* will remember the story of how Melibeus left his home one day, and on his return found his wife Prudence and his daughters beaten and wounded by three enemies. Husband and wife debate as to what should be done in such a situation. In her counsel to her husband Prudence is as prudent as she should be, and learned as well. Perhaps it was her long-winded as well as edifying discourse in the face of present disaster that commended the "little treatise" to Chaucer's interest. Certainly the *cadre* of the story is unique. Yet in the idea of humiliation and the comfort supplied by the philosophical lady, one can see how the inspiration of Boethius was made practical, and a work of art translated in a sense from Boethius into entertaining mediocrity. A pleasant scene is that in which Prudence, according to Chaucer's version, "delibered and took avys in hirself" how she could solve their great difficulty. She proceeds to call in their adversaries and appeal to their better nature, touching on the benefits of peace and the harms of war. "And whan they herden the goodliche wordes of dame Prudence, they weren so supprised and ravysshed, and hadden so greet joye of hire that wonder was to telle. 'A, lady,' quod they, 'ye han shewed unto us the blessynge of swetnesse. . . .'"[1] Thus may one achieve peace, domestic as well as foreign! This narrative Chaucer assigned to himself on the Canterbury pilgrimage, presumably for its sobering effect after the impudence of his *Tale of Sir Thopas*. He took it perhaps from the Latin of Albertano and certainly from a French translation sometimes attributed to Jean de Meun. A slightly dif-

[1] *Complete Works,* ed. Robinson, p. 221 (vii, 1726 ff.).

ferent text of this French version was included in the
treatise which the Ménagier of Paris wrote so delightfully
for his young wife in 1392-1394 to prepare her for her
second husband should she marry again.

Another work of consolation has been ascribed to the
Spanish Pedro de Luna (c. 1328-1422), one time anti-
pope Benedict XIII who was deposed by the Council of
Constance. Something of the sort he may have written,
as scribes and tradition testify. But the Latin text attributed to him is one of the compilations from Johannes of
Dambach, with few differences from the original. Like
the earlier treatise it has fifteen main divisions, in which
most of the material is lifted bodily from Johannes with
little rearrangement but without the allegorical framework. The scribe himself admits that the work may have
been composed by someone in Pedro's behalf, and it is
easy to imagine how people came to think that Pedro was
responsible for such an anatomy of melancholies. His
life was under great duress in the ecclesiastical upheaval
of his day. His fame was widespread, however, and
soon a Spanish translation of the book appeared. In this
material, Boethius is not forgotten but often quoted as in
the original, and in the Spanish preface is named as "el
noble é costante baron."

In the same period Alain Chartier offered hope for the
social situation in his uncompleted *Espérance ou Consolation des Trois Vertus* (published 1429), discussing in
prose and verse the corruptions of the clergy and other
ills, and offering the remedy of a more truly Christian life.
Alain like many another blames Fortune for all that is
wrong. Understanding (Entendement), who tells the
author to have recourse to God, here performs the func-
tion assigned to Reason in some allegories; and Hope
(Espérance) counsels Understanding to seek God's grace.
Intellect, we infer, needs illumination. Social treatises
of one sort or another are fairly common in the period,
and often bear a slight resemblance to the *Consolatio* in
the use of a figure like Reason or Sapience or Prudence

vaguely parallel to Philosophia. Thus the *Songe de Pestilence* (1374-1377), written in prose and verse with a complicated allegory introducing Ratio, Sapience, Prudence, and various others, might be considered here. But the history of such figures in medieval literature is far from simple, and they cannot be derived from the personification in Boethius with any great likelihood.

Similarly the general motif of blaming Fortune for social or personal discomfort is enormously popular. Boethius showed the way in which it might be treated lyrically and even dramatically; he supplied numerous formulae for describing the goddess; he suggested proper remedies for vanquishing or annihilating her. It is hardly an exaggeration to say that in the *Consolatio* all the details of the conventional portrait of Fortune in medieval literature found a beginning. One cannot hope to stop her wheel; if the goddess cease to be fickle, she ceases to be Fortune; she puts one up, another down: ideas like these in great number were first expressed for the Middle Ages by Boethius, and then passed round in common currency. Thus we eventually get the rich collection of material, to take one example, in Machaut's *Remède de Fortune.* How significant it is that there Machaut says of the goddess:

> Mais Boëces si nous raconte
> Qu'on ne doit mie faire conte
> De ses anuis.[1]

They never forgot who it was that so successfully gave Her Majesty away! Or we find debates between Fortune and some other personification—Virtue, Poverty, Love, and the like—for which the *Consolatio* really offers an initial impulse, like that of the (eleventh-century or earlier) *Altercatio Fortune et Philosophie,* a short but pithy affair in twenty-four distichs. Fortune claims the earth, but Philosophy offers heaven. Fortune rules things of the body; Philosophy, those of the soul. Fortune bestows the

---

[1] *Rem.,* 982-984 (*Œuvres,* ed. Hoepffner, II, p. 36).

Plate 5, Boethius and Fortune

goods of life; Philosophy teaches how to discriminate between what is good and what is evil.   And so on, almost an
epitome of the discussion in Boethius!   The Marquis of
Santillana (in the early fifteenth century) presents a dialogue in Spanish verse in his *Bías contra Fortuna*, according
to which Bías defends his poverty against Fortune and
prefers the life of reason to her gifts.   Fregoso's *Dialogo
di Fortuna* (1521) sets forth in verse the power of the
goddess and suggests a remedy in the instruction of Truth,
incidentally touching on the problem of free will.   But
such matter is embodied in almost countless poems and treatises and longer or shorter works, in which Fortune causes
tragedy or contends with Reason, Understanding, or some
other figure.   Personal troubles or social evil, the charge is
the same.   The theme is almost universal, and the lines of
interrelationship among the documents that treat it are
too involved for us to give a fair representation here of
the way in which the tradition developed.   Like Eustache
Deschamps we know where it began:

> En Boece, de consolacion
> Trouverez-vous de Fortune l'assault,
> Ses blandices et sa decepcion. . . .[1]

Against this tide of complaint rose the doctrine of moral
responsibility in brief discussion or stern treatise or in the
argument of the scholastics, which derives, at least in part,
from the same astonishing source.

Among the books thus far described we have occasionally noticed one where the author was prompted to write
because of his own sufferings in prison or exile.   Pier della
Vigna, who wrote the *Consolatio Nostri Exemplo*, was
blinded and imprisoned, and eventually he committed sui-
cide.   He is the bleeding bush in Dante's *Inferno*, who
tells how he formerly "held both keys" of the heart of
Frederick II.[2]   Johannes of Dambach in his preface
compares his own case with that of Boethius, telling us

---

[1] *Bal.*, clxxxi (*Œuvres Complètes*, ed. De Queux de Saint-Hilaire, I, p. 316).
[2] *Inf.*, xiii, 58-59.

that he himself was "cast out from the place of his own home."[1] Albertano of Brescia, we know, had been imprisoned in the conflict between the emperor and the pope, although it was several years afterward that he wrote his *Liber Consolationis*. Alberto della Piagentina, we recall, made his translation of Boethius when he was imprisoned at Venice. There are a number of other treatises which seem to have had similar beginnings. Alienated by the rapacious Berengar and his extremely disagreeable wife Willa, Liutprand of Cremona (†972) went into voluntary exile, and comforted himself by writing a history of his own times. The *Antapodosis* or "book of retribution," which he set down in prose and verse during 958-962, was composed partly to revenge himself on his enemies. It refers to Boethius, quotes him, and uses some of his metrical forms. The tone of Liutprand's work, however, entirely unlike that of the *Consolatio*, can hardly be described as free from envy, hatred, and malice. Its purpose is often to include the gossip of history. As the author himself declares:

The aim and object of this work is to reveal, declare and stigmatize the doings of this Berengar, who now is not king but rather despot of Italy, and of his wife Willa, who because of her boundless tyranny is rightly called a second Jezebel, and because of her insatiate greed for plunder a Lamia vampire. Such shafts of falsehood, such extravagance of robbery, such efforts of wickedness have they gratuitously used against me and my household, my kinsmen and dependents, as neither tongue avails to express nor pen to record. Let this present page then be to them antapodosis, that is, repayment.[2]

In a wholly different temper Hildebert of Lavardin (1056-1133) wrote his long poem *De Exsilio Suo* on the troubles of his harassed life. Tormented by problems of the clergy in the diocese of Le Mans, persecuted by Wil-

---

[1] *Cons. Theol.* [7 *ro*]: "a proprie mansionis loco eiectus, quandam exilii speciem sustinens; prefatum opus aggressus."
[2] Trans. Wright, *The Works of Liudprand* (Broadway Med. Libr.), p. 109. For the Latin, see the Appendix to this chapter.

liam Rufus, and involved in strife with King Louis in the
diocese of Tours, he was wearied but steadily urbane. He
became a distinguished figure in the literary world as well
as a most important Churchman. As a master of classical
style he achieved a wide reputation, and his letters became
familiar as models of their kind. Yet the world that he
knew was filled with turmoil and with the disruption of
human affairs that appears in his poem. Once, he tells us
there, he was in good estate, and indeed thought it strange
that all went so well:

> Mirabar sic te, sic te, Fortuna, fidelem:
> Mirabar stabilem, que leuis esse soles.[1]

Then came the grievous reversal:

> Has ludit Fortuna uices, regesque superbos
> Aut seruos humiles non sinit esse diu.
> Illa dolosa comes, sola leuitate fidelis,
> Non inpune fauet aut sine fine premit.

Her countenance once bland was transformed. Now all
is stormy and harsh. But the moral deduced nevertheless
is that God actually rules everything:

> Ille simul semel et solus preuidit et egit
> Cuncta, nec ille aliter uidit agitque aliter.
>
> .   .   .   .
>
> Ipse manens, dum cuncta mouet, mortalibus egris
> Consulit atque ubi sit spes statuenda docet.

The allusion to the unmoved mover of the universe nicely
gathers up a conspicuous theme of Aristotle and Boethius.
M. Hauréau found in the work certain expressions alien
to the spirit of the remoter antiquity. Perhaps diatribes
against Fortune are not in general marked with what we
think of as classical restraint, but Hildebert's poem has its
own dignity none the less.

A more tempestuous outburst, written also in elegiacs,

---

[1] For the complete text see Werner, *Beiträge zur Kunde der lat. Lit. des Mittelalters,* pp. 95-97 (f. 42 ᵛ).

is the *Elegia de Diversitate Fortunae et Philosophiae Consolatione* by Henry of Settimello of the latter part of the twelfth century. The author, a priest, had been a man of some affluence in a worldly way, but now he has lost all his money and must go begging. He recalls the sufferings of others, including Boethius, and his plaint echoes the *Lamentations* of Jeremiah, which he must often have heard in the liturgy of Holy Week:

> Quomodo sola sedet probitas! flet, ingemit, aleph,
>   facta uelut uidua que prius uxor erat.
> Cui de te, fortuna, querar? cui? nescio. . . .[1]

The ironic turns here mark his bitterness. Whither, he asks, shall he fly? He cannot stand, and on his couch he suffers. Thus Fortune revolves men about on her wheel. In the second book a closer similarity to the *Consolatio* begins to be apparent. The author calls on Fortuna, who replies in self-defense. He attacks her in turn; and while the manner of the dialogue becomes less like that of Boethius as they exchange abuse, Fortune's account of herself is much in the vein of her imagined words in the older treatise. In the third book appears Philosophy, whose stature varies in the familiar way, and who is accompanied by the Seven Arts, a motif we have already found in Adelard's *De Eodem et Diuerso*, in the allegory of Petrus of Compostella, and in Simund de Freine's *Roman*. Philosophy rebukes the author for his blindness, and reminds him that Fortune only follows her accustomed method:

> Nonne meus Seuerinus inani iure peremptus
>   carcere Papie non patienda tulit?
>
> .   .   .   .   .
>
> Quid referam multos, quorum sine crimine uita
>   uerbera Fortune non patienda tulit.

The examples of great men all remind us that Fortune brings tragedy in her train. Philosophy scolds the author

---

[1] *Henrici Septimellensis Elegia—sive de Miseria,* ed. Marigo, 29 ff.

roundly; in contrast one appreciates the measured restraint of her speeches in the *Consolatio*. But, asks Henry, will things improve in this world: virtue goes into exile and vice triumphs; what chance is there of hope for better things? In the fourth book Philosophy offers her remedies. Strength of character is the cure for ill fortune; stand firm and be of good cheer; let Fortune go on as she likes; seek virtue, flee from vice, and trust in the goodness of God. With such counsel Philosophy bids farewell to the author, and he in turn ends the poem, taking gracious leave of the Bishop of Florence to whom it is dedicated. The work became popular; it was quoted, and furnished with a commentary. It had due influence on Peter of Eboli, who in about the same period wrote an elegiac poem on the campaigns of Henry VI and incidentally the maleficence of Fortune and the hope offered by Sapientia.

In 1276 Pierre de la Broche, a barber of Louis IX (better known as St. Louis) and a favourite of his son, was hanged for calumny of the queen, Marie of Brabant. In poetry at least his sufferings were attributed, one may say inevitably, to the caprice of Fortune. One lyric refers to him thus:

> J'oi l'autr'ier d'un homme moult forment reprochier
> Qu'il seut des esperons les granz chevaus brochier.
> Quant le senti Fortune de l'un des piez clochier,
> Si le fist trébuchier de plus haut c'un clochier.[1]

"The other day I heard of a man much reproached because he knew how to stick great steeds with his spurs. When Fortune caught him limping with one foot, she made him fall from higher than a clock-tower."

How perfectly the man was suited for a theme of this sort! If ever the sharp contrasts of the Middle Ages offered the right opportunity it was here in the case of this commoner and barber, raised to the position of minister to a king, and alas! plunged again into misery through the

---

[1] "Le Dit Moniot de Fortune," in Jubinal's *Nouveau Recueil*, I, 196. Cf. the note on the stanza.

malice of Fortune! In this vein, if we may judge by the fragment left to us, was composed a dialogue conducted by Pierre with Reason and Fortune. There is no great originality in the piece except in the application of the theme to the present tragedy. Fortune, according to Pierre, has sold him riches and dignity only too dearly. Now all is turned to his harm. Reason announces that Fortune herself is at hand to speak in her own defense. The fickle goddess has her say, reminding Pierre of the condition from which she raised him and rebuking him for pride. It is his disloyalty to his earthly lord, she avers, that has brought him so low. In the exchange of speeches she accuses him of defaming the Queen; iniquity, she points out, has brought its own reward. Reason then pronounces sentence:

> Pierres, bien as Fortune oïe,
> Qui se desfent moult sagement. . . .

He has indeed heard Fortune, who defends herself wisely, and for his treachery he is doomed to receive suffering:

> Qui mal fet, ce dist l'Escripture,
> Mal trovera: c'est ma créance.[1]

Seldom, in allegory at least, does Fortune come off so triumphantly with the support of Reason. All this follows no doubt the tradition of Boethius but only in a general way.

A similar motif runs through the Anglo-Norman poem of the early fourteenth century[2] written by Edward II, or by a strong sympathizer, to lament his imprisonment. This begins as follows:

> En tenps de iver me survynt damage,
> Fortune trop m'ad traversé:
> Eure m' est faili tut mon age.
> Bien sovent l[e]ay esprové:

---

[1] For the fragment see Monmerqué and Michel, *Théâtre Français,* 208 ff. The quotations are taken from pp. 214-215.

[2] *Mod. Lang. Rev.,* XVI (1921), pp. 34-46.

En mond n'ad si bel ne si sage,
[Ne] si curtois ne si preysé,
Si eur(e) ne lui court de avantage,
Que il ne serra pur fol clamé.

"In the winter injury came upon me. Fortune too much has thwarted me. Luck has failed me all my life. Full often have I found it so: in the world is none so fair nor so wise, nor so courteous nor so highly prized, that, if luck does not run to his advantage, he will not be acclaimed as a fool."

Strikingly similar to this poem again, at least in some respects, is the fourteenth-century Middle English *Somer Soneday*, which also lays the blame on Fortune for a king's downfall. In the same connection one is inevitably reminded of Petrarch's consolation delivered orally to King John of France on the occasion of that monarch's liberation from an English prison in 1360. It was to be expected that Petrarch should attribute the misadventure to Fortune's caprice, but his suggestion was taken seriously and later he had to give account of himself for his use of such a pagan figure. One recalls as well his long treatise *De Remediis Utriusque Fortunae*, which with the use of dialogue offers antidotes for the effects of good fortune as well as for those of bad. Here Ratio debates with Gaudium and Spes, on the one hand, and with Dolour and Metus, on the other. Hope of long life, beauty of body, intelligence, eloquence, virtue, sweet odours and songs are discussed, as well as imprisonment, losses, and other forms of distress. The book, which derives from Seneca as well as from Boethius, bears some slight resemblance to the *Consolatio* of Johannes of Dambach. It was widely known and ran through some twenty editions.

Many accounts of the rise and fall of kings on Fortune's wheel found favor in the Middle Ages, showing some trace of influence from Boethius. Even Boccaccio's *De Casibus Virorum Illustrium* should be mentioned, a compendious work in which we learn of a whole succession of royal tragedies as well as others. Here the story of

Boethius himself appears, just before that of King Arthur.
By this extraordinary production Chaucer was partly
guided in his *Monk's Tale;* but in this instance the Knight,
and perhaps Chaucer's own patience, cut the story short.
Boccaccio's entire work, however, was translated into
French by Laurent de Premierfait; and this version
served as the basis of Lydgate's *Fall of Princes,* a monument of edification and re-edited of late as three solid
volumes chiefly important to the antiquarian. It is an
interesting feature that here Boethius is celebrated mostly
as a social hero, although his writings and sanctity are
recalled:

> For comoun proffit he was onto the toun
> In mateeres that groundid wer on riht
> Verray protectour and stedfast champioun
> Ageyn too tirauntis, which of force & myht
> Hadde in the poraille [the poverty-stricken]
>   oppressid many a wiht
> Be exacciouns and pillages gunne of newe
> Vpon the comouns, ful fals & riht vntrewe.[1]

Guillaume de Machaut's *Confort d'Ami* was written in
4004 lines of octosyllabic couplets to console the King of
Navarre, who had been imprisoned in 1356 by John of
France. What the King has lost, says Machaut, were
only the gifts of Fortune. Search the "livre de Boesse"
to find out about that kind of thing!

So the catalogue may go on, with as little hope of fin-
ishing as Chaucer's *Monk's Tale,* full of sound and fury
and occasionally poetry as well. When James I of Scots
languished in an English prison, he took a book to read
upon and pass the time away, and we may guess what it
was:

> . . . the name is clepit properly
> Boece, eftere him þat was the compiloure,
> Schewing [gude] counsele of philosophye,
> Compilit by that noble senatoure
> Off Rome, quhilom þat was the warldis floure. . . .

[1] *Fall of Princes,* viii, 2633-2639, ed. Bergen (III, 897).

who "Foriugit was to pou*er*t in exile." [1] In his very sufferings Boethius found security:

> And so the vertew of his ʒouth before
> Was in his age the ground of his delytis:
> Fortune the bak him t*u*rnyt, and therefore
> He makith ioye and confort, þ*at* he quit is
> Off their*e* vnsekir warldis appetitis;
> And so aworth he takith his penance,
> And of his vertew maid it suffisance:
>
> With mony a noble reso*un*, as him likit,
> Enditing in his fäir*e* Latyne tong,
> So full of fruyte, and rethor[ik]ly pykit,
> Quhich to declare my sc[e]le is ouer ʒonge. . . . [2]

This is fine praise for a man dead, lo, these many years! In a remarkable poem, *The Kingis Quair*, from which these lines are quoted, the King tells of his own miseries, for which he spends much time blaming Fortune, just as Charles d'Orléans poetically inveighed against the same lady during his term of imprisonment in England. King James has a vision in which he sees the wheel on which the Goddess turns lovers, bringing them to good estate or to woe. It is a slippery affair, and many failed footing thereon, while some were whirled to an ugly pit beneath. Something of a debate on free will is introduced in a discourse conducted by Dame Minerva, who is not unlike Philosophy. This truly fine work inspired the *King's Tragedy* of Dante Gabriel Rossetti. It is also possible that *The Kingis Quair* was itself partly inspired by such a poem as Baudouin de Condé's *Li Prisons d'Amours*. The idea of a prison of love, however, in which Fortune constrains her victims, has doubtless at most a tenuous connexion with the story of Boethius. It would be interesting but impossible at the present time to follow the motif in its various literary forms—for example in Froissart's *Prison Amoureuse*, where, as with Machaut's *Voir Dit*,

---

[1] *The Kingis Quair*, ed. Lawson, pp. 2-3.
[2] *Ibid.*, pp. 4-5.

the narrative is in verse and the epistles in prose; but in most cases resemblance to the *Consolatio* is pretty remote.

Despite the claim of James I to have read the Latin original, we may suspect that the "Boece" which he pondered over in prison was Chaucer's translation. Certainly that was the book which was consulted by Thomas Usk, who, perhaps for shiftiness in politics and for siding with the young Richard II as against the Duke of Gloucester, tasted a prison term and was finally put to death for treason. He wrote his *Testament of Love* in self-defense, a book long assigned to Chaucer but identified as Usk's by the acrostic in the initial letters of the chapters. Brembre, who was executed for the same crime, was a friend of Chaucer's. In the *Testament* there are borrowings from the poet's works and a direct reference to his *Troilus and Criseyde*. The work is in many ways a strange production, somewhat cluttered and heavy. It is a "testament" in the sense of a confession of faith. The author represents himself in prison, bewailing his chance and lamenting the loss of his pearl, Margaryte, who symbolizes among other things divine grace and Holy Church. Once, we infer, he was suspected of Lollardry, but now he wishes to make his orthodoxy plain to every reader. Into his foul dungeon comes a lady, the seemliest and most goodly to his sight that ever appeared. She is divine Love, who like Philosophia, loves wisdom and sets Thomas right concerning his present distress and many incidental questions, including that of fate and free will. Thus "In this boke be many privy thinges wimpled and folde; unneth shul leude [ignorant] men the plites [folds] unwinde." [1] Esoteric the book is indeed, or at least sometimes difficult to follow; Usk treats everything in full. Incidentally his search for his precious pearl seems once or twice reminiscent of the Middle English poem the *Pearl*, and throws a curious light on its interpretation.

Very different in the annals of prison literature, and altogether French in temper and framework, is *Les For-*

[1] *Test.*, 76-77 (ed. Skeat, *Complete Works of Geoffrey Chaucer*, VII, 144).

tunes et Adversitez de Jean Regnier, which by its colophon is also entitled a *Livre de la Prison.* Jean Regnier, whose name appears in acrostic, was imprisoned 1432-1433, and in another work, a "Balade morale que le prisonnier fit," he gloomily uses the *Ubi sunt* formula to ask: "Ou est Boece et Chaton et Thobie?"[1] *Les Fortunes et Adversitez* is a long complaint with lays interspersed, blaming Fortune and calling on God and the Virgin Mary for aid. Espérance sends Jean news that help will eventually come to him. He laments the evils that he beholds destined for France. Several ladies, for whom he makes lays, pay him a visit. Desconfort, leading in Despoir, comes to see him; but at last he is cheered by the sight of Réconfort, who is accompanied by Espoir, and who tells him the story of Job and also that of the penitent thief. Various balades are inserted for the great feast days, and serve an ornamental purpose. Jean takes long leave of the world:

> A Beauvais, droit devant sainct Pierre,
> Ou je suis enfermé en pierre. . . .[2]

Did he see the magnificent wheel of Fortune on the wall of the parish Church of St. Étienne not far away?

But all this seems petty in its elegance. Fortune has a broader canvas than this to work on. The great Jean Gerson (1363-1429), Chancellor of the University of Paris, philosopher, champion of woman in the controversy started by Christine de Pisan, and notable Churchman who took a conspicuous part in the Council of Constance, suffered exile from France at the hands of the Duke of Burgundy. Ruthlessly Gerson had pursued with indictments certain followers of Burgundy because they were implicated in the murder of the Duke of Orléans. He carried the vigour of his onslaught even into the Council of Constance, where presumably he hoped that godly men would stand him in good stead; but the Council failed to

---

[1] *Les Fortunes,* etc., ed. E. Droz (*Soc. Anc. Textes Fr.*), p. 179.
[2] ll. 4287-4288.

lend him much support. In this humiliation he wrote a direct imitation of Boethius, his *De Consolatione Theologiae* in four books of prose and verse treating of the slings and arrows of outrageous Fortune. In a dialogue conducted between Volucer and Monicus we find discussion of the problem of God's will and human free will, the power of chance, and the hope to be discovered in goodness and God. Volucer in a general way represents the active life, and Monicus the contemplative. But why, asks Monicus, in obtaining consolation against the power of chance, against the empty felicity of the world, would not that dialogue of Philosophy and Boethius suffice "which is composed in a style altogether elegant, brief and distinguished, containing most weighty doctrines."[1] Volucer explains, however, that Theology is superior to Philosophy, as grace is to nature, or the mistress to her handmaid, the master to his disciple, eternity to time, intelligence to ratiocination, and the things which are not seen to those which are. The verse uses the metrical forms of Boethius, and the temper of the work is not unworthy of its spiritual ancestor.

One wonders, however, whether the ghost of Boethius was present at the Council of Constance. We remember the case of Pedro de Luna, competing for the highest position of all and completely frustrated therein, deriving his consolation at second hand through Johannes of Dambach. There were others, notably Theodorich Vrie and Jacobus de Teramo, who dealt with the corruptions of the Church in works touched by the influence of the original *Consolatio*. In an *Historia Concilii Constantiensis* in eight books of prose and verse Theodorich Vrie presents a dialogue of Christ and his bride Ecclesia showing the evil inheritance the Church received from Cain, and incidentally referring to the grievous story of Pedro de Luna. Another name for the work is *De Consolatione Ecclesiae*.

---

[1] ". . . qui prorsus eleganti stilo, breui *et* splendido compositus est, sententias grauissimas in se tenens." *Gersonii Opera Omnia*, ed. Du Pin, I, col. 132 (I, pr. ii).

In his *Consolatio Peccatorum* or *Processus Beliali* Jacobus de Teramo gives us the burlesque account of the lawsuit in which Belial prosecuted Christ as an interloper in His harrowing of Hell. Here there is little reflection of Boethius except in the name. Incidentally, Gerson finally achieved the personal title of Doctor Consolatorius, which may have comforted him.

About a hundred years later an Englishman no less famous and of a quality not unlike Gerson's was writing a similar treatise in the Tower of London. In 1534 Sir Thomas More "made" his *Dyalogue of Comforte agaynste Tribulacyon* after he was imprisoned for refusing to compromise his religion to the advantage if not the respectability of Henry VIII. It was written for his children and his friends, and the martyr's courage appears in the playful tone with which some of it is conceived. It purports to be a translation through French from a Latin treatise composed by a Hungarian. In general character it bears more resemblance to Gerson's work than to that of Boethius, and indeed it quotes from another book of the great Frenchman. In three parts it offers the prose dialogue of Anthony and Vincent on the evils suffered in their poor country from the harsh and brutal Turk, who at times obviously carries suggestions of Henry of England and his policies. The suggestions, however, are not quite explicit. Thus with reference to religious difficulties More observes:

. . . but if we tourne as they dooe, and forsake our Sauiour too, and then (for there is no borne Turke so cruell to christen folke, as is *th*e false christen that falleth from the fayth) we shall stand in peril (if we perseuer in *th*e trueth) to be more hardelye handeled, and dye more cruell death by our own countrey men at home, then if we wer taken he*n*ce and caried into Turkye.[1]

The remedy for all ills, according to More, is to be found in religion. The philosophers of old are not quite ade-

[1] *Workes*, ed. Rastell, pp. 1140H-1141A.

quate to help us; for they failed to refer "the finall ende
of theyr coumforte vnto God." [1]   The charges against the
Turk are unsparingly bitter, and one sees that the writer
contemplates martyrdom serenely for the ancient faith in
England.   Four centuries after his death he has been
canonized as a saint.   It is a truly noble book, recently
described by an authority on More as "one of his greatest
works." [2]   It too is a worthy child of the tradition to which
it belongs, in its dignity and also in its special type of
humour not unlike the original *Consolatio*.   Very different is the temper of the *Spiritual Consolation*, written by
Bishop John Fisher (also in the Tower) for his sister
Elizabeth.   Fisher was canonized with More.   Although
he knew Boethius, his work is only a brief and lugubri-
ous complaint or plea for repentance.

At this point it may be interesting to recall a much
earlier work by More, the *Wordes of ffortune to yͤ
people: the Boke of the fayre Gentyl woman, that no man
shulde put his truste or confydence in*.   In this poetical
collection, in stanzas of rime royal, the discourse of Fortune gives a conventional picture of her character and
methods, omitting few if any of the motifs known to
the tradition of her literature.   But it is vividly managed
for all that.   The remedy for injuries received from the
goddess is a familiar one: love virtue, it alone is free.
Another document in much the same sort is the anony-
mous *Complaint against Fortune* in the Shirley manuscript, also in stanzas of rime royal, a little recalling the
verses of Henry of Settimello though not deliberately
reminiscent.   Whoever wrote it holds converse with
Fortune in the usual style:

> Fortune alas. alas what haue I gylt
> In prison thus to lye here desolate
> Art thou the better to haue [me] thus yspylt.
> Nay nay god wote. . . . [3]

---

[1] *Workes*, ed. Rastell, p. 1142C.
[2] Routh, *Sir Thomas More and his Friends 1477-1535*, p. 211. Note pp. 22
and 126 for indications of More's interest in Boethius.
[3] *Anglia* XXXII (1909), 484 ff.

Rather uniquely Fortune here admits that the author is really guiltless of the crime that brought him to prison; but she insists unanswerably that he is punished thus for his other sins.   The humble author offers a prayer to God to protect the Church and to make people virtuous.

We cannot follow in detail the manner in which Boethius was received at the Renaissance.   In Italy the great Rienzi named a son after him.   A century later Politian asks: "Who is keener in dialectic than Boethius, or subtler in mathematics, or more satisfying in philosophy, or more sublime in theology?" [1]   Girolamo Cardano (1501-1576), famous for mathematics and astrology, wrote a work in three books of prose *De Consolatione* urging that the true remedy for ills is found in the interior life: in the use of the mind and in the love of virtue.   This was translated into English by Thomas Bedingfield, better known for his rendering of Machiavelli's Florentine History.   Another English version of Cardano appeared about a century later. Like Sir Thomas More confined to the Tower, John Leslie (1527-1596), Bishop of Ross, composed a work called *Piae afflicti Animi Consolationes, divinaque Remedia,* which was later translated into French with another book of his, *Animi tranquilli Munimentum et Conservatio.* Bishop Leslie's crime was complicity in the attempt to restore Mary Queen of Scots to the throne of England, and he dedicated the work in its original form to her.   It was he, in fact, who arranged to have the papal bull which deposed Elizabeth nailed to the door of the Bishop of London.   Our afflictions, he holds, come from God and not from Fortune.   The consolation which he offers is Christian doctrine, with the advice to be ever instant in prayer, and to fix one's desires on the eternal life.   Thus, for different reasons, Bishop Leslie and Queen Elizabeth both seem to have derived some help from Boethius.   The Belgian Justus Lipsius wrote his *De Constantia* (published

---

[1] "Nam quis Boetio uel in dialecticis acutior? uel subtilior in mathematicis? uel in philosophia locupletior? uel in theologia sublimior?" Politian, *Opera Omnia, Liber Misc.* cap. i, Sig. B 3ʳᵒ, ll. 24-26.

1583-1584), a treatise which belongs in the list of books which offer remedies for grief. Lipsius had suffered the loss of his property through pillage in the civil war in his country. The theme of his work, in two books, is that public as well as private ills derive from fate. Necessity, which comes ultimately from God, rules everything and permits no escape: "Necessitatis non aliud effugium est, quam uelle quod ipsa cogat"[1]—the Renaissance method of saying "In His will is our peace." One must bow, accordingly, to what is inevitable. These ills are external. Charmingly cultivate your garden and seek wisdom. Thus did the stoic retreat within himself, while More had discussed the sins of fear and advised contemplation of the joys of heaven. Yet one may urge that something of both types of remedy is prompted by the original argument of Boethius.

So we might continue our study of the tradition, and Dr. Houghton in his unpublished dissertation has followed it in part in the seventeenth century. Prisoners in that period apparently consoled themselves in a similar way. The father of that Sir Harry Coningsby who translated the *Consolatio* was confined in the Tower and then in Peter House. Doubtless it was for this reason that the son was led to his task; in his preface he tells of his father's sufferings. So too Sir Richard Graham, Lord Preston, another illustrious translator, was sentenced to death for high treason, and spent due time in the Tower and in Newgate. Edward Barlow, priest and prisoner, entertained himself in jail by reading the *Consolatio*. Some eleven hundred years, therefore, after the time of Boethius a natural impulse still led men in disaster or suffering to see a parallel to their own fortune in the story of the *Consolatio*, and to draw refreshment for their souls from its philosophy. This point is the more interesting when we recall the fact that Aristotelianism was on the wane at the time. Boethius must have held his own as a

[1] *De Const.* I, cap. xxi, p. 57.

Platonist or as a moralist, or just for the good sense of his discussion.

Down through the centuries, then, a multitude of readers tried to render the *Consolatio* accessible to others in some form or other, perhaps in the attempt to utilize its effective scheme of presentation or again with the wish to preach its healing doctrine. Impressively in fact as well as in name it was a source of consolation. Boethius clearly stood for much more than an intellectual figure. Among men there are those who going through the vale of misery use it for a well, and the pools are filled with water.

CONCLUSION

WHAT IS POSITIVELY KNOWN about the life of Boethius, we have already observed, is at best meagre. But if a man may show himself in his influence upon others, something of a portrait of the author of the various textbooks and treatises, and especially of the *Consolatio Philosophiae,* is spread before us in the array of details with which we have been occupied. Traits that do not loom large in authorship but that count heavily in making up the total effect of personality may, it is true, be missed. But the learning, the diligence, the logic, the sense of symmetry, are all here together with charity and sympathy and courage. After all, Martianus Capella offered the Seven Liberal Arts, but—to put it in medieval fashion—Boethius added the Four Cardinal Virtues. Even humour is here, in the way Fortune holds forth and Philosophy disciplines in the *Consolatio* and then in countless appearances in subsequent literature. And the poetry of the *carmina,* an inspiration to numerous verses mundane and celestial, is more than just a criticism of life:

> Sunt etenim pennae uolucres mihi
> Quae celsa conscendant poli.
> Quas sibi cum uelox mens induit,
> Terras perosa despicit. . . .[1]

King Alfred or his follower wrote: "Ic hæbbe fiðru fugle swiftran . . ."[2] and later Dante spoke of Beatrice as:

> . . . quella pia, che guidò le penne
> De le mie ali a così alto volo.[3]

---

[1] *Cons. Philos.* IV, m. i:
"For I have swift and nimble wings which will ascend the lofty skies,
With which when thy quick mind is clad, it will the loathèd earth despise . . ." (Loeb trans., p. 303.)

[2] Krapp, *The Paris Psalter and the Meters of Boethius,* p. 188 (No. 24).

[3] *Par.* xxv, 49-50. She furnished the plumes, *ibid.,* xv, 53-54.

Chaucer, soaring in the clutches of his indefatigable
teacher, the eagle, sees the spacious firmament on high
and comments thus:

> And thoo thoughte y upon Boece,
> That writ, "A thought may flee so hye
> Wyth fetheres of Philosophye,
> To passen everych element. . . ." [1]

Matters intellectual and moral engaged the interest of
Boethius, but he had further insight. How many others
rose upon these same pinions into the realm of the imagination?

From the tradition of his life in medieval accounts, both
in the *Vitae* appearing with his works and in other references, we have seen that he was regarded as a saint and as
an intellectual figure. But as a saint his cult was re-
strained; and the average modern may take satisfaction in
observing that through all the eulogy and amid the blunders the image is clearest of a man of character. We forget to-day that the calendar of saints is inclusive, and that
here Boethius may find a place with men like Thomas
Aquinas and Albertus Magnus and Thomas More. After
decapitation, according to legend, he carried his head in
his hands, but he did not have to lose it completely. Nor
was his learning forgotten, certainly not by those who
commented on his works, or translated or imitated them,
or used them as textbooks and heard lectures on them at
Oxford or on the left bank of the Seine. His own martyrdom lent force to the reality of his convictions in the
Consolatio, and the idealism of that in turn added significance to his other treatises. The suspected taint of heresy,
for which Bruno of Corvey found fault with his Platonism, seems not to have been discovered by many readers
nor to have vitiated his influence. Alfred found him "a
man most truly wise," concerned for the religion of his
country; the author of the Provençal *Boece* saw him on
his knees in prayer; Gerbert of Aurillac celebrated his

[1] *House of Fame,* 972-975 (*Complete Works,* ed. Robinson, p. 341).

"intellect divine"; Boccaccio wrote of his undying fame among the philosophers; [1] in the seventeenth century he is regarded as a martyr for the old religion, and almost in our own day Leo XIII sanctioned his cult for the diocese of Pavia. From his own time onwards he is steadily praised for sanctity and sense.

We need hardly repeat here what has been already dealt with—and then in summary fashion—regarding the importance of his books in medieval education. The enormous number of manuscripts and the fact that they were widely used in the universities tell their own story. How often the historians who treat of instruction in the various arts have had to say that in this art or that the basis for work was the textbook furnished by Boethius! As an authority on arithmetic he appears in an allegory of Honorius of Autun, in the *Apocalypsis* of Bishop Golias, and probably in the sculpture of Chartres Cathedral. For Henri d'Andeli's *Battle of the Seven Arts* he was preeminent in logic. Chaucer knew him best as a philosopher and an authority on music. Quotations from his works were in the writings and on the lips of many conspicuous men throughout the whole period. Writers of note translated the *Consolatio* and borrowed from it. Still others copied its form or substance. How then may one even approximate an accurate analysis of the influence that Boethius exerted on his fellow men, when his offering was so rich and so varied?

A full analysis would of course be impossible, but an attempt to indicate some of its general outlines may be worth while. Anything of the sort must naturally be quite tentative, and yet it need not be entirely impressionistic. The conclusions that result are in part like those that sprang from a consideration of the life or the legend. Here too we find sanctity and sense. The *Consolatio* and the *Opuscula Sacra* carried the idealism and the religion of their author. What then of the intellectual content of the works as a whole? We need not stop to consider the

[1] *De Casibus*, VIII, xviii.

soundness of the mathematics or the musical theory or the science of the textbooks. Our problem is briefly to determine what is the nature of the philosophy of Boethius wherever he sets it forth, if indeed we may discover some points that suggest a general harmony in its scheme. In the textbooks we notice, of course, his concern for mankind and his belief in the intellectual life. But what was the substance of the intellectual life he offered?

It is the fashion to-day to trace elements of Neoplatonism in all true religion and idealistic philosophy. That Boethius derived help from the Neoplatonists cannot be denied, but the fact must not receive too much emphasis. He made considerable use of their commentaries on Aristotle. His approach to the *Categories* was through the *Introduction* of Porphyry. Whether or not they gave him the initial idea of reconciling Aristotle with Plato or at least of relating the two in his study, they reminded him of the method. Moreover, they furnished him with important material. His discussion of divine prescience and human free will in the *Consolatio* is indebted to a treatise of Proclus; and his description of the orb of destiny of which Providence is the centre probably comes from Plotinus. These matters had a wide influence through his mediation, at least in part, and affected medieval thought. But he went further than Neoplatonism; and Proclus and Plotinus themselves, perhaps, led him back to Aristotle and Plato.

The doctrine of reminiscence in Plato is reflected in the *Consolatio*, notably in the following lines:

> Quod si Platonis musa personat uerum,
> Quod quisque discit immemor recordatur.[1]

More important, however, is the description of the frame of the universe in III, m. ix, which achieved wide attention as Platonic. In both instances it seems likely that the

---

[1] *Cons. Philos.*, III, m. xi, 15-16:
"If Plato's heavenly muse the truth us tell,
We learning things remember them anew." (Loeb trans., p. 287.)

approach of Boethius was through the commentary of
Proclus on the *Timaeus*. The discussion in Plotinus of
the divine centre round which (as centre of all centres)
souls revolve must have reminded Boethius of Aristotle's
figure of that centre of stability which is God. His frequent references to love as ordering and controlling the
universe is Platonic, and so is the idea of each element
seeking its proper region; but it is hard to tell whether he
derived this material from Plato or the Neoplatonists.
In his theory of weight he was led by both, perhaps, to
Aristotle.

It is chiefly as an Aristotelian, we may be sure, that he
influenced the Middle Ages. His textbooks on logic carried this doctrine. Even when he seems a Stoic in his
attitude toward destiny in the *Consolatio,* he moves on to
the position regarding free will which is truly Aristotle's;
and from that same embodiment of good sense he took the
theory of conditional necessity which enabled him completely to escape from determinism. His Fortune or his
mobile Fate may justly be regarded as a personification of
Aristotle's "incidental cause" which is ultimately subservient to a rational deity. With these points clear, it is
certain that as a moralist he achieved his greatest power
from the same source; and perhaps it is not too much to
say that in his argument the very tone has a moderation
and quiet cogency which is like Aristotle's scientific detach-
ment. In Boethius's metaphysics, in his view of the divine
simplicity and peace, he has followed apparently all three
of his chief sources; but in such matters he does not stop
there.

The devotion of the Neoplatonists is intellectual when
they lift their gaze to the divine Principle. Their worship is marked with fervour but hardly with what we ordinarily mean by love, except as one adores what is supreme.
When the Greeks refer to God as father it is simply as
creator. Love with them is an attraction for what is desirable, in which—as indeed in their consideration of the

armma qui quonda stu
dio florente peregi
flebilis heu mestos cogo

Plate 6, Boethius, Philosophy, and the Poetical Muses

divine Principle—the whole question of Personality is neglected and omitted. The famous definition of personality which Boethius gave to the philosophers [1] shows his evaluation of the importance of that factor. As a Christian he believed in a personal God, a Deity that cherished human personality. With him, accordingly, love is something more than the Platonic lure. Comparisons may be arbitrary; but with this fact recognized let us compare a passage in Plotinus with a similar one in Boethius. Plotinus, we may note, is less austere than Plato:

Thus the Supreme as containing no otherness is ever present with us; we with it when we put otherness away. It is not that the Supreme reaches out to us seeking our communion: we reach towards the Supreme; it is we that become present . . . when we look, our Term is attained; this is rest; this is the end of singing ill; effectively before Him, we lift a choral song full of God.

In this choiring, the soul looks upon the wellspring of Life, wellspring also of Intellect, beginning of Being, fount of Good, root of Soul. It is not that these are poured out from the Supreme lessening it as if it were a thing of mass . . . so long as the sun shines, so long there will be light.[2]

The passage from Boethius is, to be sure, not a disquisition; it is poetry:

Thou with like cause doest make the souls and lesser lives,
Fix them in chariots swift, and widely scatterest
O'er heaven and earth; then at Thy fatherly behest
They stream, like fire returning, back to Thee, their God.
Dear Father, let my mind Thy hallowed seat ascend,
Let me behold the spring of grace and find Thy light,
That I on Thee may fix my soul's well cleared sight,
Cast off the earthly weight wherewith I am opprest,
Shine as Thou art most bright, Thou only calm and rest

---

[1] *Contra Eut.* iii, 4-5: "naturae rationabilis indiuidua substantia."
[2] *Enneades,* VI, ix, 8-9 (trans. Mackenna and Page, *Plotinus on the One and Good,* pp. 248-249).

To pious men whose end is to behold Thy ray,
Who their beginning art, their guide, their bound, and way.[1]

In thus addressing God as the Way, the Truth, and the
Life, Boethius introduces a quality similar to that which
appears in the rendering of Neoplatonism by the pseudo-
Dionysius. This Supreme Being does reach out to us
seeking our communion. These verses seem closer to
Christian hymns than to Greek poetry. Touched with
Platonism they doubtless are, but with something more.

The full moral and philosophical influence of Boethius
carried, of course, only with those writers who produced
something like a complete translation of the *Consolatio*.
That is, King Alfred, Jean de Meun, Chaucer, Walton,
and the rest. Here approximately the same doctrine was
conveyed to others even if the idiom was different. Alfred
had other books translated by his followers, but this particular work he seems to have preferred to do himself.
Jean de Meun and Chaucer borrowed great sections of the
Consolatio for their own poetry, but they also took the
trouble to make workmanlike translations of the whole
treatise. In Chaucer's use of passages in his *Troilus and
Criseyde* he dignifies the poem with a philosophical background, and at times shows the spiritual leaven of Boethius
at its subtle work. Modern critics sometimes regard such
lines as the medieval intrusion of the sententious, and thus
they miss an important quality in the poetry. Surely one
cannot thus set aside Troilus's hymn to love (III,
1744 ff.); it is quite arbitrary therefore to dispose in that

---

[1] III, m. ix, 18-28 (Loeb trans., pp. 265-267). Cf. the Latin:

Tu causis animas paribus uitasque minores
Prouehis et leuibus sublimes curribus aptans
In caelum terramque seris quas lege benigna
Ad te conuersas reduci facis igne reuerti.
Da pater augustam menti conscendere sedem,
Da fontem lustrare boni, da luce reperta
In te conspicuos animi defigere uisus.
Dissice terrenae nebulas et pondera molis
Atque tuo splendore mica! Tu namque serenum,
Tu requies tranquilla piis, te cernere finis,
Principium, uector, dux, semita, terminus idem.

way of other lines from Boethius for which one may have less taste. In particular the magnificent conclusion gathers up the whole experience of the poem and interprets it. I dwell on this point lest the modern disdain for the sententious lead us entirely to disregard the moral and spiritual influence of Boethius because of nothing greater, on our part, than critical prejudice.

If the doctrine of the *Consolatio* had a profound effect in Chaucer's case, I believe that the form of it had in Dante's. The dialogue between the prisoner and Lady Philosophy prepared the way for Dante's instruction conducted by Beatrice and by Virgil. In many instances writers of the period borrowed from the scheme of Boethius without catching anything of his spirit. This is more or less true in the numerous debates with Fortune, in the many remote *Consolationes,* and in the works which took advantage of the variety gained by alternating prose and verse. But with Dante we find a purpose and a spirit that harmonizes with that of the "sainted soul" he takes pains to celebrate. The very passage I have quoted above from III, m. ix is like a summary of the *Paradiso.* With Dante as with Boethius the love that is common to all is the love which turns the sun and the other stars:

> Hic est cunctis communis amor
> Repetuntque boni fine teneri,
> Quia non aliter durare queant,
> Nisi conuerso rursus amore
> Refluant causae quae dedit esse.[1]

But the influence of Boethius is not limited to perfect representations of his thought or artistic plan. He was

---

[1] *Cons. Philos.*, IV, m. vi, 44-48:
> This powerful love
> Is common unto all,
> Which for desire of good do move
> Back to the springs from whence they first did fall.
> No worldly thing
> Can a continuance have
> Unless love back again it bring
> Unto the cause which first the essence gave.
> (Loeb trans., p. 357.)

the first among medieval writers to set forth the picture of the Goddess Fortune and her wheel with anything like a full and proper characterization. Henceforth those who wrote dialogues of the kind, short or long, or who composed apostrophes or complaints to her, are in some measure indebted to the *Consolatio*. Hildebert of Lavardin, Henry of Settimello, the Spanish Marquis of Santillana, one thinks of many in this company. Even the briefest allusions to Fortune really show outlying ripples of the same great rhythmic course. Manuscript illuminations and sculpture continue the tradition of the figure. Moreover the influence from the *carmina* shows another channel, where the use of metres, the quotation of lines, the borrowing of ideas, going from one author to another in crosscurrents, sometimes, of indebtedness, have great significance. The poem on the Former Age (*Cons.* II, m. v) was widely popular; the verses on nobility (II, m. vii and III, m. vi) were often quoted. But we cannot pause to discuss the influence of Boethius in the matter of lyric power or quality, inviting as the subject is. In spite of Lady Philosophy's repudiation of the "sweet poison" of the Muses, the breath of poetry truly informed his verse, and his poems were not easily forgotten in the Middle Ages.

In some part of the medieval world, then, one could have heard these lyrics set to music; one could have gazed on a picture of Fortune and her wheel in stone from the same tradition; one could have seen students poring over the Boethian textbooks on arithmetic and logic and the other Arts, and heard great scholars lecturing on their material in all the important universities; one could have found a king translating the *Consolatio*, another reading it in prison and writing a poem from its inspiration; one could have discovered the moralists borrowing its lessons and the artists helping themselves to its motifs. Everywhere it is the same extraordinary fact, the influence of this philosopher and martyr who was put to death in the sixth century! The picture is surely without parallel.

The total impression we get is that his work was good in effect; that it served to steady men, and taught them to use reason and wisdom. The greatness of Boethius in this and that realm or in the different centuries may seem to fluctuate; but the stature of his Lady Philosophy suffered change, and he is like her. Interestingly enough, after his death, he ceases to be the victim; he himself becomes the teacher and instructs the whole Middle Ages. Frequent complaints go up to Fortune for the same old causes, and he gives the answer of Philosophia. This may sometimes carry with it something of the music of Plato, but it is likely to be told in the words of Aristotle. Saintliness and good sense mark the man's path through the centuries. In the absence of more details regarding the personal habits of his life and the various things he did, this, we may fairly assume, is what he was like.

APPENDIX

APPENDIX

THE INTRODUCTION

Pages 1 ff. On the life and works of Boethius, see Usener, *Anecdoton Holderi;* Stewart, *Boethius;* Murari, *Dante e Boezio,* 3-155; Grabmann, *Die Gesch. der Scholast. Methode,* I, 148 ff.; Manitius, *Gesch. der lat. Lit. des Mittelalters,* I, 22 ff.; Geyer, *Die patristische und scholast. Philos.* (Ueberweg, *Grundriss,* zweiter Teil), 135 ff. and 669 f.; De Wulf, *Hist. de la Philos. Médiévale,* I (1934), 111-119, and 125-126; Fortescue and Smith, *Cons. Philos.,* xi ff. and 188 ff.; Rand, *Founders of the Mid. Ages,* 135 ff. and 310 ff.; and Schurr, *Die Trinitätslehre des Boethius,* xii-xxx.

Page 2. Taylor includes his study of Boethius in his chapter on "The Latin Transmitters of Antique and Patristic Thought," *Mediaeval Mind,* I, ch. v. Graf calls him "il primo degli scolastici" in *Roma nella Memoria e nelle Immag. del Medio Evo,* II (Turin, 1883), p. 322. Cf. too Frantl, *Gesch. der Logik,* II (1861), pp. 20, 108 f.; Grabmann, *Die Gesch. der scholast. Methode,* I, 148-177 ("Boethius, der letzte Römer—der erste Scholastiker"); and Rand, *Harvard Studies in Class. Philol.,* XV (1904), p. 28 ("the first of the scholastics") and *Founders of the Mid. Ages,* 156 and 317. Burdach would also have him "der Inspirator der Renaissance" ("Die humanistischen Wirkungen der Trostschrift," etc., in the *Deutsche Vierteljahrsschrift,* XI [1933], p. 533).

Pages 3-4. Bibliographical material for editions of the works of Boethius will be found in the references cited above. See Migne's *Patr. Lat.,* LXIII-LXIV (Paris, 1847); for the *Com.* on *De Interp.,* περὶ ἑρμηνείας, ed. C. Meiser, Leipzig, 1877; *Com.* on Porphyry's *Isagoge,* ed.

S. Brandt, Vienna and Leipzig, 1906; *Cons. Philos.*, ed.
Peiper; ed. Fortesque and Smith; ed. Stewart and Rand
(*Loeb Libr.*); and also ed. Weinberger (*Corpus Script.
Eccles. Lat., LXVII*). On the survival of some of the
logical books, see Haskins, *Studies in the History of
Mediaeval Science*, pp. 223 ff. On chronology see espe-
cially Brandt, "Entstehungszeit und zeitliche Folge der
Werke von Boethius," in *Philologus*, LXII (1903), 141-
154 and 234-275; and McKinlay in *Harvard Studies in
Class. Philol.*, XVIII (1907), 123 ff. On Boethius's
borrowing from the commentaries of Porphyry and
Syrianus cf. Prantl, *Gesch. der Logik*, I, 694; J. Bidez
in *Comptes rendus de l'Académie des Inscriptions et Belles-
Lettres*, L (1922), pp. 346 ff.; and *Revue belge de Philol.
et d'Hist.*, II (1923), 189 ff. For Ennodius, see the
Mon. Germ. Hist., Auct. Antiq., VII, p. 236: "tu in me,
emendatissime hominum, dignaris praedicare uirtutes,
quem in annis puerilibus sine aetatis praeiudicio industria
fecit antiquum, qui per diligentiam imples omne quod
cogitur, cui inter uitae exordia ludus est lectionis assiduitas
et deliciae sudor alienus, in cuius manibus duplicato igne
rutilat qua ueteres face fulserunt. nam quod uix maioribus
circa extremitatem uitae contigit, hoc tibi abundat in
limine." Also, p. 268: "nemo dissonantiam Atticae per-
fectionis metuat et Romanae, nec praecipua gentium bona
in societatem dubitet conuenire. unus es qui utrumque
conplecteris, et quidquid uiritim distributum poterat
satis esse, auidus maximarum rerum possessor in-
cludis."

Page 4. On the method of the *Consolatio*, see Usener,
Anecdoton Holderi, pp. 51-52; Rand, in *Harvard Studies
in Class. Philol.*, XV (1904), 1 ff.; Klingner, *De Boethii
Cons. Philos.*, 1-120, reviewed by Rand, *Am. Journ. of
Philology*, XLIV (1923), 86-87; Patch, *Speculum* IV
(1929), 62 ff.; VIII (1933), 41 ff.; and X (1935),
393 ff.; and Rand, *Founders of the Mid. Ages*, p. 149
(". . . I am concerned to prove that Boethius was not a

Neoplatonist . . .") and pp. 159 ff. Cf. *Camb. Med. Hist.*, I (N. Y., 1911), p. 579.

CHAPTER I

Pages 8-9. For the idea of Boethius as a magician cf. Bonnaud, *Speculum*, IV (1929), pp. 200-201. With regard to Elpis or Helpis, see Obbarius, *Cons. Phil.*, pp. xii-xiii, n. 16; Semeria, *Il cristianesimo di S. Boezio rivendicato*, pp. 13-14; Murari, *Dante e Boezio*, pp. 60 ff. Murari derives the name from a mistaken reading of the *Consolatio*, II, pr. iii, 20 ff. and from an epitaph in San Pietro in Cieldoro (see Peiper, *Philos. Cons.* p. xxxvi). On the idea of study at Athens, see Murari, *op. cit.*, 13-14, and 59-60; and Bonnaud in *Speculum*, IV (1929), 198 ff.

On the *Vitae*, see Peiper, *op. cit.*, pp. xxix-xxxv; M. Esposito, *Hermathena*, XVII (1913), pp. 109-114 (*Vita* in a MS. in Corpus Christi College, Oxford, dated xi cent.); Schepss, *Handschriftliche Studien z. Boethius De Cons. Phil.*, 39 ff.; also *Archiv. f. d. Studium d. neueren Spr.*, XCIV (1895), p. 156. For the legend see Murari, *Dante e Boezio*, pp. 57 ff. and Graf, *Roma nella Memoria e nelle Immag. del Medio Evo*, Turin, 1923, pp. 622 ff.

Page 9. In the introduction to his edition of the *Anonymus Valesii*, p. lxxvii, Cessi questions the attribution to the Bishop Maximian. He puts the date very early, and suggests that the author was perhaps an eyewitness of what he describes, *ibid.*, p. clxvii. See, for another edition, Mommsen's in *MGH., Auct. Antiq.* IX, pp. 306-328. Stewart (*Boethius*, p. 33) interprets Theodoric's message to the Emperor as political retaliation, but for summary discussion of the whole matter see Rand, *Founders of the Mid. Ages*, pp. 322-323.

Page 12. For the message to the Emperor in Alfred's prefatory account cf. the *Vitae* in Peiper, *Philos. Cons.* pp. xxxi and xxxv; for the murder of Pope John, *ibid.*, p. xxxv. See Peiper's note on Alfred's version, *ibid.*, p. xxx.

Page 13. On the Provençal account of Boethius, cf. the *Vitae* in Peiper, *op. cit.*, pp. xxx and xxxii, and see Stewart, *Boethius*, pp. 178 ff. On the reference to the feigned letters, see Ebert, *Allgem. Gesch. d. Lit. d. Mittelalters im Abendlande*, III (1887), 359, n. 4.

Page 15. Note 1, an account of the Church and the inscription may be found in the *Anonymi Ticinensis*, ed. Maiocchi and Quintavalle, pp. 12-13, which indicates that the verses quoted by Gualla are incomplete omitting several after the second line. A longer version (Graf, *Roma nella Mem. e nelle Immag. del M.E.*, p. 633, n. 36; *Anon. Tic.*, 13, n. 1) at least approximating the fuller form that originally appeared on the tomb is printed in Allegranza's *De Sepulcris Christianis*, p. 49, from the end of a codex written in 1390. Murari, *Dante e Boezio*, p. 112, cites an act of 1665 recording a chapel at S. Pietro in Cieldoro dedicated to S. Severino Boezio, and another of 1576 referring to the altar in his name. On the veneration of the relics at the tomb, see Graf, *op. cit.*, pp. 630 ff.; for records see *Acta Sanctorum, Maii*, VI, 704 ff. On the martyrdom of Boethius see the material collected by Murari, *op. cit.*, pp. 114 f., especially the distich of Monza (vi century—see Biraghi, *Boezio Filosofo, Teologo, Martire*, etc., pp. 36-37). Cf. Nitzsch, *Das System des Boethius*, pp. 13 ff. For the idea of his decapitation, see *Gestorum Pontif. Roman.*, I (1898), *MGH.*, p. 136, Ioannes I (523-526); and for the motif of his carrying his head in his hands, the *Anon. Tic.*, p. 13 and n. 2; Baronius, *Annals*, A.D. 526, XVII, (vol. IX, Lucca, 1741, p. 354); and Rota, *Cons. Phil.*, pref. [sig. a 5ᵛ]. For the decree which sanctioned the cult at Pavia see the *Acta S. Sedis*, XVI (1898), pp. 302-303, and Fortescue and Smith, *Cons. Philos.*, pp. 186-187. For further details on his cult, see Capsoni, *Mem. istor. d. città di Pavia*, III (1788), xci, pp. 107-108, and Bosisio, *Intorno al Luogo del Supplizio*. Details on the matter of the burial of the relics may be found in Fortescue and Smith, *Cons.*

Phil., pp. xxii-xxiv, where the translation to their present location in 1923 is reported from a communication received by the editor.

Pages 16-17.   On the restraint of the cult, see Graf, *Roma nella Memoria e nelle Immag. del M.E.*, p. 643. For the legend of Theodoric see *ibid.*, pp. 643 ff. On the translation of Caussin's *Holy Court* and its use, see Hodgkin in *Italy and Her Invaders*, III, pp. 573-575. It was published 1626-1638. Other editions followed in 1638, 1650, 1663, and 1678.

Page 18.   Bruno of Corvey's commentary on the *CP.*, III, m. ix, is edited by Cardinal Mai, *Classicorum Auctorum e Vaticanis Codicibus*, III, pp. 331-345; for John of Salisbury, see the *Policrat.*, vii, 15. Cf. Obbarius, *Cons. Philos.*, Jena, 1843, xxviii ff.; Graf, *op. cit.*, pp. 615 ff. and p. 622, n. 20; Murari, *Dante e Boezio*, pp. 116 ff.; Fortescue and Smith, *op. cit.*, pp. xxv ff. and 191-192. On the religion of Boethius, see also Usener, *Anec. Hold.*; Nitzsch, *Das System des Boethius*; Rand, *Harvard Studies in Class. Philol.*, XV (1904).

CHAPTER II

Page 22.   On the number of MSS. see Schepss, "Zu Boethius," in *Commentationes Woelfflinianae*, p. 277, and Engelbrecht, [*Wiener*] *Sitzungsberichte*, CXLIV (1901), pp. 1-60. For Geoffrey's *Historia*, see Griscom's edition, p. 19, and for the *Roman de la Rose* Langlois's, I, p. 32.

Page 22.   For the MSS. in medieval libraries see Laistner, *Thought and Letters in Western Europe*, pp. 180 ff.; Lehmann, *Mittelalterliche Bibliothekskataloge Deutschlands und der Schweiz*, I, 87, 250, etc.; and also Gottlieb, *Ueber mittelalterliche Bibliotheken*, p. 162 (Durham); p. 31 (Engelberg i. d. Schweiz before 1175 had the *Cons.*); p. 92 (Chateaudun); cf. pp. 294, 443, etc. Also cf. Manitius, *Rheinisches Museum für Philol.*, n. s. XLVII (1892), *Ergänzungsheft*, pp. 130-135. At Peterborough were several: see James, *Lists of MSS. Formerly in Peterborough Abbey Library (Supplts. to Trans. Bibl. Soc.*, No. 5), p. 46, No. 119, etc. The *Cons.* was at Llanthony Priory (in the suburbs of Gloucester) in the hands of a schoolmaster, see *Speculum*, III (1928), pp. 587 ff. For Rievaux, see Wright and Halliwell, *Reliq. Antiq.*, II (1843), pp. 185, 187; translated in Benham's *English Lit. from Widsith to the Death of Chaucer*, pp. 437, 439. Cf. generally Delisle, *Cabinet des manuscrits*, I (1868), 510-511; II (1874), 429, 447, etc.; III (1881), 63, 86-87 (Sorbonne); Faucon, *La Librairie des Papes d'Avignon*, I (1886),11, 64, 70, etc.; II (1887), 13, 33, 135, etc.; *Catal. Général des MSS. des Bibl. Publ. des Départements*, I, 232, No. 439; 233, No. 441 (Laon); Montfaucon, *Bibl. Bibliothecarum Manuscriptorum Nova*, II (1739), 1295, etc. For Paris see the *Disciplina Scholarium*, in which textbooks of Boethius are required (Migne, *Patr. Lat.*, LXIV, 1223-1238). This pseudo-Boethian document issued from Paris in the xiii cent. See Haskins, *Med. Culture*, p. 73 and n. l. and the *Compendium . . . of the Univ. of Paris*, ed. Burke, p. 33. For Chartres, see Clerval's *Les Écoles de Chartres*, pp. 26, 110, etc. and Fulbert of Chartres (Migne, *op. cit.*, CXLI) col. 284. For St. Gall, see Gottlieb, *op. cit.*, p. 26; Scherrer, *Verzeichniss der Handschriften der Stiftsbibl.*, Nos. 816, 818, 825, etc.; Lehmann, *op. cit.*, I, 87, and 89 (Grimald's library).

West's translation of Alcuin is quoted by Benham, *op. cit.*, pp. 63-68, with notes. On the passage cf. *Neues Archiv*, XI (1886), 553; also note James, *Fasciculus J. W. Clark Dicatus*, pp. 2-96, "Catal. of the Library of the Augustin. Friars at York" (for Boethius, 30, 48, 64, 74, from the xiv and xv centuries); and Leach, *Educational Charters and Documents*, pp. 10 ff. For Leofric's gift to Exeter see *The Exeter Book of Old Eng. Poetry*, p. 28 and n. 101.

Page 23.   For the clerk who would lend *De Musica* see *Epist. Karol. Aevi*, IV, *MGH.*, *Epist.* VI, Berlin, 1925, p. 197 (No. 32).   For Servatus Lupus see his *Correspondance*, ed. Levillain, pp. 110 and 214 ff.   For Dr. Dee's books see James, *Lists of MSS. Formerly Owned by Dr. John Dee*, (*Supplts. to Trans. Bibl. Soc.*, No. 1) p. 21, No. 47; p. 27, No. 114.   Cf. also James, *MSS. in the Library at Lambeth Palace*, pp. 17-18, and James, *Descriptive Catalogue of the MSS . . . Lambeth Palace*, Part I (1930), pp. 106-108 (No. 67).   On the supposed Boccaccio autograph MS. of the *Consolatio* see Hortis, *Studj sulle Opere Latine*, p. 341; cf. Narducci, *Intorno all' autenticità di un codice Vaticano contenente il trattato di B.*, and Hecker, *Boccaccio-Funde*, pp. 28-29, n. 2.

Page 24.   On musical settings for some of the *carmina* see de Coussemaker, *Hist. de l'Harmonie au M.A.*, pp. 100-102 and 151 (I, m. v; IV, m. vii, composed by the ninth century or earlier, perhaps by Boethius); Manitius, *Gesch. der lat. Lit. des M.A.*, I, p. 33 (in the psalter of Louis the German); also the Dutch version of 1585 by Coornhert.

On echoes of Boethius see Manitius, *Gesch. der lat. Lit.*, I, pp. 622 ff. (Hrotsvitha); Migne, *Patr. Lat.*, CXXVI, 303 (Hincmar); CXCIII, 1006 (Gerhoh); CCV, 251, 252, 301 (Petr. Cantor); CCXII, 717 (Helinandus); CCX, 732, 856, 865, 866 (Alanus de Insulis); CXCIX, 622 (John of Salisbury); also CLXXX, 12-13 (Hermann Tornac.); CCVI, 155, 212, 245, 300, 345 (Thos. Cisterc.) etc.   For Abailard's use of Boethius see Sikes, *Peter Abailard*, pp. 50 and *passim*. For Walter Map, *De Nugis Cur.*, I, i; V, vii; William of Malmesbury, *Gesta Reg.*, ii, section 167 (*Rolls Series*, I,

p. 195); Roger Bacon, *Opus Majus*, ed. Bridges, II, 66, 244, etc.; Holkot, *Opus super sap. Salomonis*, lect. xcv and cvii. Note echoes in the passage from Valla cited by Fortescue and Smith, *Cons. Philos.*, pp. 182-183. For poetic echoes also [*Wiener*] *Sitzungsberichte*, CXVII (1888), xii, 24-26, and CXXI (1890), vii, 14-18. Manitius, *op. cit.*, I, 186, notes that Columban uses a verse measure from Boethius; 313, that Walafrid Strabo was similarly influenced. Consult his indices for other references, and see Patch, *The Goddess Fortuna in Med. Lit., passim.* Cf. De Wulf's *Philos. and Civiliz.*, p. 57: "Throughout the twelfth century the philosophers are unanimous in repeating the words of Boethius: *persona est . . .*" etc. Cf. C. C. J. Webb, *God and Personality*, Aberdeen, 1919, pp. 47 f.

For Albertus Magnus, see *Physic.* II, ii, cap. xx (vol. III, pp. 155-156). Cf. Thorndike, *Hist. of Magic and Exper. Science*, II, 589; Haskins, *Studies in the Hist. of Med. Science*, p. 239.

Pages 24-25. On Jean de Meun, see Langlois, *Origines et Sources*, pp. 136-138, 185-186, and Galpin *Publ. Mod. Lang. Assoc.*, XXIV (1909), pp. 337 ff. For the poem itself see Langlois's edition, *Soc. Anc. Textes Fr.*, 5052 ff. and 17302 ff. For Brunetto Latini, cf. Baur, *Boetius und Dante*, p. 9. For Dante, see Murari, *Dante e Boezio*, p. 230, n. 1; 231 ff.; 365 ff., etc., and Fortescue and Smith, *op. cit.*, pp. 201 ff. For Boccaccio see *Comento sopra Dante*, (*Opere* XI), 156; *Gen. Deorum*, trans. Betussi, pp. 11*vo.* etc., (Latin, p. 9); *De Casibus*, VIII, xviii. In his famous defense of Poetry in the *Genealogia* he discusses what Boethius has to say in apparent contempt of the Muses, 246*vo.*-247, (Latin, p. 382); cf. Hortis, *Studj sulle Opere Latine*, pp. 195, 196, and 208, and Osgood, *Boccaccio on Poetry*, pp. 94 ff. Note also the description of Philosophy, *Gen. Deorum*, 229*vo.*-230 (Latin, pp. 358-359); Osgood, *op. cit.*, pp. 32-33, notes p. 153.

For Chaucer, cf. below pp. 149 and 156; and see Jefferson, *Chaucer and the Cons. Philos.*, and Stewart, *Boethius*, pp. 260 ff. For Lydgate, see the *Fall of Princes;* cf. also *Troy Book*, iv, 3008 ff., and his use in *Reson and Sens.* of *Les Échecs Amoureux* (cf. *Mod. Lang. Notes*, XXIX [1914], 197 and Sieper, *Les Échecs Amoureux*, 130 ff., 211 ff.) Gavin Douglas acknowledges indebtedness, *Poetical Works*, IV, p. 6, 12 ff.

For Christine de Pisan, see *Œuvres*, ed. M. Roy (*Soc. Anc. Textes Fr.*) I, 97; II, 297, etc. For Pontano, *Opera Omnia*, pp. 139 *vo.*-140; and Pico della Miran., *Opera*, I, 170-171, 215. For others see Thorndike, *Magic and Exper. Science*, II, 407 (Barthol. Anglicus); Baehrens, *Poet. Lat. Min.*, V, 419; G. Reisch, *Margarita Philos.*, VIII, xvi; Deschamps, cited below. Stewart, *Boethius*, pp. 163 ff. suggests that the *Beowulf* shows influence in its treatment of Wyrd as subordinate to God and in its use of free will. The parallel passages he cites are not convincing to me: 1059-1060, cf. *Cons. Phil.*, II, pr. i, 47; 1060-1062, cf. *ibid.*, II, pr. iv, 66-67.

The Latin of Otto of Freising reads as follows: "Cum iuxta Boetium in omnibus philosophiae disciplinis ediscendis atque tractandis summum uitae positum solamen existimem, uestrae nobilitatis personam eo familiarius ac iocundius amplector. . . ." *Ottonis Episc. Frisingensis Chron.*, ed. Hofmeister, p. 4, ll. 3-6; also *Mon. Germ. Histor.*, ed. Pertz, *Scriptores*, XX, p. 117. See also Hofmeister, *op. cit.*, p. 229, 31 ff., and the *Gesta Friderici*, I, section 5. Note Peiper's references, *Philos. Cons.*, pp. lxiv f.

Page 26. Cf. Weinberger, *Philos. Cons.*, pp. xxv-xxvii. For the edition of 1473 see Brunet's *Manuel*, I, 301; Graesse, *Trésor*, I, 463; *Gesamtkatalog der Wiegendrucke*, IV (1930), 342. The first collected edition is noted in the *Gesamtkatalog*, IV, 296-297. Graesse speaks of the *Cons. Phil.* as "imprimé probablement à Savigliano en 1470." Cf. Vernazza, *Osservazioni tipo-*

grafiche sopra libri impr. in Piemonte nel sec. xv.; and
see the *Gesamtkatalog,* IV, 300. Fortescue and Smith,
Cons. Philos., p. 192, give 1476 as the date for Coburger's
first edition.
For the later editions see Brunet's *Manuel,* I, 301 ff.;
Graesse, *Trésor,* I, 462 ff.; Bateson, *Catal. of the Library
of Syon Monastery,* p. 26 (also cf. p. 18 for the *Arithm.*)
Gesamtkatalog der Wiegendrucke has more than fifty
entries before 1500 and still more with translation added:
IV, 300 ff. Fortescue and Smith, *op. cit.,* pp. 192 ff.,
give later editions, to which add H. R. James, in the Universal Library, 1897. For Swift's copy of Vallinus, see
Harold Williams, *Dean Swift's Library, Catal. Facs.,* p.
2. With regard to S.E.M. see the *Review of English
Studies,* VII (1931), pp. 160-167 (Walter E. Houghton,
Jr.,) "S.E.M.—'Translator' of Boethius": "The whole
volume, therefore, is not a translation, but the first edition
of the *De Consolatione* to be published in England,"
p. 160.

Page 27.   On the two early commentaries on the *Cons.*
see Schepss, *Handschriftliche Studien,* p. 32, and *Archiv f.
d. Stud. d. neueren Sprachen,* XCIV (1895), pp. 149 ff.
(with reference to Alfred's use of two types: that
represented in the one bound in a tenth cent. MS. written
by Froumund, and that in the marginal scholia in MS.
Monacensis 19452. These derive originally from one,
which Naumann maintains is that of Remigius.)   For the
commentary of Remigius of Auxerre see Geyer [Ueber-
weg], *Grundriss,* II, *Die patristische und scholast. Philos.,*
179; Manitius, *Gesch.,* II, 809; Naumann, *Quellen und
Forschungen,* CXXI (1913), pp. 1-23, "Notkers Boethius,
Untersuchungen," etc.; and Stewart, *The Journal of
Theological Studies,* XVII (1916), pp. 22-42. Naumann believes in the existence of another and independent
one.   For a commentary by John the Scot, see the an-
nouncement of a discovery by Dr. Silk in *Revue Néoscolastique de Philos.,* XXXVI (1934), p. 77; and for

the text itself, *Saeculi Noni Auctoris in Boetii Cons. Philos. Commentarius*, ed. E. T. Silk, Rome, 1935 (*Papers and Monographs of the American Academy in Rome*, IX). For Lupus of Ferrières on the *metra* see Peiper, *Philos. Cons.*, pp. xxiv f.; Schepss, *Handschrift-liche Studien*, p. 41. For his correspondence see the edition with French translation by Levillain, in *Classiques de L'Hist. de Fr. au M.A.*; cf. pp. 44-45 (the *Arithm.*). Peiper notes another metrical study by Nicolai Perotti in the xv century, *op. cit.*, p. xxiv. See also Manitius, *Gesch.*, I, pp. 35 and 490; and III, p. 219.

The idea of a commentary written by Asser may be based on the statement of William of Malmesbury that he elucidated the text, *Gest. Reg.* ii, section 122 (*Rolls Series*, I, p. 131), and *Gesta Pontif.*, ii, section 80 (*Rolls Series*, p. 177). Cf. Bardenhewer, *Patr.*, 557. Schepss believes, however, that Asser only made use of the com-mentaries then in existence, *Archiv*, XCIV, p. 159. For the commentary of Bruno of Corvey see Migne, *Patr. Lat.*, LXIV, 1239 ff. and Mai, *Class. Auct.*, III, pp. 331 ff. Cf. Schepss, *Handschriftliche Studien*, p. 21, n. 33, and p. 35, n. 11; Manitius, *Gesch.*, I, pp. 527-529 and II, pp. 744 and 747; Specht, *Gesch. des Unterrichts-wesens*, p. 341; and Murari, *Dante e Boezio*, p. 116. Murari, *op. cit.*, p. 173, cites Codex 388 of the Vienna library as containing a commentary on III, m. ix, by Adalbold Bishop of Utrecht (†1027); cf. Manitius, *op. cit.*, II, p. 747, and III, pp. 218-219.

For the material on the commentaries of William of Conches and Nicholas Trivet see *Notices et Extraits des MSS. de la Bibl. Impér.*, XX, part ii (Paris, 1862), pp. 40-82, reprinted in *Excursions Historiques et Philos-ophiques à travers le M.A.*, "Des Commentaires Inédits de G. de Conches et de N. Triveth," etc., Jourdain, pp. 29-68. Cf. also Poole's *Illustrations of the Hist. of Med. Thought*, pp. 124 ff.; Hurter, *Nomencl. Liter.*, II (1906), cols. 104-105, 579-580. Clerval, *Les Écoles de Chartres*, p. 182; Manitius, *Gesch.*, I, p. 35; *Kirchen-*

lexikon, XII, 98; and *Publ. Mod. Lang. Assoc.*, XVIII (1903), pp. 173 ff. (for Chaucer's use of Trivet). Chaucer's use of Trivet is also discussed further in Chapter IV.

Page 28. For the pseudo-Aquinas, see Peiper, *Philos. Cons.*, p. xliv; Manitius, *Gesch.*, I, p. 35. Cave, *Script. eccles. hist.*, II, Append., pp. 11-12, favours the authorship of Thomas Iorsius (Joyce); cf. Fortescue and Smith, *Cons. Philos.*, p. 192. For its popularity note the entries in the *Gesamtkatalog der Wiegendrucke*, IV (1930), 304 ff. On the pseudo-Grosseteste commentary see Hauréau, *Hist. de la philos. scolastique*, II, 1 (1880), 175; Poole and Bateson, *Index Britanniae Scriptorum*, etc., *John Bale's Index*, p. 376 (*Anecdota Oxoniensia*, IX); Murari, *Dante e Boezio*, pp. 198-199; Baur, *Die Philos. Werke des Robert Grosseteste*, pp. 46 * ff. For other commentaries see Murari, *op. cit.*, p. 186 (Alfred de Morlay, xii cent.); p. 199 (Whetley). For William Whetley's at Lincoln Grammar School, see Leach, *The Schools of Med. England*, pp. 192-193. Whetley also wrote a commentary on the pseudo-Boethian *Disc. Scholar.* Cf. *Bale's Index*, p. 151. See also Graf, *Roma nella Memoria e nelle Immag. del. M.E.*, p. 619 (Malabranca da Orvieto); Manitius, *Gesch.*, I, p. 35, (William of Aragon, John of Saxony, and Pierre d'Ailly); Peiper, *op. cit.*, pp. xli ff.

For commentaries on the *Opuscula Sacra* see Rand, *Johannes Scottus* (in *Quellen und Untersuch.*, I, 2); the ascription is opposed by Cappuyns, "Le plus ancien commentaire des 'O.S.' et son origine," in *Recherches de Théol. ancienne et med.*, III (1931), pp. 237 ff. who argues that the work was written by Remigius of Auxerre influenced by the works of John the Scot. He is answered by Rand in *Revue Néoscolastique de Philos.*, XXXVI (1934), 67 ff. Cf. Manitius, *Gesch.*, I, pp. 330 f., 337, and 518; Jansen, *Der Kommentar des Clarenbaldus von Arras*, etc., (*Breslauer Studien* 8), pp.

15-31; Peiper, *op. cit.*, pp. xlvi ff. For a com. on *De Trin.* by Bede see Migne, *Patr. Lat.*, LXIII, 567; for one by Geoffrey of Auxerre († 1180), Murari, *op. cit.*, p. 186; Bardenhewer, *Patrol.*, p. 557. See generally Schurr's *Die Trinitätslehre des Boethius.*

Page 29. On the trial of Gilbert de la Porrée see Poole's *Illustrations of the Hist. of Med. Thought*, pp. 133 ff., where a full and careful account may be found; also Poole, *Ioannis Saresberiensis Histor. Pontif.*, pp. xxxvi ff.; and Manitius, *Gesch.*, III, pp. 210-213. For material by contemporaries: the *Hist. Pontif.*, pp. 16 ff., cc. 8 ff. (John of Salisbury); *Mon. Germ. Histor.*, *Scriptores*, XX, pp. 376 ff., (Otto of Freising). The commentary that caused the trouble is printed in Migne, *Patr. Lat.*, LXIV, 1255 ff. For the second preface see Poole, *Illus.*, pp. 367 ff.; *Hist. Pontif.*, pp. 98-99. On the fact that John of Salisbury heard Gilbert lecture see Haskins, *Ren. of the Twelfth Cent.*, p. 374, and Poole, *Illus.*, p. 210, translating the *Metalogicus.* See also Haskins, *op. cit.*, p. 353; Clerval, *Les Écoles de Chartres*, pp. 168 and 185; Peiper, *Philos. Cons.*, p. xliv.

The Latin of John of Salisbury's tribute runs as follows: "Erat enim uir ingenii perspicacissimi, legerat plurima, et ut ex animi sententia loquar, circiter annos lx. expenderat in legendo et tritura litterarum, sic in disciplinis liberalibus eruditus, ut eum in uniuersis nemo precederet, credebatur ipse pocius in uniuersis precedere uniuersos." *Hist. Pontif.*, cap. 8, p. 17, 27—p. 18, 2. For Gilbert's tribute to Boethius see the Epitaph, Hauréau, *Hist. de la philos. scol.*, I, p. 470, and Murari, *Dante e Boezio*, p. 185.

Page 30. On Clarenbaldus, see Jansen, *Der Kommentar des Clarenbaldus*, pp. 3-148; Manitius, *Gesch.*, III, pp. 240-241; Poole, *Illustrations*, pp. 370 ff.; Clerval, *Les Écoles de Chartres*, p. 193. On the commentary of Thomas Aquinas see Grabmann, *Thomas Aquinas, His*

Personality and Thought, trans. Michel, p. 24. Silk's
remarks on the commentaries appear in the *Trans.
Proceed. Amer. Philol. Assoc.,* LXII (1931), pp.
xxxvii f.

Page 31. Rashdall's remarks may be found in his *Universities of Europe,* I, pp. 34-35. Specht agrees, *Gesch.
des Unterrichtswesens,* p. 123, adding Isidore and St.
Augustine. But Isidore derives somewhat from Boethius.
Manitius, *Gesch.,* II, p. 10, observes that in the eleventh
century France and Germany relied on Martianus Capella
and Boethius, while Monte Cassino had recourse to Varro.
West in *Alcuin and the Rise of the Christian Schools,*
p. 25, says that the dialectics of Cassiodorus derive in part
from Varro but chiefly from Boethius: "It is really
Boethius made easy for beginners." Cf. also Roger,
L'Enseignement des Lettres classiques, p. 182.

Exactly what Otloh says is as follows: "Peritos autem
dico magis illos, qui in Sacra Scriptura, quam qui in Dialectica sunt instructi. Nam dialecticos quosdam ita simplices
inueni, ut omnia Sacrae Scripturae dicta iuxta dialecticae
auctoritatem constringenda esse decernerent: magisque
Boëtio quam Sanctis Scriptoribus in plurimis dictis crederent. Unde et eundem Boëtium secuti, me reprehendebant, quod personae nomen, alicui, nisi substantiae rationali,
ascriberem." Pez, *Thes. Anecd.,* III, pt. 2, cols. 144-145.
Cf. Specht, *Gesch. des Unterrichtsw.,* p. 126; and *Mon.
Germ. Hist., Scriptores,* IV, p. 521, n. 12. For women's
study of the authors mentioned, see Specht, *op. cit.,* p.
269.

Page 32. On Robert of Torigny and the "antiquior
translatio," see Haskins, *Studies in the Hist. of Med.
Science,* pp. 227 ff., revised from the same author's "Mediaeval Versions of the Posterior Analytics," *Harvard
Studies in Classical Philol.,* XXV (1914), 87 ff. For the
general situation cf. Rashdall, *Univ. of Europe,* I, 350
and II,² 744; Taylor, *Med. Mind,* I, p. 92 and n. 3; II,

p. 277, n. 1.   A similar explanation is offered by Specht, *Gesch. des Unterrichtswesens*, pp. 123-124: "Der Name Aristoteles wird zwar viel genannt und hoch gepriesen, jedoch seine logischen Schriften waren nur in den lateinischen Uebersetzungen des Konsuls Manlius Boetius bekannt. Von letzteren wurden aber vorzüglich nur die Kategorien und das Buch *de interpretatione* in den Schulen gelesen, weil sie der Uebersetzer mit Kommentaren erläutert und bereits schulmässig hergerichtet hatte, alle anderen dagegen blieben zum grössten Teil gänzlich unbeachtet. Eines der hauptsächlichsten logischen Schulbücher war die *Isagoge* des Porphyrius, eine Einleitung in die Kategorien des Aristoteles, in der lateinischen Uebersetzung des Boetius. Das Buch fehlte selten in den Bibliotheken."

Page 32.   On the *Timaeus* and the *Consolatio*, and the Platonism of Boethius, see Thorndike, *Hist. of Magic and Exper. Science*, I, pp. 620 f.; Klingner, *De Boethii Cons. Philos.*, 38 ff., and *passim*; Burdach, "Die humanistischen Wirkungen der Trostschrift," pp. 535 ff.   Cf. Bruno of Corvey's notes on *Cons.* III, m. ix, in his commentary discussed above; and note the quotation from Laurentius Valla (xv cent.) in Migne, *Patr. Lat.*, LXIII, col. 570. On the question of Neoplatonism, cf. Clerval, *Écoles de Chartres*, p. 118; Dodds, *Proclus, The Elements of Theology*, pp. 228 and 321; cf. *Speculum*, IV (1929), pp. 62 ff., and VIII (1933), pp. 41 ff.

Page 33.   On secular education see Rashdall's *Univ. of Europe*, I, p. 35; Specht, *Gesch. des Unterrichtswesens*, p. 103 (Tegernsee); Roger, *L'Enseignement des Lettres classiques*.   A letter of the monk Froumund tells of the diligent study at Tegernsee of Statius, Persius, Juvenal, Horace, Cicero, and Boethius, Pez, *Thes. Anecd.*, VI, pt. 1, 163-167; cf. Specht, *op. cit.*, p. 369.

On rhetoric and logic see Baldwin, *Med. Rhetoric and Poetic*, pp. 100-103 and *passim*; Norton, *Readings in the Hist. of Education*, p. 79 (cf. pp. 40-41, on the reading of Abailard and John of Salisbury); Rashdall, *op. cit.*, I, pp. 36-37; Specht, *op. cit.*, p. 123; Manitius, *Gesch.*, II, p. 11; Burdach "Die humanistischen Wirkungen der Trostschrift," pp. 557 f.; and *Classical Philol.*, XXVIII (1933), 75. According to Haskins (*Studies in the Hist. of Med. Science*, p. 66), Hermann of Carinthia (xii cent.) knew logic only through Boethius. For Roger Bacon's reference to the *Disc. Schol.* see *Opus Majus*, ed. Bridges, I, p. 85. For the *Disciplina* itself see Migne, *Patr. Lat.*, LXIV, 1223 ff. Cf. Haskins, *Med. Culture*, p. 73 and n. 1; Lehmann, *Pseudo-antike Literatur des Mittelalters*, pp. 27 f., and E. M. Sanford, "De Disc. Scholar.," *Classical Journal*, XXVIII (1932-1933), pp. 82 ff.

Page 33. The *Battle of the Seven Arts* was written in the second quarter of the xiii cent. D'Andeli was a Norman or Picard well acquainted with the University of Paris. See Paetow's edition of the allegory, Berkeley, California, 1914, for the summary and the quotations cited.

Page 34. On Boethius in dialectic see Prantl, *Gesch. der Logik im Abendlande*, I, pp. 679 ff. and II, pp. 8-9; Meier, *Gesch. der Schule von St. Gallen*, p. 111; Mallet, *Hist. of the Univ. of Oxford*, I, p. 7, n. 1; Manitius, *Gesch.*, I, p. 30; Murari, *Dante e Boezio*, p. 169; De Wulf, *Hist. Philos. Méd.*, I (1934), 114 ff.

Pages 34-35. For Gerbert of Aurillac's study see Taylor, *Med. Mind*, I, pp. 291 ff.; II, 342; Specht, *Gesch. des Unterrichtswesens*, p. 124; Murari, *Dante e Boezio*, pp. 173-174. For the argument on the division of philosophy into practical and theoretical see Richer's *Historiae*, ed. Waitz, *Scriptores Rerum German.*, III, c. 60, p. 107: "Tunc quoque Gerbertus: 'Cum hoc,' inquit, 'magni constet, utpote diuinarum et humanarum rerum comprehensio ueritatis, tamen, ut nec nos ignauiae arguamur et auditorum aliqui proficere possint, secundum Vitruuii [Vic-

torini?] atque Boetii diuisionem dicere non pigebit. Est
enim philosophia genus. Cuius species sunt practice et
theoretice." See also c. 46 and c. 65. Note also the Annals of Verdun, 992 (1014), *Annales Minores*, vi, 8,
Mon. Germ. Hist., Script., IV: "Girbertus Aquitanicus
monachus studio et sapientia claruit, in tantum ut ab
Ottone archiepiscopus Ravennatium et postea papa Ro-
manus daretur, et multa studia ueterum philosophorum
renouauit, post Boetium apud Latinos insignis habitus."
Cf. *Lettres de Gerbert*, ed. Havet, pp. 112, 172, etc. On
Boethius and the classification of the sciences, see Baur,
*Gundissalinus (Beiträge zur Gesch. der Philos. des Mit-
telalters*, IV, 2-3), pp. 11 and 350-352.

The sentence which gave rise to the controversy between
realists and nominalists is as follows: "Mox de generibus
ac speciebus illud quidem, siue subsistunt siue in solis
nudisque intellectibus posita sunt siue subsistentia corpo-
ralia sunt an incorporalia et utrum separata a sensibilibus
an insensibilibus posita et circa ea constantia, dicere
recusabo." "Altissimum enim," he continues, "est hu-
iusmodi negotium et maioris egens iniquisitionis." In
Isagogen Porph., i, 10 (Brandt, p. 159), and Migne, *Patr.
Lat.*, LXIV, col. 82, A-B (see 78-85). See Mallet, *Hist.
of the Univ. of Oxford*, I, p. 12; Prantl, *Gesch. der
Logik*, II, pp. 45 ff.; Rashdall, *Univ. of Europe*, I, p. 39;
Grabmann, *Gesch. der schol. Methode*, I, 152 (for his
place in the development of scholasticism, see the whole
discussion, pp. 148-176); Murari, *Dante e Boezio*, pp.
182 ff. The real debate apparently begins with Roscellinus in the xi cent. Cf. Puccinotti, *Il Boezio ed altri
scritti storici e filosofici*, pp. 25 ff., on the idea that Boethius originated the conceptualism of Abailard. Cf.
Stewart, *Boethius*, pp. 247 ff. For Abailard see Sikes,
Peter Abailard, 103 ff. and 272 ff. That Boethius was a
realist, however, appears in *De Trin.*, ii, 42 ff.—see Rand,
Boethius, the Theol. Tractates, etc. (*Loeb Libr.*), p. 10
and n. b; and *Founders of the M. A.*, pp. 145 f. and 314,
n. 20. For the Philosophy of Boethius in sculpture see

Mâle, *Relig. Art in France, XIII Cent.*, trans. Nussey, pp. 90 ff., and figures 45-46.

Page 36. On the *Arithmetic* see West, *Alcuin and the Rise of the Christian Schools*, p. 25 and p. 150 (Rabanus quotes Boethius in his *Computus*); Norton, *Readings in the Hist. of Education*, p. 79 and pp. 135 ff.; Haskins, *Studies in the Hist. of Med. Science*, pp. 84, 91, 134, 374. See the MS. prepared for Otto III, *Lettres de Gerbert*, ed. Havet, p. 172 and notes 2 and 3. Note the material cited in Bonnaud's article, *Speculum*, IV (1929), 202-205. Cf. Migne, *Patr. Lat.*, XC (Bede, *Didasc. dubia et spuria*), 641 and CVII (Rhabanus), 671-672; Roger Bacon, *Opus Majus*, ed. Bridges, I, p. 99. See Brauer, *Die Bücherei von St. Gallen und das althochdeutsche Schrifttum* (*Hermaea* XVII), pp. 18 and 33; Weidmann, *Gesch. der Bibl. von St. Gallen*, p. 365. Anstey, *Mun. Acad.*, I, 286; II, 413 (use at Oxford); Haskins, *Harvard Studies in Classical Philol.*, XX (1909), p. 92 (at Paris). For a somewhat patronizing reference, see the *Atlantic Monthly*, CLVI (1935), pp. 64 ff.

Page 36. Clerval's observation is found on p. 125, *Écoles de Chartres:* "Les traités élémentaires en usage réduisaient à ceux de Boèce, parmi les anciens, et, parmi les modernes, aux écrits de Gerbert. . . ." Cf. p. 126. Also see Manitius, *Gesch.*, I, p. 26; the *Paphnutius* (scene i) and *Sapientia* (scene iii) of Hrotsvitha.

Page 37. Many MSS. of the *Apocalypsis* of Golias were available in the xiii and xiv centuries. See Strecker, *Die Apokalypse des Golias*, p. 3, and Raby, *Secular Latin Poetry*, II, 191 and 214 ff. For the figure under Arithmetic at Chartres, see Mâle, *Relig. Art in France, XIII Cent.*, p. 89. For the royal entries, see Withington, *English Pageantry*, I, p. 145; p. 167 and n. 5. Cf. also *Lettres de Gerbert*, ed. Havet, pp. 6 f. and 117 f.

For Boethius in the field of geometry see Clerval,

Écoles de Chartres, p. 125; Specht, *Gesch. des Unter-richtswesens,* p. 144; Hankel, *Zur Gesch. der Math.,* pp. 302, 314; Manitius, *Gesch.,* I, p. 286; Scherrer, *Verzeichnis der Handschriften,* pp. 281 ff.; *Isis,* XIX (1933), p. 189.

Pages 38-39. Cf. T. Gérold, *La Musique au Moyen Âge,* Paris, 1932, pp. 66-67, and the same author's *Les Pères de l'Église et la Musique,* Strasbourg, 1932, p. 159. On *De Musica,* see Meier, *Gesch. der Schule von St. Gallen,* pp. 115 f.; Clerval, *Écoles de Chartres,* p. 127; Rashdall, *Univ. of Europe,* II², p. 457; Haskins, *Studies in the Hist. of Med. Science,* p. 374; Manitius, *Gesch.,* I, pp. 27 and 631; Norton, *Readings in the Hist. of Educ.,* p. 79; Bonnaud, *Speculum,* IV (1929), 202.

For Walter of Speyer see the *Vita et Passio St. Christophori (de Studio,* I, 92-106), ed. Harster, pp. 21 ff.; Specht, *Gesch.,* p. 100; Gottlieb, *Ueber mittelalterliche Bibl.,* p. 442. For St. Gall see Ekkehard's testimony, *Zeits. f. deutsches Altertum,* XIV (1869), p. 27. Cf. the *Casus S. Galli:* "In membris uero spiritualis sic effloruit disciplina, ut non solum Benedicti regulam et institutionem, uerum eciam philosophiam totamque ad unguem usque inuestigarint theoriam Platonis, Socratis, Aristotelis, Ypocratis, Boetii omnes inuestigauerunt riuulos, adeo ut in suis metris philosophos non solum, sed et poetriam fuerint, quod arduum esse negocium et praecipue modernis, qui aliquam poetrie nouerunt uiam, perpendere satis est facile,"—ed. von Arx, *Mon. Germ. Hist., Scriptores,* II, 165-166; cf. Peiper, *Philos. Cons.,* pp. lxi f.   See Prantl, *Gesch. der Logik,* II, p. 47; and Clark, *St. Gall,* pp. 103 and 277.   On the Abbott Grimald see Meier, *Gesch. der Schule von S. G.,* 44 ff.; Weidmann, *Gesch. der Bibl.,* pp. 396 ff.; Lehmann, *Mittelalterliche Bibliothekskat. Deutschlands,* etc., I, 89; Specht, *Gesch. des Unterrichtswesens,* pp. 314 f.   Cf. Hartmut, Meier, *op. cit.,* 48. Note where Ermenrich in his letter to Grimald speaks of having imitated Boethius: "In priori quidem opere Anitium

Boetium sum imitatus, in isto uero Prosperi nostri morem ex parte secutus," *Epistola*, ed. Dümmler, p. 35. On Notker Labeo see *Die Schriften* edited by Piper, and the discussion in Chapter III above; cf. also Brauer, *Die Bücherei von St. Gallen* (*Hermaea* XVII), pp. 18, 33, 75, and Clark, *op. cit.*, 115 (who notes in the Zurich library a compendium in dialogue form somewhat like Notker's *Rhetoric*). Cf. Wackernagel, *Zeits. f. deutsches Altertum*, IV (1844), pp. 463 ff. Geoffrey de Vinsauf uses quotations in his *De Arte Versificandi*, see Faral, *Les Arts Poétiques*, p. 273, item 13 (from the *Cons.*). For the *Arithm.* at St. Gall see Specht, *op. cit.*, p. 130; *De Musica*, see Meier, *Gesch. der Schule von S. G.*, pp. 115 f.

Page 39. For the requirements at the universities see: **Paris**, Denifle and Chatelain, *Chartularium*, I, 78 and 278; Abelson, *The Seven Liberal Arts*; Rashdall, *Univ. of Europe*, I, p. 434; Norton, *Readings*, p. 135; Paetow, "The Arts Course at Med. Univ.," *Univ. of Illinois Bulletin*, VII (Jan. 9, 1910), No. 19, p. 68; Haskins, *Studies in the Hist. of Science*, pp. 239, 356 ff. ("an unofficial enumeration of the books then in use in the schools of Paris"); Haskins, *Harvard Studies in Classical Philol.*, XX (1909), p. 92 ("A List of Textbooks from the Close of the Twelfth Century," by some attributed to John of Garland, here assigned by Haskins to Alexander Neckam). **Chartres**, Clerval, *Écoles de Chartres*, pp. 110, 117, 222-223 (according to the *Eptateuchon*, 1141-1155, of Thierry, who wrote two books of commentary on the *Arithm.*), etc. Note the reference, p. 398, to the borrowing of books, including Boethius. **Montpellier**, Paetow, "The Arts Course," etc., *Univ. Illinois Bull.*, VII, No. 19, pp. 64-65; Fournier, *Statuts et privilèges*, II, 278. **Toulouse**, Paetow, "The Arts Course," etc., *Univ. Illinois Bull.*, VII, No. 19, p. 96, plate. **Oxford**, Anstey, *Mun. Acad.*, I, 34 (1267); 243 (1408); 286 (1431); II, 413. The first of these (I, p. 34) shows conditions after the New Logic was discovered and read: ". . . quod omnes libros ueteris logicæ ad minus bis audierint, exceptis libris Boethii, quos semel sufficiat audiuisse, præter quartum librum *Topicorum* Boethii, quem audiuisse non astringantur." Translated in Benham's *English Lit.*, etc., p. 411; Leach, *Educ. Charters*, pp. 191 ff. See also Rashdall, *op. cit.*, I, p. 443 and II², pp. 455 ff.; Norton, *op. cit.*, pp. 135 ff.; Paetow, "The Arts Course," etc., *Univ. Ill. Bull.*, VII, No. 19, pp. 69-70; Wordsworth, *Ancient Kalendar of the Univ. of Oxford*, pp. 33 and 109; Mallet, *Hist. Univ. Oxford*, I, pp. 6-7; Haskins, *Studies in the Hist. of Science*, p. 239 (Roger Bacon speaks of lectures on Boethius). Vienna, Ashbach, *Gesch. der Wiener Univ.*, I, pp. 86 ff.; Paderborn, *Vita Meinwerci*, Pertz, *Mon. Germ. Hist.*, *Script.*, XI, 111 ff. The story of what was found in the room of Master T. Cooper is in Anstey, *Mun. Acad.*, II, p. 516. Here too I may note the list of books in the Tours MS. (MS. xiii cent.; list, xiii-xiv cent.) including Boethius, *Speculum*, IV (1929), p. 265; cf. also *Mélanges Mandonnet*, II (Paris, 1930), 261 ff. (*Bibl. Thomiste*, 14).

Pages 39-40. For Alcuin see West's *Alcuin and the Rise of the Christian Schools*, pp. 92 ff.; Roger, *L'Enseignement des Lettres classiques*, 318; Manitius, *Gesch.*, I, p. 286. To Thomas Aquinas has been assigned the treatise *De Fato*, probably spurious—see Thorndike's *Magic and Exper. Science*, II, pp. 613 f. This work shows influence from the *Cons. Philos.* For Michael Scot, see Haskins, *Studies in the Hist. of Med. Science*, pp. 284 and 288; Thorndike, *op. cit.*, II, p. 322. For Roger Bacon see his *Opus Majus*, ed. Bridges, I, p. 67 (III, i); trans. Burke, I, p. 76. Bacon, however, quotes from the *Disc. Schol.* as evidence that Boethius placed emphasis on the knowledge of terms (Bridges, I, p. 85), and perhaps his inferences are based on that document and hence of less value. For Grosseteste, see Thorndike, *op. cit.*, II, p. 450, for his approval of the philosophy of Boethius; on Neckam, Haskins, *Stud. Hist Med. Science*, pp. 239 and 356 ff. Cf. also *De Laudibus, dist.* v, 191-192 (*Rolls Series*, p. 444).

Page 40. Two passages from John of Salisbury may be quoted:

"Qui uero librum hunc diligentius perscrutatur, non modo Ciceronis et Boetii topicos ab his septem uoluminibus erutos deprehendet, sed librum diuisionum, qui compendio uerborum, et elegantia sensuum, inter opera Boetii, quae ad logicam spectant, singularem gratiam nactus est." *Metal.* III, ix (Migne, *Patr. Lat.*, CXCIX, 909).

"Si michi non credis, liber *de Cons. Phil.* reuoluatur attentius et planum erit haec in contrarium cedere. Et licet liber ille Verbum non exprimat incarnatum, tamen apud eos qui ratione nituntur non mediocris auctoritate est, cum ad reprimendum quamlibet exulceratae mentis dolorem congrua cuique medicamenta conficiat. Nec iudaeus quidem nec graecus sub praetextu religionis medicinae declinet usum, cum sapientibus in fide et in perfidia desipientibus sic uiuidae rationis confectio artificiosa proficiat, ut nulla religio quod miscet abhominari audeat, nisi qui rationis expers est. Sine difficultate profundus est in sententiis, in uerbis sine leuitate conspicuus, orator uehemens, efficax demonstrator; ad id quod sequendum est nunc prolabitur suadens, nunc quasi stimulo necessitatis impellens." *Policrat.* vii, 15 (ed. Webb, II, pp. 155-156; also Migne, *op. cit.*, CXCIX, 672 B-C). For the influence of Boethius see Schaarschmidt, *Johannes Saresberiensis*, pp. 119-121 and 305-307, etc.

For lists of eulogies see Migne, *op. cit.*, LXIII, 563 ff.; Peiper, *Philos. Cons.*, pp. xxxv ff.; Fortescue and Smith, *Cons. Philos.*, pp. 173 ff.; Graf, *Roma nella Memoria*, etc., pp. 616 ff.

Page 41. Thorndike correctly states in *Magic and Exper. Science*, II, p. 589, regarding Albertus Magnus: "The

keynote of his solution is found in the definition of Boethius that 'Fate is the disposition inherent in movable things by which Providence binds each by its order.'"
See "The Tradition of the Goddess Fortuna in Med. Philos. and Lit.," pp. 197 ff., in *Smith College Studies in Mod. Lang.*, III, No. 4, 1922; and for references to Fortune derived from Boethius cf. Chapter IV above on imitations of the *Cons.* For the matter on free will in Boethius see also the *Com. in Librum Arist.* περὶ ἑρμηνείας, ed. Meiser, II, pp. 193-194.

Page 42.   Thorndike also indicates the influence on William of Auvergne, *op. cit.*, II, p. 366.   Cf. further Wedel, *The Med. Attitude Toward Astrology*, pp. 138 ff.   For influence in various matters in Dante see *Par.* v, 19-24; vii, 64-72; *De Mon*, I, 12; Murari, *Dante e Boezio*, pp. 291 ff.; 301 ff.; 365 ff.

Pages 43-44.   Chaucer uses material on democratic ideals in *Gentilesse* as well.   For "commun profit" see the *Journ. Eng. Germ. Philol.*, XXIX (1930), pp. 381 ff. Deschamps deals with the question of wealth in *Bal.* cccxix (*Œuvres*, III, pp. 10-12); dcccclxxii (V, pp. 209-210) shows his interest in Boethius.   For other material pertinent to the influence of Boethius in his works, see *Bal.* cxc (II, p. 7); clxxxi (I, pp. 316-317); cccxiv, lay xi (II, pp. 344 ff.); *Cplt. de l'Église* (VII, p. 297); XI, pp. 158 and 211.   On the idea of a natural sympathy in Dante for Boethius in exile see Murari, *Dante e Boezio*, pp. 229 ff. and 308 ff.; and the similarity of Beatrice to Philosophia, 238 ff. and 255 ff.; and Baur, *Boetius und Dante*, p. 10.

On Chaucer's use see Jefferson, *Chaucer and the Cons. Philos.*, and the discussion in Chapter III above; also *Mod. Lang. Rev.*, XXII (1927), pp. 377 ff.

Page 45.   For Boethius in the *florilegia* see Haskins, *Ren. of the Twelfth Cent.*, pp. 113-114; also *Classical*

Philol., XXIII (1928), 131; XXVII (1932), 31, 33 (n. 2), and 39.

CHAPTER III

Page 46.   Johnson's version of III, m. ix, is quoted in the *Life*, I, 96. It has been furnished with a musical setting (from the Genevan Psalter) in the *Home and Community Song Book* of T. W. Surette and A. T. Davison, (Boston, [1931],) p. 144, No. 101. We also find an interesting comment of Johnson's in the *Life*, I, 420: " 'Speaking of Boetius, who was the favourite writer of the middle ages, he said it was very surprizing, that upon such a subject, and in such a situation, he should be *magis philosophus quàm Christianus.*' " The Index, in vol. II, confuses our author with Hector Boece.

Page 49.   For William of Malmesbury see *Gestis Reg.*, ii, section 122 (*Rolls Series*, I, p. 131): "Hic sensum librorum Boetii De Consolatione planioribus uerbis enodauit, quos rex ipse in anglicam linguam uertit." Cf. also *Gesta Pontif.*, ii, section 80 (*Rolls Series*, p. 177; and Stevenson, *Asser's Life of King Alfred*, p. lxviii. Note Burnet's remark that the Platonism of Boethius "has been a constant factor in the evolution of English literature since the ninth century A.D. . . ." *Essays and Addresses*, p. 271. For a list of Alfred's emendations and additions see Sedgefield, *King Alfred's Version*, pp. xxxi-xxxii, and his edition of the Old English, *King Alfred's Old English Version*, pp. xxv-xxxv; also Leicht, *Anglia* VII (1884), pp. 187-202.

Page 50.   On Alfred's use of the commentaries see Schepss, *Archiv für das Studium der neueren Sprachen*, XCIV (1895), pp. 149 ff.

Pages 51-52.   For the manuscripts and related questions see Chambers, Förster, and Flower, *The Exeter Book of Old*

English Poetry, p. 28, notes 95 and 101; Sedgefield, *King Alfred's Old English Version,* pp. xi ff. and *King Alfred's Version,* pp. xxv-xxvii; and Krapp, *The Paris Psalter and the Meters of Boethius,* pp. xxxv ff. For Professor Napier's fragment see the *Zeitschrift für deutsches Altertum,* XXXI (1887), pp. 52-54, containing parts of xiv, 3, and xvi, 1. An account of the controversy about Alfred's authorship of the *metra* is found in Sedgefield, *King Alfred's Old Eng. Version,* pp. xxiii-xxiv and xxxvii-xli; also in the same author's *King Alfred's Version,* pp. xxvii-xxxi. To these may be added the brief argument in the *Camb. Hist. of Eng. Lit.,* I, pp. 112-113 (by P. G. Thomas); Fehlauer, *Die engl. Übersetzungen von Boethius' "De Cons. Philos.,"* pp. 21 ff.; and Krapp, *The Paris Psalter,* pp. xlv ff. (with bibliog. pp. liii ff.). See further G. F. Browne, *King Alfred's Books,* London, 1920, pp. 263-390; also Heusinkveld and Bashe, *Bibliographical Guide to Old English,* pp. 62 and 105 f.

Page 54.   For foreign versions of Alfred's work, see Sedgefield, *King Alfred's Old Eng. Version,* pp. xxi-xxiii. For modern editions see that of the metres in Grein's *Bibliothek,* III, 247-303, and Krapp's *The Paris Psalter* (note editions cited, pp. li-lii). Tupper's verses appear in the *Whole Works of King Alfred the Great* (Jubilee edition), I, pp. 164-249.

On Notker Labeo one may consult Murari, *Dante e Boezio,* pp. 176-177; J. M. Clark, *The Abbey of St. Gall* (cf. *Speculum,* II [1927], pp. 354-356; on Greek at St. Gall see Laistner, *Thought and Letters in Western Europe,* pp. 193 ff.); Piper, *Die Schriften Notkers,* pp. 1-363; Brauer, *Die Bücherei von St. Gallen und das althochdeutsche Schrifttum;* Graff, *Althochdeutsche, dem Anfange des 11ten Jahrh.;* Hoffmann, *Der mittelalterliche Mensch, gesehen aus Welt und Umwelt Notkers des Deutschen;* Scherrer, *Verzeichniss der Handschriften der Stiftsbibl. von St. Gallen;* Lohmeyer, *Vergil im deutschen Geistesleben bis auf Notker III;* and, for a recent edition, Sehrt and Starck, *Notkers des Deutschen Werke*, Halle, 1933—.

Pages 56-56.   For *De Sancta Trinitate* see Ehrismann, *Gesch. der deutschen Lit.*, I, 412, n. 1.

Page 56.   On Notker's work see Braune, *Über die Quantität der althochdeutschen Endsilben;* Henrici, *Sprachmischung in älterer Dichtung Deutschlands;* Hoffmann, *Die Mischprosa Notkers des Deutschen,* diss.; Hoffmann, *Die Mischprosa Notkers des Deutschen (Palaestra LVIII);* Junghans, *Die Mischprosa Willirams;* Schaumann, *Studien zu Notkers Mischprosa;* Wunderlich, *Beiträge zur Syntax des Notker'schen Boethius;* Lindahl, *Vollständiges Glossar zu Notkers Boethius De Cons. Philos., Buch I.* On sources, Kelle, *Über die Grundlage, auf der Notkers Erklärung von Boethius De Cons. Phil. beruht,* ([*Münchener*] *Sitzungsberichte,* 1896, heft iii), pp. 349-356; Naaber, *Die Quellen von Notkers "Boethius De Cons. Phil.";* Naumann, *Notkers Boethius, Untersuchungen über Quelle und Stil,* pp. 24 ff.; cf. also *Mod. Lang. Rev.* XXX (1935), 183 ff. For much of my bibliography on Notker I am indebted to the generous advice of Professor Taylor Starck of Harvard University.

Page 57.   For the comparison of the versions of Notker and King Alfred see also Stewart, *Boethius,* p. 194.

Page 58.   For the testimony of Ekkehard IV, see the poem *In natale S. Otmari;* the passage is printed in Kelle's *Gesch. der deutschen Lit.,* I (1892), 394. See also von Arx's text *Mon. Germ. Hist., Scriptores,* II, 57-58, and cf. *Zeits. für deutsches Altertum,* XIV (1869), p. 13 and note.

For the version of Peter von Kastel, see Peiper, *Phil. Cons.,* p. lii; Stewart, *Boethius,* pp. 237 f.; Pez, *Thes. Anecd. Nov.,* IV (1723), p. xxiv; A. Coburger, Nürnberg, 1473, "Das puech von dem trost der weisshait des maisters Boecij," Graesse, I, 465; *Gesamtkatalog der Wiegendrucke*, IV, 342 (showing that the "Coburger, 1473" is Peter's; cf. Stewart, *loc. cit.*), 344. For other German versions see Bömer, *Zs. für deutsches Altertum*, L (1908), 149-158; "Boecius der hochberümpt Meister und Poet von dem trost der weiszheit," "Getruckt vnnd vollendet durch Johannem Schot zu Strassburg," 1500, *B.M. Catal.*; van Helmont's translation Sulzbach, 1667, published anonymously, the poetical parts written by Knorr von Rosenroth together with a biography of Boethius and a preface; the biog. and pref. are omitted in the edition of Lüneburg, 1697. See on the two last items *Beyträge zur critischen Historie der deutschen Sprache*, I (1732), 9-10, 448-453. For most of this material on van Helmont I am indebted to the kind offices of Professor J. H. Hanford and his student Miss Dorothy Mason at the Western Reserve University. For van Helmont, however, see also M. H. Nicolson, *Conway Letters* (New Haven, 1930), pp. 309 ff. and *Yale Review*, n. s., XVIII (1929), pp. 347 ff.

Page 63. The prose version vied with another in prose and verse for Jean de Meun's authorship. Scholarly dispute on the subject occupied Paul Meyer and Léopold Delisle and even Stewart for some years. See Stewart's *Boethius*, pp. 200 ff.; *Romania* XX (1891), 329 f.; *Hist. Litt.*, XXVIII (1881), 408 ff.; Delisle, *Anciennes Trad. Fr. de la Cons.*; Langlois, *Romania* XLII (1913), pp. 331 ff. Still another (xv century) version was confused with that of Jean de Meun. See Stewart, *op. cit.*, p. 203, and notes on the Colard Mansion version below.

Page 64. The title for Renaut's work is here taken from the Magdeburg MS., which incidentally is not a reliable one. For Frère Renaut, see Stewart, *Boethius*, 213 f.; *Romania* XX (1891), 329; Långfors, *Les Incipit des Poèmes Fr.*, p. 144 (noting twenty-three MSS.); Nagel, *Die altfranzösische Übersetzung der C.P. des*

B. von Renaut, diss.; Nagel, "Die altfr. übersetzung der Cons. des B.," *Zeits. für roman. Philol.,* XV (1891), 1-23; Gröber's *Grundriss,* I (second ed. 1933), pp. 79 and 259. I have not seen G. Bertoni's *Notice sur deux MSS. d'une traduct. fr. de la Cons. de Boèce,* Fribourg, 1910, to which I have found reference. The quotations in the text are taken from the fine MS. in the Yale Library, written about 1400. I am indebted to Dr. Silk for checking them for me. For Renaut's digressions see for example "L'istoire d'un homme. . . ." noted by Bertoni, *Zs. für roman. Philol.,* XXXIV (1910), pp. 368 f.

Page 65. On other French translations see Delisle, *Anc. Trad. Fr. de la Cons.;* and pp. 16 f. for the prose version by an Italian author. Paulin Paris, *Les MSS. Fr.,* VI, 343 f. identified him with Alberto della Piagentina. Cf. also Peiper, *Phil. Cons.,* p. liii. See further the translation by Pierre de Paris (xiii-xiv cent.), Langlois, *Notices et Extraits des MSS.,* XXXIII, 2nd part, 1889, pp. 261 ff. (MS. Vat. 4788); and Stewart, 206 f.; also that of Jehan de Cis (xiv cent.), Paulin Paris, *op. cit.,* V, 55 ff., and Stewart, *Boethius,* pp. 212 f.; one long attributed to Charles d'Orléans, but now to a Benedictine monk, Delisle, *Inventaire . . . des MSS. fr. de la Bibl. Nat.,* II, 317 ff.; Brunet, *La France litt. au XVe Siècle,* p. 28; Stewart, *op. cit.,* pp. 208 ff. See also Delisle, *op. cit.,* I, 103; Gröber, *Grundriss,* II, ii (1897), 104-105; Stewart, *op. cit.,* p. 212.

For Colard Mansion's version see MacFarlane, *Antoine Vérard,* pp. 18-19, No. 37; Brunet, *La France litt. au XVe Siècle,* pp. 27-28; Stewart, *op. cit.,* p. 203. Brunet (followed by Stewart) suggests that the edition of 1477 printed by Colard Mansion may have been written by Mansion himself. This was compiled by Regnier de sainct Trudon, and translated "par vn honneste Clerc desole querant sa consolation en la translation de cestui liure." See Peiper, *Philos. Cons.,* liii; Graesse, I, 466;

Gesamtkatalog der Wiegendr., IV, 346.   The paraphrase
of Leibnitz is found in Foucher de Careil, *Lettres et
Opuscules inédits de Leibniz*, pp. 265-273.   For other
versions see Graesse, I, 466; Fortescue and Smith, *Cons.
Philos.*, p. 196.

On the translation attributed to Brunetto Latini, note
that the idea appears even in Peiper, *Philos. Cons.*, p. liv
and Manitius, *Gesch.* I, 34.   Cf. Graesse, I, 466; Murari,
Dante e Boezio, 203; and Stewart, *Boethius*, pp. 232 ff.
For Alberto della Piagentina's version, see the edition
published at Florence, 1735, and that at Naples, 1856;
cf. Milanesi, *Il Boezio e L'Arrighetto*, pp. 3-273; Battaglia, *Il Boezio e L'Arrighetto*, pp. 13-209 (see also the
introduction, pp. viii ff.); and Zambrini, *Opere Volgari a
Stampa dei Sec. XIII e XIV*.   For other Italian versions,
see Peiper, *op. cit.*, p. lv (with ref. to the trans. of III, m.
ix, by Lorenzo de' Medici); Fortescue and Smith, *Cons.
Philos.*, pp. 195-196; Milanesi, *op. cit.*, pp. xix-xxxi,
lxxix-cv; and Argelati, *Biblioteca degli Volgarizzatori*, I
(Milan, 1767), pp. 163 ff.

For the Catalan see the *Gesamtkatalog der Wiegendr.*,
IV, 348-349; for the Spanish of Ginebreda, Graesse, I,
466; *Gesamtkat.*, IV, 349-351.   For other translations
than Ginebreda's see Graesse, I, 466-467; *B.M. Catalogue*; etc.   For the Flemish and Dutch, see Graesse, I,
465, and VII, Supplt., 99; *Gesamtkat.*, IV, 343-344.
Coornhert's is listed in the *B.M. Catalogue*.

Page 66.   The Greek of Planudes gives the verse in the
appropriate metres, as noted by Stewart, *Boethius*, pp. 234-
235.   The verse was first published by Weber, *Carmina
Græce*, Darmstadt, 1833; the entire work appeared in the
edition of Bétant, Geneva, 1871.   For versions in Hebrew,
Hungarian, and Polish, see Peiper, *Philos. Cons.*, p. lvi;
Fortescue and Smith, *Cons. Philos.*, 198; Graesse, I, 467;
B.M. Catalogue; etc.   On the tradition of Chaucer as a
moralist, cf. *Philol. Quarterly*, XIII (1934), 82 f. and
Modern Philology, XXXI (1933), 165 ff.   For Hoc-

cleve's allusion see *Eng. Verse between Chaucer and Surrey. . . .*, E. P. Hammond (Durham, N. C., 1927), p. 74.

Page 67. The use of Trivet's commentary was pointed out by Miss Petersen, *Publ. Mod. Lang. Assoc.*, XVIII (1903), pp. 173-193. For Chaucer's use of the French and the Latin, see Lowes, *Romanic Rev.*, VIII (1917), pp. 383 ff.; Jefferson, *Chaucer and the Cons. Philos. of Boethius*, pp. 1-15; and Silk, Yale diss., 1929, unpubl.

Page 68. Jefferson, *op. cit.*, pp. 133 ff., notes the passages influenced by Boethius. For Chaucer's use of material from the *Consolatio* in revising the story of the *Teseide* see *Essays in Memory of Barrett Wendell*, p. 102. For his use of Fortune in general see *Mod. Lang. Rev.*, XXII (1927), 377 ff., and on the *Troilus, Speculum*, VI (1931), 225 ff.

Page 72. Liddell, [*London*] *Academy*, XLIX (1896), pp. 199-200, deals with the pirated version, found in Bodl. MS. Auct. F. 3. 5. See also Skeat, *Works of Geoffrey Chaucer*, II, p. xviii.

Lydgate's supposititious version is listed in Bale, *Index Brit. Script.*, p. 231; and Peiper, *Philos. Cons.*, p. lv. MacCracken, *The Minor Poems of John Lydgate*, Part I, p. xxxvii, n. 11, suggests confusion with Chaucer's version "but more probably" with Walton's. For the latter see Science's edition, p. xliii: a manuscript note attributes Walton's version to Lydgate. This is found in only one manuscript, and is written in a hand much later than that of the scribe. Pemberton, *Queen Elizabeth's Englishings*, p. viii and note 1, with regard to Queen Elizabeth's MS. in the Record Office, says: "A modern note in the MS. appears to refer to a translation of Boethius by Lidgate printed by Tottel, 1554, folio, under the title of *A Treatise excellent and commodious showing the Fall of Sundry most notable Princes*." The work here re-

ferred to, now edited by Bergen, (*EETS.*, *E.S.*, CXXI-
CXXIV,) has of course nothing to do with a translation
of the *Consolatio;* but here again confusion is possible.
Lydgate's version is, however, still noted as a fact by
Manitius, *Gesch. der Lat. Lit.*, I, p. 33; Raby, *Hist. of
Christian-Latin Poetry*, p. 114; and by the *Encycl. Brit.*,
eleventh ed., IV, p. 117.

Page 73. For the material from the tradition of the
damnation of Theodoric see Science's edition, sts. 29-30.
The hermit's vision is in Gregory's dialogue: see Migne,
Patr. Lat., LXXVII, cols. 367-370 (*Dial.* IV, xxx).

Pages 74-75. On Science's edition of Walton, note the review in the [*London*] *Times Lit. Supplt.*, Oct. 10, 1929,
p. 780. Cf. Schümmer, *John Waltons metrische Übersetzung der C.P.*, (*Bonner Studien zur engl. Phil.*, VI),
a study of the MSS. and an essay toward a critical text.
About a third of the whole translation was the basis of
Schümmer's investigations, according to Science, p. v.
For Richard's modifications see Science's edition, pp.
xxv ff.; Schümmer, *op. cit.*, pp. 1 ff. Science (p. xxx)
remarks that "Richard's work, then, as editor and printer
resulted in an almost entirely new exposition of the text."
Caxton's edition of Chaucer may explain why a translation of Boethius has been attributed to the printer himself.
See Pemberton, *Queen Elizabeth's Englishings*, p. xii.

Page 75. Fehlauer in his *Die engl. Übersetzungen*, p.
62, suspects that Colville was a clergyman, because of the
tone of the Prologue. The translation is signed "George
Colvile, alias Coldewell." Bax's spelling of the name is
kept in the present discussion. The author is practically
unknown, although he is said to have been at Oxford.
See Anthony à Wood, *Athen. Oxon.*, I (1813), 48. For
his use of Chaucer see Fehlauer, *op. cit.*, 63 ff., showing
influence from Caxton's edition; cf. *Beibl. Anglia*, VIII
(1897-1898), 322. Fehlauer thinks that Colville did

not rely on Chaucer "in so plumper Weise wie z. B. Walton." The style he finds "viel leichter und flüssiger . . . als der Chaucers." For influence and comparison see Bax's edition, p. 35, and Chaucer, *Boece*, II, pr. iii. Cf. also Queen Elizabeth's rendering (Pemberton, *op. cit.*, p. 25), which here appears to good advantage.

Page 77. Material for Chaloner's life is found in the *DNB*. s.v. Chaloner, Sir Thomas, the elder. His metrical versions of the *carmina*, found in the Public Record Office in manuscript, are printed in Pemberton's *Queen Elizabeth's Englishings*, Appendix, pp. 150-160. Fehlauer, *Die engl. Übersetzungen*, p. 98, says they are "recht annehmbare Leistungen auf dem Gebiete der Übersetzungs—wie auf dem der Dichtkunst." Also: "Versmass und Reim sind mit peinlicher Genauigkeit und mit grossem Geschick behandelt, ohne dass dem Sinne des Originals Gewalt angetan worden ist." He interprets the reference to a prose version as meaning Colville's, p. 97.

Pages 78-79. For the assertions about Queen Elizabeth's speed in translation and for the text see Pemberton *Queen Elizabeth's Englishings*, (*EETS.*, CXIII), pp. viii and 1-120. Also cf. Nichols, *Progresses*, III, 564. Of her work Fehlauer, *Die engl. Übersetzungen*, p. 84, says: "Die Königin Elisabeth hat uns eine Übertragung geliefert, in der wir Wort für Wort gesetzt finden; auf diese Weise konnte es ihr nicht gelingen, den Geist und die Schönheiten des lateinischen Werkes in die englische Sprache zu übertragen."

Page 80. For the discussion of material in the seventeenth century I have leaned heavily on Houghton's *English Translations of Boethius's CP. in the Seventeenth Century*, Yale diss., 1931, unpubl. For Phineas Fletcher note also Douglas Bush, *Mythol. and the Ren. Tradition*, pp. 170-171. For Bracegirdle, see Houghton, *op. cit.*, pp. 33 ff.; Fehlauer, *Die engl. Übersetzungen*, pp. 95-97.

Some of his verse is quoted by Flügel in *Anglia* XIV (1892), pp. 499-501. It is found in B.M. Addit. MS. 11401.

Page 82. For John Thorie see Wood, *Athen. Oxon.*, I (1813), 624. On Michael Walpole see the article in the *DNB.* which anticipates Houghton in assigning the book to him although it does not identify it as "I.T." 's.; and see Houghton, *op. cit.*, pp. 50 ff.

Page 84. Fanshawe is treated by Houghton, *op. cit.*, 81 ff. Cf. p. 91: "The young poet has, in fact, achieved to a remarkable degree the almost impossible task of following his text faithfully and still retaining the spirit of the original." For Coningsby see Sedgefield, *King Alfred's Version*, pp. xlvi-xlviii, and Houghton, *op. cit.*, 103 ff. For Elys see Houghton, *op. cit.*, pp. 124 ff. The title reads "Summum bonum, or An explication of the divine goodness in the words of the most renowned Boetius. Translated by a lover of Truth and Virtue." It appeared at Oxford, "printed by H. Hall for Ric. Davis, 1674." The authorship is discussed by G. B. Dolson and Houghton in the *Review of Eng. Studies*, X (1934), 71 ff. See Fehlauer, *Die engl. Übersetzungen*, pp. 4 f. and 99 ff. for later versions. On Preston's see Houghton, *op. cit.*, 147 ff.

Page 85. The curious volume of "S.E.M." 's is carefully examined and the authorship identified by Houghton in his article, " 'S.E.M.'—'Translator' of Boethius," *Rev. Engl. Studies*, VII (1931), pp. 160-167. The book has been listed by W. C. Hazlitt and others as a translation. It does contain a few translations of short passages, largely taken from Walpole.

Page 86. Miss Waddell's charming renderings are printed in her *Med. Latin Lyrics*, pp. 48-57: V, m. iii; III, m. xii, 29-58; IV, m. vi, 1-18; IV, m. vii, 32-35.

See for Jones *The Romanesque Lyric,* by Allen and Jones, p. 249: II, m. iii.

Chapter IV

Pages 88-89. On the use of prose and verse cf. Reinhard's study, *Speculum,* I (1926), 157 ff. For *De Rectoribus Christianis* of Sedulius Scottus see Hellmann's edition, 19 ff.; also Migne, *Patr. Lat.,* CIII, 291-332. Cf. Raby, *Christian-Latin Poetry,* p. 196; also the same author's *Hist. of Secular Lat. Poetry,* I, 242 ff.; Murari, *Dante e Boezio,* p. 187. For his use of Boethius, see Manitius, *Geschichte,* I, p. 320.

Dudo's *Historia Normannorum* is edited by Lair; it is also in Migne, *Patr. Lat.,* CXLI, 609-758. Selections may be found in *Mon. Germ. Hist., Scriptores,* IV, 93-106, ed. G. Waitz. Peiper, *Phil. Cons.,* lviii, points out the use of Boethius's metres; also Manitius, *Geschichte,* II, pp. 259, 261, 262.

For Bernard Silvester and his *De Mundi Uniuersitate siue Megacosmus et Microcosmus,* see the edition of Barach and Wrobel. For an outline of the work cf. Raby, *Sec. Lat. Poetry,* II, 8 ff. Manitius points out his use of Boethius's metres, *Geschichte,* III, p. 207.

Adelard's *De Eodem et Diuerso* is edited by Willner in the *Beitr. zur Gesch. der Philos. des Mittelalters,* IV, Heft 1, 1-112. See further Geyer (Ueberweg's *Grundriss*), II, 226 ff., 231 f.; and Haskins, *Studies in the Hist. of Med. Science,* 36. Philosophy appears with the Arts (including Boethius among the philosophers) in a painting described in Boccaccio's *Amorosa Visione,* iv (*Opere,* ed. Moutier, XIV, 18-20).

Page 89. For the *Fons Philosophie* of Godfrey of St. Victor see the edition of Charma (*Mémoires de la soc. des antiq. de Norm.,* XXVII, pp. 21 ff.); the poem is outlined in Raby's *Sec. Lat. Poetry,* II, pp. 13 f. and Manitius, *Gesch.,* III, 778-779. On the formulation of

the Seven Liberal Arts see the *Eng. Hist. Review,* V
(1890), 417 ff.; on their use in painting, Leitschuh,
Gesch. der Karol. Malerei, pp. 59, 269, etc.; and K.
Künstle, *Ikonographie der christliche Kunst,* I (Freiburg
i. Br., 1928), pp. 145-156. For the handmaids of Philocosmia cf. *Cons. Philos.,* III, pr. ii, 47-48, a passage that
impressed itself on Roger Bacon: see his *Opus Majus,* ed.
Bridges, II, 367.

Page 90. Both works of Alanus de Insulis are in Migne,
Patr. Lat., CCX, 431 ff., and in Wright's *Anglo-Latin Satirical Poets,* II, pp. 268 ff. For outlines see Raby, *Sec.
Lat. Poetry,* II, 15 ff.; and *Christian-Latin Poetry,* 298 ff.
De Planctu Naturae is translated into English in the *Yale
Studies in English,* XXXVI, "The Complaint of Nature," by Moffat. Cf. Langlois's statement: "Si le
Roman de la Rose rappelait au souvenir de Jean de Meun
le traité de Boèce, il devait lui rappeler plus naturelle-
ment encore le *de Planctu Naturæ,* dont le cadre est
identique, jusque dans l'exécution des détails, à celui de
la Consolation, et dont le sujet a des affinités avec celui
du poème de Guillaume de Lorris, puisque les plaintes
de Nature ont pour objet le mépris dans lequel sont
tombées les lois naturelles de l'amour, et que Alain met
en scène, en les personnifiant, les vices qui favorisent la
luxure et les vertus qui la combattent. Plus de cinq mille
vers du roman sont inspirés du *de Planctu Naturæ.*" In
Petit de Julleville's *Hist. de la Langue et de la Litt. fr.,*
II², *Moyen Age,* p. 125. See also Langlois, *Origines et
Sources du Rom. de la Rose,* pp. 95-96, 186, and *passim.*
We cannot trace the indebtedness among these authors
further at this time.

Page 91. For the *Visión Delectable* of Alfonso de la
Torre see the *Bibl. de Aut. Españ.,* XXXVI (Madrid,
1871), 339-402. Cf. Post, *Med. Spanish Allegory,*
256 ff. The work was written at the request of the Prior
of Navarre for the instruction of Prince Don Carlos de
Viana, son of Juan II. See Mérimée, *Hist. of Spanish*

Lit., trans. Morley, p. 120. For the fluctuation of Reason's height see the *Bibl. de Aut. Españ.*, XXXVI, p. 352. For early examples of the figure see the *Iliad* iv, 442-443, and the *Aeneid* iv, 176-177. Cf. the *Roman de Fauvel*, ed. Långfors, *SATF.*, ii, 2445-2482, for an account of Boethius, and 2328-2331 for the picture of Fortune. Chaucer's portrait of Fame in the *House of Fame* may derive in this respect (1365-1376) from the *Aeneid*.

Page 91. On Dante, see Murari, *Dante e Boezio*, 229 ff. and *passim*, and Burdach, "Die humanistischen Wirkungen der Trostschrift," pp. 537 ff.

Page 92. Johannes Trithemius speaks of Ekkehard's work as "opus insigne ad imitatione*m* Boetij gemino stylo compactum ad instructionem *et* consolationem monachorum ualde utile. . . ." See Gesner, *Bibl. Instituta, etc.*, (Zurich, 1583,) 210, and Oudin, *Commentarius de Script. Eccles. Antiquis*, II, cols. 1099-1100; also Fortescue and Smith, *Cons. Philos.*, 199; Murari, *Dante e Boezio*, 188. For other "Consolations" see Auer, *Johannes von Dambach und die Trostbücher vom 11. bis zum 16. Jahrhundert*, 233 ff.; Peiper, *Philos. Cons.*, lix.

For the MSS. of Lawrence of Durham's treatise see Manitius, *Geschichte*, III, 818, and *Publ. of the Surtees Soc.*, LXX (1880 for 1878), *Dialogi Laurentii Dunelmensis*, p. xxxvi. The work is described in the latter, pp. xxxvi-xxxviii, and a brief specimen of the verse is printed in Raby's *Secular Latin Poetry*, II, 108. See also Manitius, *Geschichte*, III, 818-819.

Pages 92-93. For Pier della Vigna's *Consolatio* see Fabricius, *Bibl. Latina*, V (1858), 270b, and for Johannes of Dambach's work, *ibid.*, IV, 431; and Auer, *Johannes von Dambach*, etc. Cf. Hurter, *Nomenclator liter. theol. cath.*, II, section 339, pp. 663-664. For a perfect copy of the *Consolatio Theologiae*, I have examined the edition printed at Speyer, 1478, in the Pierpont Morgan Library (New York City). For the supposedly original *Consolatio* by Matthew of Krakow see Auer, *op. cit.*, pp. 197 ff. The work is a compilation from Johannes. Isidore of Seville's *Synonyma* is published in Migne's *Patr. Lat.*, LXXXIII, cols. 825 ff. Note "Sic exsilio trusus sum, sic exsilio damnatus sum," (831B), and the end: "Tu enim es dux uitae, tu magistra uirtutis. . . . Tu es quae a recto nunquam discedis," (868B). Cf. Cañal, *San Isidoro*, 52-53.

The *De Consolatione Rationis* of Petrus of Compostella is edited by Soto in the *Beitr. zur Gesch. der Philos. des Mittelalters*, VIII, iv, 1-151. Cf. Post, *Med. Spanish Allegory*, pp. 115-116; and Manitius, *Geschichte*, III, 154 f. Post notes the relation of the work of Petrus to the *Synonyma* of Isidore. The author may be Petrus Micha.

Page 94. Chaucer's *Tale of Melibee* is most recently edited in Robinson's *Complete Works of Geoffrey Chaucer*, 201-224, and for bibl. see 846-847. See for the Latin text the edition of Sundby, Chaucer Society publications, 1873 (note reference to Boethius, p. 90); for translations see *ibid.*, pp. xviii ff., including French, German, and Dutch. On the French text used by Chaucer cf. *Publ. Mod. Lang. Assoc.*, L (1935), 92 ff.

Page 95. A Spanish *Consolaciones* supposedly based on Pedro de Luna's version is edited by Don Pascual de Gayangos in the *Bibl. de Aut. Españ.*, LI, pp. 563-602. See Auer's *Johannes von Dambach*, etc., 210 ff.; Antonio, *Biblioteca Hispania Vetus*, II, x, cap. iii, 209 ff. I have compared several parts of the above Spanish text (which seems to correspond to that described in Auer, p. 212) with the Paris 1493 Latin, and I fail to understand Auer's note (p. 208, 18a) that the Spanish versions "wollen keine Übersetzungen sein." With the exception of the rearrangement of material in a few books (cf. Auer, 303) the Spanish seems remarkably close to the Latin.

The Harvard copy of the 1493 Latin, however, and the
Spanish both lack the preface with the allegorical framework, and belong in the class of "Exzerpten."

Page 95. For Alain Chartier's *Espérance* see his
Œuvres, ed. Du Chesne, 261-390. The *Songe de Pesti-
lence* is edited by Tilander, *Les Livres du Roy Modus*,
SATF., II, 1-228. For the date see I, pp. xlv-xlvi.

Page 96. For detailed treatment of the tradition of
Fortune see *The Goddess Fortuna in Medieval Literature*, by Patch, with the references included. For the
Altercatio Fortune et Philosophie see Walther, *Das
Streitgedicht*, p. 108 and pp. 232-234; and for the other
debates the [*Kittredge*] *Anniversary Papers*, pp. 448-
450; and Walther, *op. cit.*, p. 109. Fregoso's *Dialogo*
was published at Venice in 1531. Cf. Patch, *Smith College Studies in Modern Languages*, III (1922), No. 4,
pp. 224-225. For Guillaume de Machaut's interest in
Boethius see his *Œuvres*, ed. Hoepffner, *SATF.*, II, pp.
xix ff. His *Remède de Fortune* appears in the same volume,
pp. 1-157.

Page 97. For Santillana's poem see the edition of his
works by de los Ríos, pp. 145 ff. Cf. Post, *Med. Spanish
Allegory*, pp. 230-231. The *proemio* shows that the
work was offered as a "consolation" to the Conde de Alva.
One may compare the prose dialogue with Fortune by
Ulrich von Hutten, *Schriften*, ed. Böcking, IV (1860),
pp. 75 ff.

Pages 97-98. On the prison theme one may note the
Libellus Penarum by Benedictus de Pileo (born c. 1365)
described by Sabbadini, *Le Scoperte dei Codici*, pp. 152-
154. For Albertano of Brescia see Sundby, *Liber Consol.
et Consilii*, p. xi. The Latin of Liutprand is as follows: "Intentio huius operis ad hoc respicit, ut Beren-
garii huius, qui nunc in Italia non regnat sed tyranizat,

atque uxoris eius Willae, quae ob inmensitatem tyran-
nidis secunda Iezabel, et ob rapinarum insacietatem Lamia
proprio apellatur uocabulo, actus designet, ostendat, et
clamitet. Tanta enim mendatiorum iacula, tanta rapinarum dispendia, tanta impietatis molimina in me et
domum meam, cognationem et familiam, gratis exercuere,
quanta nec lingua proferre nec calamus praeualet scribere.
Sit igitur praesens pagina antapódosis, hoc est retribu-
tio. . . ." Becker, *Die Werke Liudprands*, p. 73, 26 ff.
(III, i). Note the reference to Boethius p. 4. For the
influence of Boethius see Peiper, *Philos. Cons.*, lvi-lix.
I have not seen Koepke's *De Vita et Scriptis Liudprandi*,
etc. Further bibliographical notes are in Raby's *Secular
Latin Poetry*, I, 283 ff.

Pages 98-99. On Hildebert see the study of Dieudonné,
Paris, 1898 (note pp. 115 ff. on the letters). For Hildebert's *De Exsilio Suo* see Hauréau, *Les Mélanges
Poétiques*, pp. 80-86; Migne, *Patr. Lat.*, CLXXI, cols.
1418 ff.; Werner, *Beitr. zur Kunde der lat. Lit.*, pp.
95-97. Cf. *Hist. Litt. de la Fr.*, XI (1759), 250-412.
For the remarks of Hauréau, see *op. cit.*, p. 85; "Il
y a des locutions et des constructions qui n'appartiennent
pas à la bonne antiquité. Mais, d'autre part, il y a de
belles pensées, exprimées dans un style d'une remarquable
noblesse, et qui, suffisamment développées, ne le sont
pas avec une prolixité répréhensible."

Page 100. See *Henrici Septimellensis Elegia—sive de
Miseria*, ed. Marigo (Padua, 1926); cf. for the Italian,
Il Boezio e L'Arrighetto nelle versioni del Trecento, ed.
Battaglia, pp. 213-254; see also the edition in Migne,
Patr. Lat., CCIV, 843-868. Cf. further Bonaventura,
"Arrigo da Settimello," in *Studi Medievali*, IV (1913),
110 ff.; Torraca, *L'Elegia di Arrigo da Settimello*, (*Atti
R. Accad. . . . di Napoli*, n. s., X, 1928, 257 ff.);
Strecker, *Studi Medievali*, n. s., II (1929), 110 ff.; and
Raby, *Secular Latin Poetry*, II, 163-164. For the

Italian rendering see Bonaventura, *op. cit.*, 165 ff. and 178 ff.

Page 101. For the influence on Peter of Eboli see Raby, *Christian-Latin Poetry*, p. 293; and for Eboli's poem Muratori's *Rerum Ital. Scriptores*, XXXI, i, ed. Rota (cf. pp. xxxvi-xxxvii); also *Fonti per la Storia d'Italia*, XXXIX, ed. Siragusa.

Page 102. The play may also be found in *La Complainte et le Jeu de Pierre de la Broce*, ed. Jubinal, pp. 29 ff. Jubinal prints a *Complainte* of the hero which is composed in the manner of the sixteenth-century broadsides, *ibid.*, 23 ff.

Pages 102-103. The Anglo-Norman poem on Edward II is referred to in Fabyan's *New Chronicle*. *Somer Soneday* is edited by Brown, *Studies in Engl. Philol. . . . in Honor of F. Klaeber* (Minneapolis, 1929), pp. 362 ff.

Page 103. The episode in which Petrarch consoled the King is discussed in *Smith College Studies in Mod. Lang.*, III (1922), No. 4, p. 208; see also Barbeu du Rocher, *Mémoires de l'Académie des Inscript.*, 2d series, III, 189 ff. Petrarch's *De Remediis* appears in Dassaminiato's vernacular rendering in the *Collezione di Opere Inedite o Rare*. See Gröber's *Grundriss*, I (2d ed., 1933), 143, for an Old French rendering.

Page 104. For a comparison of Lydgate's version with Boccaccio's and Laurent de Premierfait's see Bergen, *Lydgate's Fall of Princes*, IV, 324-326, etc. On Boccaccio's use of Boethius in *De Casibus* see Hortis, *Studj sulle Opere Latine*, pp. 473-475. For Chaucer see *Complete Works*, ed. Robinson, notes, pp. 852 ff. The definition of tragedy is discussed in the note on 1973 ff., p. 852. Guillaume de Machaut's *Confort d'Ami* is edited by Hœpffner, *Œuvres, SATF.*, III, 1 ff.; see the reference to Boethius, 1904 ff.

Page 105. For *The Kingis Quair* see also Skeat's edition, *STS.*, Edinburgh and London, 1911. Baudouin de Condé's *Prisons d'Amours* is edited with the *Dits et Contes*, Scheler, I, 267 ff. For the theme of Fortune and the prison see Patch, *Goddess Fortuna in Med. Lit.*, 67 ff. and 161 ff.; Post, *Med. Spanish Allegory*, 79 ff.; and Neilson, *Origins and Sources of the Court of Love*, 66 and 191 (and see 142-143, for the influence of Boethius on the poetry of love). Froissart's *Prison Amoureuse* is in the *Œuvres*, ed. Scheler, I (1870), 211 ff.

Page 106. Usk's *Testament of Love* is printed in Skeat's volume *Chaucerian and Other Pieces*, pp. 1-145 (supplementary to his edition of Chaucer). The symbolism of Usk's pearl is noted in Osgood's edition of the *Pearl*, p. 83 (cf. p. xxii); the question of a parallel of the poem to the situation in the *Consolatio*, of course only in the vaguest manner, is referred to on pp. xxxiii f.

Page 108. Gerson's *De Consolatione Theologiae* appears in the *Opera*, ed. Du Pin, I, cols. 125-184, and was printed separately in Cologne, 1471 (". . . habet modum libri boecij de consolacione philosophie.") Volucer, we are told, stands for "intellectus discursiuus *et* ratiocinatiuus," and Monicus for "intellectus meditatiuus *et* inquisitiuus." The speech of Volucer, cols. 132-133, is as follows: "Noli mirari Monice, si Theologia Philosophiae praeficitur, quoniam sicut naturam gratia, sicut ancillam Domina, discipulam magistra, sicut tempus aeternitas, sicut ratiocinationem intelligentia, sicut uisibilia ea quae non uidentur; sic Theologia Philosophiam exuperat, quam non abiicit; sed in obsequium sumit.   Est autem lex diuinitatis *et* ordo. . . ." For other "Consolations" touching on the corruption of the Church, see Auer, *Johannes von Dambach*, etc., 247 ff.; and von der Hardt, *Rerum Concilii Oecum. Const.*, I (I), 223. Vrie's *Historia* in eight books of prose and verse is printed in volume I of von der

Hardt's work.   Pedro de Luna is dealt with in cols. 203-214.   Spargo, *Virgil, the Necromancer*, pp. 41 f. (with note 46) has some material on Jacobus de Teramo; but the *Consolatio Peccatorum* of Jacobus shows little influence from Boethius other than in name.

Pages 109-110.   More's *Dyalogue* is in Rastell's edition of the *Workes*, 1139-1264.   The *Wordes of ffortune* (cf. *Workes*, sig. C 5 vo. ff. [for sig. B 5 vo.], "Certain meters in english written by master Thomas More in hys youth" etc.) are printed by Flügel, "Liedersammlungen des xvi. Jahrhunderts" etc., *Anglia* XXVI (1903), 139 ff. (see 139, n. 1).   On More and the prison theme cf. also *Amer. Journal of Philol.*, XLIII (1922), 168-169. Fisher's *Spiritual Consolation* is printed in the *Early Eng. Text Soc.*, E. S., XXVII, 349-363; see the same volume, p. 290, for a quotation of his from Boethius.

Page 111.   Leslie's *Piae afflicti Animi Consolationes, diuinaque Remedia*, was published in Paris, 1574.   I have not seen it.   My account is based on a careful description furnished to me by Miss Natalie Starr, who examined the copy in the British Museum.   On Leslie see the account in the *DNB*.   *De Consolatione Libri Tres*, 1624, is the edition of Cardano's work I have examined.

Page 111.   For Lipsius I have consulted *Iusti Lipsi, De Constantia*, 3d edition, Frankfurt, 1590.   Basil Anderton translated a little of the treatise in his *Sketches from a Library Window*, pp. 1 ff.: "A Stoic in his Garden."   See *De Constant.* I, cap. xv, p. 43: "A deo enim eiusque decretis Necessitas, nec aliud haec Ἀνάγκη, vt Græcus philosophus definit. . . ."   Note the tribute of Lipsius to Boethius printed in Migne, *Patr. Lat.*, LXIII, 574.   For other material on the way Boethius was received at the time of the Renaissance see Burdach, "Die humanistischen Wirkungen des Trostschrift," etc., especially pp. 546 ff. For the fact that Rienzi named his son Boethius see Burdach and Piur, *Briefwechsel des Cola di Rienzo*, 205 f., No. 50 (*Vom Mittelalter zur Reformation*, II, 3). For other documents in the tradition of the "consolation" see di Giovanni, *Severino Boezio Filosofo e i Suoi Imitatori*, 130 ff.

Conclusion

Page 116. The Latin of Boccaccio, (*De Casibus*, VIII, xviii,) runs as follows: "Ex altera uero studiorum suorum singularis gloria, qua eius immixtum philosophis nomen labentibus sæculis, in dies lucidius, inter tam eximiæ rerum magistræ professores, refulget."

Page 117. Bibliography for a study of the sources of the *Consolatio* has been given earlier for the Introduction. Here I may note simply the material on Platonic reminiscence in Klingner's *De Boethii Cons. Philos.*, pp. 32 ff.

Page 119. On Boethius's definition of Personality see De Wulf's *Hist. de la Philos. Médiévale*, I, 117, and above p. 134. Also cf. Schurr, *Die Trinitätslehre des Boethius*, 19 ff. It was adopted by Thomas Aquinas in the *Summa*, I, *quaest*. xxix, i. The Greek of Plotinus runs as follows:

«ἐκεῖνο μὲν οὖν μὴ ἔχον ἑτερότητα ἀεὶ πάρεστιν, ἡμεῖς δὲ ὅταν μὴ ἔχωμεν· κἀκεῖνο μὲν ἡμῶν οὐκ ἐφίεται, ὥστε περὶ ἡμᾶς εἶναι, ἡμεῖς δὲ ἐκείνου, ὥστε ἡμᾶς περὶ ἐκεῖνο . . . οὐκ ἀεὶ δὲ εἰς αὐτό, ἀλλ᾽ ὅταν εἰς αὐτὸ ἴδωμεν, τότε ἡμῖν τέλος καὶ ἀνάπαυλα καὶ τὸ μὴ ἀπᾴδειν χορεύουσιν ὄντως περὶ αὐτὸ χορείαν ἔνθεον.

«9. ἐν δὲ ταύτῃ τῇ χορείᾳ καθορᾷ πηγὴν μὲν ζωῆς, πηγὴν δὲ νοῦ, ἀρχὴν ὄντος, ἀγαθοῦ αἰτίαν, ῥίζαν ψυχῆς· οὐκ ἐκχεομένων ἀπ᾽ αὐτοῦ ἐκείνων, εἶτ᾽ ἐλαττούντων· οὐ γὰρ ὄγκος· . . . οἷον εἰ μένοντος ἡλίου καὶ τὸ φῶς μένει.»

Enneades, VI, ix, 8-9 (ed. Volkmann, II [1884], p. 520).

ADDENDA AND CORRIGENDA

Page 144, note on page 37. For Boethius on astrology one may also consult Bonnaud's article, "Notes sur l'Astrologie Latine au VI° Siecle," in *Revue belge de Philologie et d'Histoire*, X (1931), 557-577.

Page 149, note on page 41. Boethius on Fate and Fortune is discussed extensively by Vincenzo Cioffari in his *Fortune and Fate from Democritus to St. Thomas Aquinas*, New York, 1935. Cioffari has misunderstood certain points in the present author's studies, doubtless in part because of their misleading presentation.

Page 155, note on page 65. According to Gröber's *Grundriss*, II, ii (Strassburg, 1897), 104, Ginebreda revised and completed the Catalan version of Saplan. This rendering in turn was translated into Spanish.

Page 161, note on page 89. A translation of the *Anticlaudianus* is published, with an introduction, by W. H. Cornog in his *The Anticlaudian of Alain de Lille . . .*, Philadelphia, 1935.

Page 165, note on page 100. Further material on Henry of Settimello may be found in the *Giornale Storico*, LXXXVI (1925), 196-199; LXXXIX (1927), 325-329; XCIII (1929), 1-64; XCVI (1930), 39-64.

BIBLIOGRAPHY [1]

Abelson, P. *The Seven Liberal Arts*, New York, 1906.

Acta Sanctae Sedis . . . , 41 vols., Rome, 1865-1908.

Adamson, J. W. "Education," in *Mediaeval Contributions to Modern Civilisation*, ed. F. J. C. Hearnshaw, with a Preface by Ernest Barker, New York, 1922, pp. 190-211.

Adelard of Bath. *Traktat de Eodem et Diuerso*, ed. H. Willner, Münster i. W., 1906. In *Beiträge zur Geschichte der Philos. des Mittelalters*, IV, i.

[Albertano of Brescia.] *Albertani Brixensis* Liber Consolationis et Consilii, ed. Thor Sundby, London, 1873. In *Chaucer Soc. Publ.*, second ser., 8.

Albertus Magnus. *Opera Omnia*, 38 vols., Paris, 1890-1899. Vol. III (1890), *Liber Physicorum*.

Alcuin. [*Versus de Patribus Regibus et Sanctis Euboricensis Ecclesiae*], ed. E. Dümmler, in *Poetae Latini Aevi Carolini*, I (Berlin, 1881, *Mon. German. Histor.*), pp. 169 ff.

Alexander Neckam. *De Laudibus Diuinae Sapientiae*, London, 1863. *Rolls Series*.

Alfred's Old English Version of Boethius . . . , *King*, ed. W. J. Sedgefield, Oxford, 1899.

Alfred the Great, The Whole Works of King. Edited by J. A. Giles (Jubilee ed.), 3 vols. in 2, London, 1858.

Allegranza, G. *De Sepulcris Christianis* . . . , Milan, 1773.

Allen, P. S., and Jones, H. M. *The Romanesque Lyric, Studies in Its Background and Development from Petronius to the Cambridge Songs, 50-1050*, Chapel Hill, N. C. 1928.

[*Annals of Verdun*.] *Annales Virdunenses a 822-1024*, ed. G. Waitz, in *Scriptores*, IV (Hanover, 1841, *Mon. German. Histor.*), pp. 7-8.

Anstey, H. *Munimenta Academica* . . . , 2 vols., London, 1868. *Rolls Series*.

Antonio, Nicolás. *Biblioteca Hispania Vetus*, 2 vols., Madrid, 1788.

[1] The list in general includes works cited more than once.

Argelati, F.   *Biblioteca degli Volgarizzatori* . . . , 4 vols. in 5, Milan, 1767.

Arnold, Matthew, The Poems of.   With an Introduction by A. T. Quiller-Couch, Oxford edition, London, New York, etc., 1909.

Aschbach, J.   *Geschichte der Wiener Universität* . . . , 3 vols., Vienna, 1865-1888.

Asser's Life of King Alfred.   See Stevenson.

Auer, P. A.   *Johannes von Dambach und die Trostbücher vom 11. bis zum 16. Jahrhundert*, Münster i. W., 1928.   In *Beiträge zur Geschichte der Philos. und Theologie des Mittelalters*, XXVII, 1-2.

Bacon, Roger, *The Opus Majus of*.   Edited by J. H. Bridges, 2 vols., Oxford, 1897.

Bacon, Roger, *The Opus Majus of*.   Translated by R. B. Burke, 2 vols., Philadelphia, 1928.

Baehrens, E.   *Poetae Latini Minores*, 5 vols. in 2, Leipzig, 1879-1883.

Baldwin, C. S.   *Medieval Rhetoric and Poetic* . . . , New York, 1928.

Bale, John.   See Poole and Bateson.

Barbeu du Rocher, A.   *Ambassade de Pétrarque auprès du Roi Jean le Bon*, in *Academie des Inscr. et Belles-Lettres, Mémoires Présentés par Divers Savants*, second series, III (Paris, 1854), 172-228.

Bardenhewer, O.   *Patrologie*, second ed., Freiburg i. Br., 1901. *Theologische Bibliothek.*

Baronius, C.   *Annales Ecclesiastici* [*a Christo nato ad annum 1198*], ed. J. D. Mansi, 35 vols., Lucca, 1738-1759.

Bateson, M.   *Catalogue of the Library of Syon Monastery*, Cambridge [Eng.], 1928.

Battaglia, S.   *Il Boezio e L'Arrighetto* . . . , Turin, [1929]. In *Collezione di Classici Italiani*, second ser., XIV.

Baudouin de Condé and Jean de Condé.   *Dits et Contes*, ed. A. Scheler, 3 vols., Brussels, 1866-1867.

Baur, G. A. L.   *Boetius und Dante*, Leipzig, 1873.

Baur, L.   *Die philosophischen Werke des Robert Grosseteste, Bischofs von Lincoln*, Münster i. W., 1912.   In *Beiträge zur Geschichte der Philos. des Mittelalters*, IX.

Baur, L.   *Gundissalinus: De Diuisione Philosophiae*, Münster

i. W., 1903. In *Beiträge zur Geschichte der Philos. des Mittelalters*, IV, 2-3.

Benham, A. R. *English Literature from Widsith to the Death of Chaucer*, New Haven, 1916.

Bernard Silvester. *De Mundi Uniuersitate, Libri Duo, siue Megacosmus et Microcosmus*, ed. C. S. Barach and J. Wrobel, Innsbruck, 1876. In *Bibl. Philosophorum Mediae Aetatis*, I.

Bétant, E. A. *De la Cons. de la Philos., Traduction Grecque* . . . , Geneva, 1871.

Biraghi, L. *Boezio Filosofo, Teologo, Martire a Calvenzano Milanese*, Milan, 1865.

[Boccaccio, G.] *Ioannis Bocatii de Certaldo, Historiographi Clarissimi De Casibus Virorum Illustrium*, ed. J. Ziegler, Augsburg, 1544.

[Boccaccio, G. *De Genealogia Deorum*.] *Ioannis Bocatii Peri Genealogias Deorum, Libri Qvindecim* . . . , Basel, 1532.

Boccaccio, G. [*De Genealogia Deorum*, trans. G. Betussi.] *La Geneologia de Gli Dei*, Venice, 1574.

Boccaccio, G. *Opere*, ed. I. Moutier, 17 vols., Florence, 1827-1834.

Boethi, Anici Manli Severini, De Consolatione Philosophiae libri quinque, ed. A. Fortescue and G. Smith, London, 1925.

Boethii, Anicii Manlii Severini, In Isagogen Porphyrii Commentarii, ed. S. Brandt, Leipzig, 1906. *Corpus Scriptorum Ecclesiasticorum Latinorum*, XLVIII.

Boethii, Anicii Manlii Severini, Philosophiae Consolationis Libri Quinque . . . , ed. Guilelmus Weinberger, Leipzig, 1934. *Corpus Scriptorum Ecclesiasticorum Latinorum*, LXVII.

Boethius, The Theological Tractates with an English Translation, The Consolation of Philosophy with the English Translation of "I.T." (*1609*)—*revised*, ed. H. F. Stewart and E. K. Rand, London and New York, 1918. *Loeb Classical Library*.

[Boethius.] *Commentarii in Librum Aristotelis* περὶ ἑρμηνείας, ed. C. Meiser, 2 vols., Leipzig, 1877.

Boetii, Anicii Manlii Severini, Philosophiae Consolationis Libri Quinque, ed. R. Peiper, Leipzig: Teubner, 1871.

Bonnaud, R. "L'Education Scientifique de Boèce," in *Speculum*, IV (1929), pp. 198-206.

Bosisio, G. *Intorno al Luogo del Supplizio di S. Boezio* . . . , Pavia, 1855.

Boswell's Life of Johnson, Oxford edition, 2 vols., Oxford, 1904.

Brandt, S. See *Boethii*.

Braune, W. *Über die Quantität der althochdeutschen Endsilben*, in *Beiträge zur Geschichte der deutschen Sprache*, II (1875), 143 ff.

Brauer, H. *Die Bücherei von St. Gallen und das althochdeutsche Schrifttum*, Halle, 1926. In *Hermaea*, XVII.

Brunet, J.-Ch. *Manuel du Libraire*, 13 vols., Paris, 1838-1880.

Brunet, P. G. *La France littéraire au XVᵉ Siècle, ou Catalogue Raisonné des Ouvrages en Tout Genre* . . . , Paris, 1865.

Bruno Corbeiensis. *In Boethium de Cons. Philos. Commentarius*, ed. Angelus Card. Mai, in *Classicorum Auctorum e Vaticanis Codicibus Editorum*, III (Rome, 1831), pp. 331-345.

Burdach, K. "Die humanistischen Wirkungen der Trostschrift des Boethius im Mittelalter und in der Renaissance," in *Deutsche Vierteljahrsschrift für Literaturwissenschaft und Geistesgeschichte*, XI (1933), 530-558.

Burdach, K., and Piur, P. *Briefwechsel des Cola di Rienzo*, Part 3, in *Vom Mittelalter zur Reformation, Forschungen zur Geschichte der deutschen Bildung*, II, 3, Berlin, 1912. *Aufträge der königl. preussischen Akad. der Wissenschaften.*

Burke, R. B. *Compendium on the Magnificence, Dignity, and Excellence of the University of Paris* . . . , Philadelphia, 1928.

Burnet, John. *Essays and Addresses*, London, 1929.

Bush, Douglas. *Mythology and the Renaissance Tradition in English Poetry*, Minneapolis, 1932.

Camden, William. *The History of the most Renowned and Victorious Princess Elizabeth, Late Queen of England* . . . , third edition, London, 1675.

Cañal, C. *San Isidoro*, Madrid, 1897.

Capsoni, S. S. *Memorie Istoriche della Regia Città di Pavia*, 3 vols., Pavia, 1782-1788.

Cardale, J. S. *King Alfred's Anglo-Saxon Version of Boethius De Cons. Philos.: with an English translation, and notes*, London, 1829.

Cardano, Girolamo. *De Consolatione libri Tres*, [place of publication illegible], 1624. Harvard Univ. Library.

Cassiodori Senatoris Variae, ed. T. Mommsen, in *Auct. Antiq.*, XII (Berlin, 1894, *Mon. German. Histor.*), pp. 3 ff.

Cassiodorus . . . , The Letters of, tr. T. Hodgkin, London, 1886.

Casus Sancti Galli, ed. I. von Arx, in *Scriptores*, II (Hanover, 1829, *Mon. German. Histor.*), pp. 59-183.

Catalogue Général des Manuscrits des Bibliothèques Publiques des Départements, 7 vols., Paris, 1849-1885.

Caussin, N., S.J. *The Holy Court*, trans. by T[homas] H[awkins] and others, 5 vols. in one, London, 1650, [II], pp. 276 ff.

Causton, William. *Boethius. His consolation of philosophy, in five books.* London, 1730.

Cave, William. *Scriptorum Ecclesiasticorum Historia Literaria*, 2 vols., Oxford, 1740-1743.

Cessi, R. *Fragmenta Historica ab Henrico et Hadriano Valesio primum edita Anonymus Valesianus*, Città di Castello, 1913. In *Rerum Italicarum Scriptores . . . ,* L. A. Muratori (new ed. by G. Carducci and V. Fiorini), XXIV, iv.

Chartier, Alain. *Œuvres*, ed. André Du Chesne, Paris, 1617.

Chaucer, Geoffrey, The Complete Works of, ed. F. N. Robinson, Boston and New York, [1933].

Chaucer, Geoffrey, The Complete Works of, ed. W. W. Skeat, 6 vols., London, 1894-1900. Vol. VII, Supplementary vol., *Chaucerian and Other Pieces*, London, 1897.

Christine de Pisan. *Œuvres Poétiques*, ed. M. Roy, 3 vols., Paris, 1886-1896. *Soc. des Anc. Textes Français.*

Clark, J. M. *The Abbey of St. Gall as a Centre of Literature and Art*, Cambridge [Eng.], 1926.

Clerval, A. *Les Écoles de Chartres au Moyen Âge, du Ve au XVIe Siècle*, Paris, 1895. In *Mémoires de la Soc. archéol. d'Eure-et-Loir*, XI.

Colville, George, *Boethius' Cons. of Philos., Translated from the Latin by*, ed. E. B. Bax, London, 1897.

Cooper, W. F., *The Cons. of Philos. Translated by*, London, 1902. *The Temple Classics.*

Coussemaker, E. de. *Histoire de l'Harmonie au Moyen Âge*, Paris, 1852.

Dante Alighieri, The Convivio of, London, 1908. *The Temple Classics*.

Dante Alighieri, La Divina Commedia di, ed. C. H. Grandgent, revised edition, New York, [1933].

Dante Alighieri, Tutte le Opere di, . . . , ed. E. Moore, 3d edition, Oxford, 1904.

Delisle, L. *Anciennes Traductions Françaises de la Cons. de Boëce* . . . , Paris, 1873.

Delisle, L. *Le Cabinet des Manuscrits de la Bibliothèque Nationale* . . . , 4 vols., Paris, 1868-1881.

Delisle, L. *Inventaire Général et Méthodique des Manuscrits Français de la Bibliothèque Nationale*, 2 vols., Paris, 1876-1878.

Denifle, H., and Chatelain, A. *Chartularium Universitatis Parisiensis*, 4 vols., Paris, 1889-1897.

Deschamps, Eustache, Œuvres Complètes de, ed. Le Marquis de Queux de Saint-Hilaire and G. Raynaud, 11 vols., Paris, 1878-1903. *Soc. des Anc. Textes Français*.

Dieudonné, A. *Hildebert de Lavardin Évêque du Mans, Archevéque de Tours (1056-1133), Sa Vie-ses Lettres*, Paris, 1898.

Douglas, Gavin. *Poetical Works*, ed. J. Small, 4 vols., Edinburgh, 1874.

Du Bus, Gervais. See *Roman de Fauvel, Le*.

[Dudo de St. Quentin.] *De Moribus et Actis Primorum Normanniæ Ducum*, ed. J. Lair, Caen, 1865. In *Mémoires de la Soc. des Antiq. de Normandie*, ser. 3, III.

Ebert, A. *Allgemeine Geschichte der Literatur des Mittelalters im Abendlande*, 3 vols., Leipzig, 1874-1887.

Ehrismann, G. *Geschichte der deutschen Literatur* . . . , I, Munich, 1918. In *Handbuch des deutschen Unterrichts*, VI, i.

Elizabeth's Englishings of Boethius, De Cons. Phil., A.D. 1593, Queen, ed. Caroline Pemberton, London, 1899. In *Early English Text Soc.*, CXIII.

[Elys, Edmund.] *Summum bonum, or An explication of the divine goodness* . . . , Oxford, 1674.

Engelbrecht, A. "Die Consolatio Philosophiae des Boethius. Beobachtungen über den Stil des Autors und die Ueberlieferung seines Werkes." In *Sitzungsberichte der kaiserlichen*

Akademie der Wissenschaften zu Wien, Philos.-histor. Klasse, CXLIV (1901), Abh. 3, pp. 1-60.

Ennodi, Magni Felicis, Opera, ed. F. Vogel, in *Auct. Antiq.,* VII (Berlin, 1885, *Mon. German. Histor.*).

Epistolae Karolini Aevi, IV, various editors, (Berlin, 1925, *Epist.,* VI, *Mon. German. Histor.*).

Ermenrici Epistola ad Grimoldum Archicapellanum . . . , ed. E. Dümmler, Halle, 1873.

Exeter Book of Old English Poetry, The, with Introductory Chapters, ed. R. W. Chambers, M. Förster, and R. Flower, London, 1933.

Fabricius, J. A. *Bibliotheca Latina* . . . , 6 vols., Florence, 1858-1859.

Faral, E. *Les Arts Poétiques du XIIe et du XIIIe Siècle,* Paris, 1924.

Faucon, M. *La Librairie des Papes d'Avignon* . . . , 2 vols., Paris, 1886-1887. In *Bibliothèque des Écoles françaises d'Athènes et de Rome,* 43, 50.

Fehlauer, Friedrich. *Die englischen Übersetzungen von Boethius' "De Cons. Philos.,"* Berlin, 1909.

Foligno, Cesare. *Latin Thought during the Middle Ages,* Oxford, 1929.

Foucher de Careil, A. *Lettres et Opuscules inédits de Leibniz,* Paris, 1854.

Fournier, M. *Les Statuts et Privilèges des Universités Françaises* . . . , 4 vols., Paris, 1890-1894.

Fox, Samuel. *King Alfred's Anglo-Saxon Version of the Metres of Boethius, with an English translation, and notes,* London, 1835.

Froissart, Jean, Œuvres de, Poésies, ed. A. Scheler, 3 vols., Brussels, 1870-1872.

Geoffrey of Monmouth, The Historia Regum Britanniae of, . . . , ed. A. Griscom, tr. R. E. Jones, London, New York, etc., 1929.

Gerbert, Lettres de, (983-997), ed J. Havet, Paris, 1889. In *Collection de Textes pour Servir à l'Étude et à l'Enseignement de l'Histoire,* 6.

Gerbert, Œuvres de, Pape sous le Nom de Sylvestre II, ed. A. Olleris, Clermont and Paris, 1867.

Gersonii, Iohannes, Opera Omnia, ed. L. E. Du Pin, 5 vols., Antwerp, 1706.

Gesamtkatalog der Wiegendrucke . . . , vols. I—, Leipzig, 1925—.

Gesner, K. *Bibliotheca Instituta et Collecta, Deinde in Epitomen Redacta*, Zürich, 1583.

Gestorum Pontificum Romanorum, I, *Liber Pontificalis*, ed. T. Mommsen, Berlin, 1898, in *Monumenta Germaniae Historica*.

Geyer, Bernhard. *Die patristische und scholastische Philosophie*, Berlin, 1928, in Friedrich Ueberweg's *Grundriss der Geschichte der Philosophie, zweiter Teil*.

Gibbon, Edward. *The History of the Decline and Fall of the Roman Empire*, ed. J. B. Bury, 7 vols., London, 1897-1900.

Giovanni, Vincenzo di. *Severino Boezio Filosofo e i Suoi Imitatori*, Palermo, 1880.

[Godfrey of St. Victor.] *Fons Philosophie, Poème Inédit du XIIe Siècle*, ed. M. A. Charma, Caen, 1868. In *Mémoires de la Soc. des Antiq. de Normandie*, XXVII.

Gottlieb, T. *Ueber mittelalterliche Bibliotheken*, Leipzig, 1890.

Grabmann, M. *Die Geschichte der scholastischen Methode*, 2 vols., Freiburg i. Br., 1909-1911.

Grabmann, M. *Thomas Aquinas, His Personality and Thought*, trans. V. Michel, New York, 1928.

Graesse, J. G. T. *Trésor de Livres Rares et Précieux* . . . , 7 vols., Berlin, 1922.

Graf, Arturo. *Roma nella Memoria e nelle Immaginazioni del Medio Evo*, 2 vols., Turin, 1882-1883. Revised ed., Turin, 1923.

Graff, E. G. *Althochdeutsche, dem Anfange des 11ten Jahrhunderts* . . . , Berlin, 1837.

Grandgent, C. H., ed. See *Dante Alighieri*.

Grein, C. W. M. *Bibliothek der angelsächsischen Poesie*, new edition by R. P. Wülcker, 3 vols. in 5, Kassel and Leipzig, 1883-1898.

Gröber, G. *Grundriss der romanischen Philologie*, 2 vols., Strassburg, I, 1904-1906; II, 1897-1902. I (second edition by S. Hofer), Berlin and Leipzig, 1933.

Gualla, I. *Historiae suae Patriae Sanctuarii Papiae appellatae libri sex*, [Pavia, 1505?].

Guillaume de Lorris and Jean de Meun. *Le Roman de la Rose*, ed. E. Langlois, 5 vols., Paris, 1914-1924. *Soc. des Anc. Textes Français*.

Guillaume de Machaut, Œuvres de, ed. E. Hœpffner, 3 vols., Paris, 1908-1921. *Soc. des Anc. Textes Français.*

Hankel, H. *Zur Geschichte der Mathematik in Alterthum und Mittelalter,* Leipzig, 1874.

Hardt, Hermann von der. *Rerum Concilii Oecumenici Constantiensis,* 7 vols., Frankfurt and Leipzig, 1697-1742.

Haskins, C. H. *The Renaissance of the Twelfth Century,* Cambridge [Mass.], 1927.

Haskins, C. H., *Studies in Mediaeval Culture,* Oxford, 1929.

Haskins, C. H. *Studies in the History of Mediaeval Science,* Cambridge [Mass.], 1924. *Harvard Historical Studies,* XXVII.

Hauréau, B. *Histoire de la Philosophie Scolastique,* 2 vols. in 3, Paris, 1872-1880.

Hearnshaw, F. J. C. See Adamson.

Hecker, O. *Boccaccio-Funde, Stücke aus der bislang verschollenen Bibliothek des Dichters* . . . , Braunschweig, 1902.

Henri d'Andeli. See Paetow, *The Battle of the Seven Arts.*

[Henry of Settimello.] *Henrici Septimellensis Elegia—sive de Miseria* . . . , ed. A. Marigo, Padua, 1926. In *Scriptores Latini Medii Aevi Italici,* I.

Henrici, E. *Sprachmischung in älterer Dichtung Deutschlands,* Berlin, 1913.

Heusinkveld, A. H., and Bashe, E. J. *A Bibliographical Guide to Old English* . . . , Iowa City, 1931. In [*Univ. of Iowa*] *Humanistic Studies,* IV, No. 5.

Hildebert de Lavardin, Les Mélanges Poétiques d', ed. B. Hauréau, Paris, 1882.

Histoire de la Langue et de la Littérature Française. . . . See Petit de Julleville.

Hodgkin, T. *Italy and Her Invaders,* 8 vols. in 9, Oxford, 1880-1899.

Hoffmann, Paul. *Die Mischprosa Notkers des Deutschen,* I, diss., Göttingen, 1906.

Hoffmann, Paul. *Die Mischprosa Notkers des Deutschen,* Berlin, 1910. In *Palaestra,* LVIII.

Hoffmann, P. T. *Der mittelalterliche Mensch, gesehen aus Welt und Umwelt Notkers des Deutschen,* Gotha, 1922.

Holkot, R. [*Opus* . . . *super sapientiam Salamonis,* 1483.] Hain-Copinger, *8757; Procter, 2352.

Hortis, A. *Studj sulle Opere Latine del Boccaccio* . . . , Trieste, 1879.

Houghton, Jr., W. E. *English Translations of Boethius's De Cons. Philos. in the Seventeenth Century*, Yale diss. unpubl., New Haven, 1931.

Hündgen, F. *Das altprovenzalische Boëthiuslied unter Beifügung einer Uebersetzung* . . . , Oppeln, 1884.

Hurter, H. *Nomenclator Litterarius Theologiae Catholicae* . . . , 5 vols., third ed., Innsbruck, 1903-1913.

Hutten, Ulrichs von, Schriften, ed. E. Böcking, 5 vols., Leipzig, 1859-1861; 2 supplementary vols., 1869-1870.

I.T. See Walpole, Michael.

Jacobus de, [Jacopo Palladino de] Teramo. *Consolatio Peccatorum*, Cologne, 1473. Also Strassburg, 1484.

James I of Scots. *The Kingis Quair* . . . , ed. A. Lawson, London, 1910.

James I of Scots. *The Kingis Quair* . . . , ed. W. W. Skeat, Edinburgh and London, 1911. *Scottish Text Soc.*

James, H. R. *The Consolation of Philosophy of Boethius, Translated into English Prose and Verse*, London, 1897.

James, M. R. "The Catalogue of the Library of the Augustinian Friars at York . . . ," in the *Fasciculus J. W. Clark dicatus*, Cambridge [Eng.], 1909, pp. 2-96.

James, M. R. *Lists of Manuscripts Formerly Owned by Dr. John Dee* . . . , in *Supplements to the Transactions of the Bibliographical Society*, No. 1, London, 1921.

James, M. R. *Lists of Manuscripts Formerly in Peterborough Abbey Library* . . . , in *Supplements to the Transactions of the Bibliographical Soc.*, No. 5, London, 1926.

James, M. R. *The Manuscripts in the Library at Lambeth Palace*, Cambridge [Eng.], 1900. *Cambridge Antiq. Soc.*, XXXIII.

James, M. R., and Jenkins, Claude. *A Descriptive Catalogue of the Manuscripts in the Library of Lambeth Palace*, Parts I-II, Cambridge [Eng.], 1930-1932.

Jansen, W. *Der Kommentar des Clarenbaldus von Arras zu Boethius de Trinitate*, Breslau, 1926. In *Breslauer Studien*, 8.

Jean Regnier, Les Fortunes et Adversitez de, ed. E. Droz, Paris, 1923. *Soc. des Anc. Textes Français*.

Jefferson, B. L. *Chaucer and the Consolation of Philosophy of Boethius*, Princeton, 1917.

Iohannes de Tambaco [Johannes of Dambach]. *De Consolatione Theologiae*, Speyer, 1478 [Pierpont Morgan Library]. *Consolatorium Theologicum*, [Compilation], Paris, 1493 [Harvard University Library].

[John of Salisbury]. *Ioannis Saresberiensis Historiae Pontificalis Quae Supersunt*, ed. R. L. Poole, Oxford, 1927.

John of Salisbury. *Policratici sive de Nugis Curialium et Vestigiis Philosophorum libri viii* . . . , ed. C. C. J. Webb, 2 vols., Oxford, 1909.

Jourdain, C. "Des Commentaires Inédits de Guillaume de Conches et de Nicholas Triveth sur la Consolation de la Philosophie de Boèce," in *Excursions Historiques et Philosophiques à travers le Moyen Âge*, Paris, 1888, 29-68.

Jubinal, A. *La Complainte et le Jeu de Pierre de la Broce* . . . , Paris, 1835.

Jubinal, A. *Nouveau Recueil de Contes, Dits, Fabliaux* . . . , 2 vols., Paris, 1839-1842.

Junghans, F. *Die Mischprosa Willirams*, diss., Berlin, 1893.

Kelle, J. *Geschichte der deutschen Litteratur* . . . , 2 vols., Berlin, 1892-1896.

King Alfred's Old English Version of Boethius. . . . See *Alfred, King*.

Kirchenlexikon oder Encyklopädie der katholischen Theologie, ed. H. J. Wetzer and B. Welte, 2d ed., 12 vols., Freiburg i. Br., 1882-1901.

[*Kittredge*] *Anniversary Papers*, Boston and London, 1913.

Klingner, Fritz. *De Boethii Consolatione Philosophiae*, Berlin, 1921. In *Philologische Untersuchungen*, 27.

Krapp, G. P. *The Paris Psalter and the Meters of Boethius*, New York, 1932. In *Anglo-Saxon Poetic Records*, V.

Laistner, M. L. W. *Thought and Letters in Western Europe, A.D. 500 to 900*, New York, 1931.

Langlois, E. "Notices des Manuscrits Français et Provençaux de Rome antérieurs au XVI° Siècle," in *Notices et Extraits de la Bibl. Nat. et Autres Bibliothèques*, XXXIII² (1889), pp. 1 ff.

Langlois, E. *Origines et Sources du Roman de la Rose*, Paris, 1891. *Bibliothèque des Écoles Françaises d'Athènes et de Rome*, pt. 58.

Långfors, A. *Les Incipit des Poèmes Français Antérieurs au XVIe Siècle* . . . , I, Paris, [1917].

Leach, A. F. *Educational Charters and Documents, 598-1909*, Cambridge [Eng.], 1911.

Leach, A. F. *The Schools of Medieval England*, London, [1915].

Lehmann, P. *Mittelalterliche Bibliothekskataloge Deutschlands und der Schweiz*, 2 vols., Munich, 1918-1928. *Mittelalterliche Bibliothekskataloge, Preussischen Akad. der Wissenschaften in Berlin.*

Lehmann, P. *Pseudo-antike Literatur des Mittelalters*, Leipzig, 1927.

Leitschuh, F. F. *Geschichte der karolingischen Malerei: ihr Bilderkreis und seine Quellen*, Berlin, 1894.

Levillain, L. *Loup de Ferrières, Correspondance*, . . . , Paris, 1927. *Classiques de L'Histoire de France au Moyen Âge.*

Lindahl, N. *Vollständiges Glossar zu Notkers Boethius De Cons. Phil. Buch I*, diss., Uppsala, 1916.

Lipsi, Iusti, De Constantia . . . , "Tertia editio," Frankfurt, 1590.

Liudprand, Bishop of Cremona. *Antapodosis*, in *Scriptores* III (Hanover, 1839, *Mon. German. Histor.*), pp. 264-339.

Liudprand of Cremona, The works of, Antapodosis, Liber de Rebus Gestis Ottonis . . . , trans. F. A. Wright, London, 1930. *Broadway Mediaeval Library.*

Liudprands von Cremona, Die Werke, ed. J. Becker, Hanover and Leipzig, 1915. *Scriptores Rerum Germanicarum.*

Lohmeyer, H. *Vergil im deutschen Geistesleben bis auf Notker III*, Berlin, 1930. In *Germanische Studien*, 96.

Luna, Pedro de. *Libro de las Consolaciones de la Vida Humana*, ed. Don Pascual de Gayangos, in *Biblioteca de Autores Españoles desde la Formación del Lenguaje hasta Nuestros Días*, LI, Madrid, 1905, 563-602.

[Lydgate, John.] *Lydgate's Fall of Princes*, ed. H. Bergen, 4 vols., London, 1924-1927. *Early English Text Soc., extra series*, CXXI-CXXIV.

[Lydgate, John.] *Lydgate's Troy Book*, ed. H. Bergen, 3 vols. as 2, London, 1906-1910. *Early English Text Soc., extra series*, XCVII, CIII, and CVI.

Lydgate, John, The Minor Poems of, ed. H. N. MacCracken, Part I, London, 1911. *Early English Text Soc., extra series,* CVII.

Maiocchi, R., and Quintavalle, F. *Anonymi Ticinensis Liber de laudibus* . . . , Città di Castello, 1903. In *Rerum Italicarum Scriptores* . . . , L. A. Muratori, (new ed. by G. Carducci and V. Fiorini), XI, i.

Mâle, Émile. *Religious Art in France, XIII Century,* . . . , trans., D. Nussey, London, 1913.

Mallet, C. E. *A History of the University of Oxford,* 3 vols., London, [1924-1927].

Manitius, M. *Geschichte der lateinischen Literatur des Mittelalters,* 3 vols., Munich, 1911-1931. In the *Handbuch der klassischen Altertumswissenschaft,* ed. I. von Müller and W. Otto, IX, 1-3.

Manitius, M. "Philologisches aus alten Bibliothekskatalogen," in *Rheinisches Museum für Philologie,* n.s., XLVII (1892), *Ergänzungsheft,* pp. 130-135.

Map, Walter. *De Nugis Curialium,* ed. M. R. James, Oxford, 1914. *Anecdota Oxoniensia.*

McKinlay, A. P. "Stylistic Tests and the Chronology of the Works of Boethius," in *Harvard Studies in Classical Philol.,* XVIII (1907), pp. 123-156.

Meier, P. G. *Geschichte der Schule von St. Gallen im Mittelalter,* Zürich, 1885. In *Jahrbuch für schweizerische Geschichte,* X, 35-127.

Mérimée, E. *A History of Spanish Literature,* trans. S. G. Morley, New York, [1930].

Migne, J. P. *Patrologiae Cursus Completus* . . . , Latin series, 221 vols., Paris, 1844-1866.

Milanesi, Carlo. *Il Boezio e L'Arrighetto,* Florence, 1864.

Moffat, D. M. *The Complaint of Nature,* New York, 1908. In *Yale Studies in English,* XXXVI.

Monmerqué, L. J. N., and Michel, F. *Théâtre Français au Moyen Âge,* Paris, 1842.

Montfaucon, B. de. *Bibliotheca Bibliothecarum Manuscriptorum Nova* . . . , 2 vols., Paris, 1739.

More, Sir Thomas, Knyght, The Workes of, [ed. W. Rastell], London, 1557.

Murari, R. *Dante e Boezio,* Bologna, 1905.

Naaber, A. *Die Quellen von Notkers "Boethius De Cons. Philos.,"* diss., Borna and Leipzig, 1911.

Nagel, F. *Die altfranzösische Übersetzung der cons. Phil. des B. von Renaut von Louhans,* diss., Halle, 1890.

Narducci, E. *Intorno all' Autenticità di un Codice Vaticano Contenente il Trattato di Boezio* . . . , Rome, 1822. *Atti dell' Accademia dei Lincei.*

Naumann, H. "Notkers Boethius, Untersuchungen über Quellen und Stil," in *Quellen und Forschungen,* CXXI (1913), Strassburg.

Neckam, Alexander. See Alexander Neckam.

Neilson, W. A. *The Origins and Sources of the Court of Love,* Boston, 1899. In [*Harvard*] *Studies and Notes in Philol. and Lit.,* VI.

Newton, A. E. *The Amenities of Book-Collecting and Kindred Affections,* Boston, 1918.

Nichols, John. *The Progresses and Public Processions of Queen Elizabeth* . . . , 3 vols., London, 1823.

Nitzsch, F. *Das System des Boethius,* Berlin, 1860.

Norton, A. O. *Readings in the History of Education: Mediaeval Universities,* Cambridge [Eng.], 1909.

Notices et Extraits des Manuscrits de la Bibliothèque Impériale . . . , XX, part ii, Paris, 1862.

[Notker Labeo]. *Notkers des Deutschen Werke* . . . , ed. E. H. Sehrt and Taylor Starck, I, i-iii, 1933-1934. In *Altdeutsche Text Bibliothek,* 32-34.

[Notker Labeo]. *Die Schriften Notkers und seiner Schule,* ed. P. Piper, Freiburg i. Br. and Tübingen, 1882. In *Holder's German. Bücherschatz,* VIII.

Obbarius, T. *Anicii Manlii Seuerini Boethii De Consolationis Philosophiae libri quinque* . . . *recensuit* . . . , Jena, 1843.

Osgood, C. G. *Boccaccio on Poetry* . . . , Princeton, 1930.

Osgood, C. G. *The Pearl* . . . , Boston, [1906]. *Belles-Lettres Series.*

[Otto of Freising.] *Chronicon* and *Gesta Friderici I* . . . , in *Scriptores,* XX (Hanover, 1868, *Mon. German. Histor.*), pp. 83 ff. and pp. 338 ff. respectively.

[Otto of Freising.] *Ottonis Episcopi Frisingensis Chronica siue Historia de Duabus Ciuitatibus,* ed. A. Hofmeister, Hanover and Leipzig, 1912. In *Scriptores Rerum German-icarum*, V-VI.

[Otto of Freising.] *The Two Cities . . . by Otto Bishop of Freising*, trans. C. C. Mierow; ed. A. P. Evans and C. Knapp, New York, 1928.

Oudin, C. *Commentarius de Scriptoribus Ecclesiae Antiquis . . .*, 3 vols., Leipzig, 1722.

Owst, G. R. *Literature and Pulpit in Medieval England*, Cambridge [Eng.], 1933.

Paetow, L. J. "The Arts Course at Medieval Universities," in *Univ. of Illinois Bulletin*, VII, No. 19, Jan. 9, 1910.

Paetow, L. J. *The Battle of the Seven Arts . . .*, Berkeley, California, 1914.

Paris, A. Paulin, *Les Manuscrits François de. la Bibliothèque du Roi . . .*, 7 vols., Paris, 1836-1848.

Patch, H. R. *The Goddess Fortuna in Medieval Literature*, Cambridge [Mass.], 1927.

Paulus Diaconus. *Historia Langobardorum*, ed. L. Bethmann and G. Waitz, in *Scriptores Rerum Langobard. et Italic.* (Hanover, 1878, *Mon. German. Histor.*), pp. 12-187.

Peiper, R. See *Boetii*.

Pemberton, C. See *Queen Elizabeth's Englishings*.

Pertz, G. H., Mommsen, T., et al. *Monumenta Germaniae Historica*, folio series, Berlin, 1826-1896; quarto series, 1876 ff.; *Scriptores Rerum Germanicarum*, *ex MGH. recusi*, Hanover, 1839 ff.

Petit de Julleville, L. *Histoire de. la Langue et de la Littérature Française . . .*, II², Paris, 1909.

Petrarch, F. *De' Rimedii dell' Una e dell' Altra Fortuna . . .*, volg. D. Giovanni Dassaminiato, pub. C. Stolfi, 2 vols., Bologna, 1867. *Collezione di Opere Inedite o Rare.*

Petrus of Compostella. *De Consolatione Rationis*, ed. P. B. Soto, Münster i. W., 1912. In *Beiträge zur Geschichte der Philos. des Mittelalters*, VIII, iv.

Petrus of Eboli. *De Rebus Siculis Carmen*, ed. E. Rota, Città di Castello, 1904. In *Rerum Ital. Scriptores . . .*, L. A. Muratori (new ed. by G. Carducci and V. Fiorini), XXXI, i.

Petrus of Eboli. *Liber ad Honorem Augusti . . .*, ed. G. B. Siragusa, Rome, 1906. In *Fonti per la Storia d'Italia* (*Istituto Storico Italiano*), XXXIX, with plates.

Pez, B. *Thesaurus Anecdotorum Novissimus seu Veterum Monumentorum* . . . , 6 vols., Augsburg, 1721-1729.

Pico della Mirandola, G. F. *Opera*, 2 vols. in one, Basel, [1601].

Piper, P. See Notker Labeo.

Plotini Enneades . . . , ed. R. Volkmann, 2 vols. as one, Leipzig, 1883-1884.

Plotinus on the One and Good . . . , tr. S. MacKenna and B. S. Page, London, 1930. In *The Library of Philosophical Translations*, vol. V.

Politian (Angelo Ambrogini). *Opera Omnia et Alia Quaedam Lectu Digna*, Venice, 1498. Hain-Copinger *13218; Procter *5567.

Pontano, Giovanni. *Opera Omnia soluta oratione composita*, Pars ii, Florence, 1520.

Poole, R. L. *Illustrations of the History of Medieval Thought* . . . , London, 1884.

Poole, R. L., and Bateson, M. *Index Britanniae Scriptorum* . . . , *John Bale's Index* . . . , Oxford, 1902. In *Anecdota Oxoniensia*, IX.

Post, C. R. *Mediaeval Spanish Allegory*, Cambridge [Mass.], 1915. In *Harvard Studies in Compar. Lit.*, IV.

Prantl, Karl von. *Geschichte der Logik im Abendlande*, 4 vols. in 3, Leipzig, 1855-70. Vol. II (second ed.), Leipzig, 1885.

Proclus, The Elements of Theology . . . , ed. E. R. Dodds, Oxford, 1933.

Procopius. *De Bello Gothico*, ed. J. Haury, *De Bellis* . . . , II, Leipzig, 1905.

Puccinotti, F. *Il Boezio ed Altri Scritti Storici e Filosofici*, Florence, 1864.

Raby, F. J. E. *A History of Christian-Latin Poetry* . . . , Oxford, 1927.

Raby, F. J. E. *A History of Secular Latin Poetry* . . . , 2 vols., Oxford, 1934.

Rand, E. K. *Founders of the Middle Ages*, Cambridge [Mass.], 1928. Second ed., 1929.

Rand, E. K. *Johannes Scottus*, Munich, 1906. In *Quellen und Untersuchungen*, I, 2.

Rand, E. K. "On the Composition of Boethius' Consolatio Philosophiae," in *Harvard Studies in Classical Philol.*, XV (1904), 1-28.

Rashdall, H. *The Universities of Europe in the Middle Ages*, 2 vols. in 3, Oxford, 1895.

Rawlinson, Christopher. *An. Manl. Sever. Boethi Cons. Philos. libri V, Anglo-Saxonice redditi ab Alfredo . . .* , Oxford, 1698.

Reisch, Gregor. *Margarita Philosophica*, [second ed., Strassburg, 1504].

Richard de Bury, The Love of Books: The Philobiblon of, trans. E. C. Thomas, London, 1925. *The Medieval Library.*

Richeri Historiarum libri IIII, ed. G. Waitz, in *Scriptores Rerum Germanicarum*, III (second ed., Hanover, 1877, *Mon. German. Histor.*)

Ridpath, Philip. *Boethius's Cons. of Philos., Translated from the Latin . . .* , London, 1785.

Roger, M. *L'Enseignement des Lettres classiques d'Ausone à Alcuin*, Paris, 1905.

Roman de Fauvel, Le, ed. A. Långfors, Paris, 1914 (1919). *Soc. des Anc. Textes Français.*

Roman de la Rose, Le. See Guillaume de Lorris and Jean de Meun.

Rota, J. M., ed., *De Consolatione Philosophiae*, Basil, 1546.

Routh, E. M. G. *Sir Thomas More and his Friends 1477-1535*, with a Preface by Dame Elizabeth Wordsworth, Oxford, 1934.

Sabbadini, R. *Le Scoperte dei Codici Latini e Greci ne' Secoli XIV e XV . . .* , Florence, 1914. In *Biblioteca Storica del Rinascimento*, V.

Santillana, Don Iñigo Lopez de Mendoza Marqués de. *Obras*, ed. Don José Amador de Los Ríos, Madrid, 1852.

Schaarschmidt, C. *Johannes Saresberiensis nach Leben und Studien, Schriften und Philosophie*, Leipzig, 1862.

Schaumann, E. *Studien zu Notkers Mischprosa (Programm)*, Vienna, 1911.

Schepss, G. *Handschriftliche Studien zu Boethius De Cons. Philos.*, Würzburg, 1881.

Schepss, G. "Zu Boethius," in *Commentationes Woelfflinianae*, Leipzig, 1891, pp. 275-280.

Scherrer, G. *Verzeichniss der Handschriften der Stiftsbibliotheken* . . . , Halle, 1875.

Schümmer, K. *John Waltons metrische Übersetzung der Cons. Philos.*, Bonn, 1914. In *Bonner Studien zur engl. Philol.*, VI.

Schurr, V. *Die Trinitätslehre des Boethius*, Paderborn, 1935. In *Forschungen zur christlichen Literatur-und Dogmengeschichte*, XVIII, 1.

Sedgefield, W. J., *King Alfred's Old English Version.* See Alfred, King.

Sedgefield, W. J. *King Alfred's Version of the Consolations of Philosophy of Boethius Done into Modern English* . . . , Oxford, 1900.

Sedulius Scottus, ed. S. Hellmann, Munich, 1906. In *Quellen und Untersuchungen*, I, i.

Semeria, G. *Il cristianesimo di Severino Boezio Rivendicato*, Rome, 1900.

Servatus Lupus. See Levillain.

Sieper, E. *Les Échecs Amoureux, eine altfranzösische Nachahmung des Rosenromans und ihre englische Uebertragung*, Weimar, 1898.

Sikes, J. G. *Peter Abailard*, with a Preface by the Rev. A. Nairne, Cambridge [Eng.], 1932.

Silk, E. T. "The Study of Boethius' Cons. Philos. in the Middle Ages," in *Transactions and Proceedings of the Amer. Philol. Assoc.*, LXII (1931), pp. xxxvii-xxxviii.

[Simeon of Durham.] *Symeonis Dunelmensis Opera*, I, Durham, 1868. In *Publ. Surtees Soc.*, LI.

Simund de Freine, Les Œuvres de, . . . , ed. J. E. Matzke, Paris, 1909. *Soc. des Anc. Textes Français.*

Spargo, J. W. *Virgil the Necromancer, Studies in Virgilian Legends*, Cambridge [Mass.], 1934. In *Harvard Studies in Compar. Lit.*, X.

Specht, F. A. *Geschichte des Unterrichtswesens in Deutschland von den ältesten Zeiten bis zur Mitte des XIII Jahrh.*, Stuttgart, 1885.

Spurgeon, C. F. E. *Five Hundred Years of Chaucer Criticism and Allusion (1357-1900)*, I, London, 1914. In *Chaucer Soc. Publ., second ser.*, 48.

Stevenson, W. H. *Asser's Life of King Alfred*, Oxford, 1904.

Stewart, H. F. *Boethius*, Edinburgh and London, 1891.

Stewart, H. F., and Rand, E. K., *Boethius, The Theological Tractates*, etc. See *Boethius*.

Strecker, K. *Die Apokalypse des Golias*, Rome and Leipzig, 1928. In *Texte zur Kulturgeschichte des Mittelalters*, No. 5.

Taylor, A. E. *A Commentary on Plato's Timaeus*, Oxford, 1928.

Taylor, H. O. *The Mediaeval Mind*, 2 vols., London, 1914.

Thorndike, Lynn. *A History of Magic and Experimental Science during the First Thirteen Centuries of Our Era*, 2 vols., New York, 1923. Revised ed. 1929. Vols. III and IV, 1934.

Tilander, G. *Les Livres du Roy Modus et de la Royne Ratio* . . . , 2 vols., Paris, 1932. *Soc. des Anc. Textes Français.*

Torraca, F. *L'Elegia di Arrigo da Settimello*, Naples, 1927. In *Atti R. Accademia Arch. Lett. Belle Arti di Napoli*, n. s., X, 1928, 257 ff.

Torre, Alfonso de la. *Visión Delectable* . . . , in the *Biblioteca de Autores Españoles desde la Formación del Lenguaje hasta Nuestros Días*, XXXVI (Madrid, 1871), 339-402.

Ueberweg, Friedrich, *Grundriss der Geschichte der Philos.* See Geyer, B.

Usener, Hermann. *Anecdoton Holderi, ein Beitrag zur Geschichte Roms in ostgothischer Zeit.*, Bonn, 1877.

Vernazza, G. *Osservazioni Tipografiche sopra Libri Impressi in Piemonte nel Sec. XV*, Bassano, 1807.

Vita Meinwerci Episcopi Patherbrunnensis, in *Scriptores* XI (Hanover, 1854, *Mon. Germ. Histor.*), pp. 104-161.

Waddell, H. *Mediaeval Latin Lyrics*, London, 1929.

Waddell, H. *The Wandering Scholars*, Boston and New York, 1927.

[Walpole, Michael.] *Five Bookes of Philosophicall Comfort, Full of Christian consolation*, London, 1609.

[Walther of Speyer.] *Waltheri Spirensis Vita et Passio Sancti Christophori* . . . , ed. W. Harster, Munich, 1878.

Walther, H. *Das Streitgedicht in der lateinischen Literatur des Mittelalters*, Munich, 1920. In *Quellen und Untersuchungen*, V, 2.

Walton, John, Boethius: De Cons. Philos., Translated by, ed.
Mark Science, London, 1927. In *Early Engl. Text Soc.,*
CLXX.

Webb, C. C. J. *God and Personality,* Aberdeen, 1919.

Weber, C. F. *Carmina A.M.T.S. Boetii Græce conuersa*
. . . , Darmstadt, 1833.

Wedel, T. O. *The Mediæval Attitude Toward Astrology*
. . . , New Haven, 1920.

Weidmann, [Franz], "Bibliothekar." *Geschichte der Bibliothek
von St. Gallen seit ihrer Gründung um das Jahr 830 bis auf
1841* . . . , St. Gall, 1841.

Wendell, Barrett, Essays in Memory of, ed. W. R. Castle Jr.
and Paul Kaufman, Cambridge [Mass.], 1926.

Werner, Jakob. *Beiträge zur Kunde der lateinischen Literatur
des Mittelalters,* second ed., Aarau, 1905.

West, A. F. *Alcuin and the Rise of the Christian Schools,* New
York, 1892.

William of Malmesbury. *De Gestis Pontificum Anglorum Libri
Quinque,* ed. N. E. S. A. Hamilton, London, 1870. *Rolls
Series.*

William of Malmesbury, *De Gestis Regum Anglorum Libri
Quinque,* ed. W. Stubbs, 2 vols., London, 1887-1889.
Rolls Series.

Williams, Harold. *Dean Swift's Library* . . . , Cambridge
[Eng.], 1932.

Withington, Robert. *English Pageantry, An Historical Outline,*
2 vols., Cambridge [Mass.], 1918-1920.

Wood, Anthony à. *Athenæ Oxonienses* . . . , ed. P. Bliss,
4 vols., London, 1813-1820.

Wordsworth, C. *The Ancient Kalendar of the University of
Oxford* . . . , Oxford, 1904. In *Oxford Histor. Soc.,*
XLV.

Wright, T. *The Anglo-Latin Satirical Poets and Epigram-
matists of the Twelfth Century,* 2 vols., London, 1872
Rolls Series.

Wright, T. *The Latin Poems commonly attributed to Walter
Mapes,* London, 1841. *Camden Soc.*

Wright, T., and Halliwell, J. O. *Reliquiæ Antiquæ, Scraps
from Ancient Manuscripts* . . . , 2 vols. in one, London,
1841-1843.

Wulf, Maurice De. *Histoire de la Philosophie Médiévale*, I (*Des Origines justqu'à la Fin du XIIe Siècle*), Louvain and Paris, 1934.

Wulf, Maurice De. *Philosophy and Civilization in the Middle Ages*, Princeton, 1922.

Wunderlich, H. *Beiträge zur Syntax des Notker'schen Boethius*, diss., Berlin, 1883.

Zambrini, F. *Opere Volgari a Stampa dei Secoli XIII e XIV*, Bologna, 1878.

INDEX